Relational Database Systems:

How and Why

Ron Rogerson

Howard Rogerson Associates
15 Perry Hall Road
Orpington
BR6 0HT

email: ron@howard-rogerson.co.uk
Facebook: http://bit.ly/Reldbs

Main cover photo: John Voo, licence https://creativecommons.org/licenses/by/2.0/
Inset photo: © 2019 Nancy Honey

ISBN 9 780 359 518043

Preface

This book is intended as a resource for continuing professional development, and is aimed principally at the following groups of people:

- software engineers aiming to move into SQL programming or database management, and looking to gain a good grounding before training on a specific dbms;

- students of computing or computer science where an understanding of SQL/relational databases may be a prerequisite for the courses they are following or plan to follow; and

- technical managers who would like a better grasp of the work done by their staff on SQL/relational databases.

I assume that you have at least a basic understanding of operating systems and programming, but not necessarily any knowledge of any specific programming language. Although I make reference to the many opportunities for further reading on the subject, the book aims to be a self-contained resource for learning.

It gives the background to the development of relational databases, and goes on to teach basic SQL and database practice and database development, using a freely downloadable working database management system, SAP SQL Anywhere (available for Linux, Windows 7 or later, and MacOS 10.9 Mavericks or later). A series of theoretical and practical exercises allow the reader to assess his or her progress throughout.

I don't pretend to be able to make you an expert SQL programmer or database administrator; for that, additional training would be needed in the particular rdbms of choice, but I believe I can give you a flying start.

Former colleagues at the Open University will recognise the extent to which I have shamelessly borrowed from some of their excellent teaching methods. I was motivated to write this book by what their students taught me about how best to present the subject, and by its absence now from most university and college curricula. I hope I may be able to make a small contribution to filling that gap.

I've divided the book into four sections and four appendices, as follows.

In **Section I**, I introduce some basic concepts, and go on to describe briefly the reasons why relational systems became so popular, in contrast to some of the systems they replaced.

In **Section II**, I describe the theoretical ideas, including the relational model itself, which give the background to today's actual relational database systems (rdbms).

Section III takes you through the download and installation of SQL Anywhere, together with specimen databases. Through practical exercises, you will then be able to examine and manipulate those databases using SQL. You will learn how databases are scoped, developed and implemented, and the issues which arise in the real world environment, and you will go on to analyse a data requirement and translate it into a database design yourself; you will then be able to use SQL to create a new database from such a design.

Finally, in **Section IV** I discuss some additions to rdbms systems (distributed data, multimedia and data warehousing), but otherwise we do not go beyond the kind of system which (almost) adheres to the ANSI SQL-2 standard.

Section I: Introduction

Chapter 1: Some initial concepts

In this book, I use several terms which you may have encountered in other contexts where their meaning might be slightly different.

Data is just text or numbers, or, at base, just a string of binary digits. It has no inherent meaning unless it is placed in its *Context* or *Domain*

Take, for example, the data

1500	8	5	18	31	VG	55	1

Fig. 1

This is meaningless, until we add the *context*:

Time	°C max	°C min	Wind speed	Gusts	Visibility	% humidity	UV index
1500	8	5	18	31	VG	55	1

Fig. 2

when it becomes obvious that it's information about weather conditions

So *information* is *data* with *context*

A *database* is an *organised* collection of *data,* and in this book I take for granted that we are concerned only with data as a *resource shared by many users.*

A *database management system (dbms)* is a collection of software for *managing a database* (note the distinction: in common parlance people often say, for example, that Oracle is a database, when in fact it's a dbms).

A *database administrator (dba)* is a nominated person or team of people, responsible for the integrity and security of the database (as distinct from systems programming). The identification of this role is essential for successful database operation, even if it has (in smaller organisations) to be shared with other tasks.

An *application program* is a piece of software written for a *specific purpose.* For example, the patient access web site for a local doctors' surgery will enable users to access the surgery database so as to find vacant appointment slots and to book them, but may not provide any means for them to look at their own appointment and treatment history, even if that information is also stored there.

A ***database tool***, by contrast, is a piece of *general purpose* software, which enables its user to carry out any valid operation (for example, the Interactive SQL tool provided with most rdbms implementations such as SQL Anywhere, which we start to look at in Chapter 9). So, subject to appropriate permissions, a user accessing the surgery database with a database tool could potentially look at and change *any* of the data in there.

A ***user***, in database terms, is who- or what-ever is making use of a database; it could be a human at a terminal but more commonly it's an application program. So for clarity . . .

An ***end user*** is specifically a human or human organisation making use of the database, either directly or through an application program.

Data independence is something which can only be achieved through a dbms; it means the ability of a user to access the required data without being concerned with its detailed characteristics or the structure of the way it is stored, or, consequently, by any changes to those things. It comes in two flavours:

logical data independence means the ability of a user to access the data without knowing anything about its logical structure; for example, whether the date of birth of an individual is stored as a number or a string, or how many lines their address has. This means that the logical structure can be changed without having any effect on the user's access to the required data. On the other hand,

physical data independence means that the user need know nothing about how the data is physically stored, e.g. on which machine or under what operating system; it follows from this that the data could be moved around physically without any effect on the user's access.

Chapter 2: Why relational?

While the first few pages of the book look at information systems in general, the remainder (from Chapter 5 onwards) deals exclusively, as the title indicates, with the rdbms, so it's worth explaining why this is.

The main reason is simply that, despite the growth of alternatives in recent years, relational technology remains overwhelmingly the most popular choice for data storage (DB-engines 2019). The vast majority of corporate operational data systems use a relational database, and in everyday life, practically everything we touch which requires data storage, from the home personal video recorder to eBay, has a relational database hidden behind it. It is only in specialised operations that organisations choose other kinds of system for data storage.

So why, exactly, is the rdbms so popular? We may particularly ask this question once we know how inefficient a rdbms is, in pure processing terms, compared with the alternatives.

Yes, it's true: when compared with the systems that preceded them, as well as with some of the less popular alternatives around today, relational databases use much more processing power to perform basic data storage tasks.

And, up until about the mid-1980s, computer power was hugely expensive, and skilled administrative human resources were, by comparison, cheap. Desktop personal computers had yet to emerge in any numbers, and almost all serious processing was done by big mainframe machines in specialised, climate-controlled computer rooms. They were very big in terms of physical size and electrical power consumption, but puny in terms of processing power when compared with even the mobile devices we now take for granted. Even so, that was how financial and payroll systems, for example, were run, in large corporations and public authorities.

Because these machines were so expensive to buy and operate, their use could be justified only if they were fully employed all the time (compare this with the personal computers and other devices of today, which are so cheap we can afford to leave them idle most of the time).

Consequently, those mainframes were running 24/7 and almost all processing was done in "batch" mode; that is to say, work had to be submitted and given a priority level, and the results would be available only at some later time. Indeed, some of the most important programs those mainframes ran were scheduling applications, whose only function was to ensure that the various jobs were slotted in so as to give the highest priority to the most important work, while still keeping the machines going flat out.

And of course this focus on efficiency meant that the software, too, had to be as efficient as possible. Very little processing power was wasted on user interfaces, which were at best monochrome text screens, or before that just teletype, punch card or tape machines, and printers.

ICL Series 39 computer room, 1980s

Not only was the software written as simply and efficiently as possible, it was often written specifically to take advantage of the particular features of the environment where it was running. For this, we need to understand that mainframe computing was a highly proprietary business, with none of the open systems we use today. Machines from one manufacturer were completely incompatible with those of other manufacturers, and to all intents and purposes were unable to communicate with them. (For many years the largest mainframe manufacturer had three ranges of computers, each using entirely separate operating systems, and even two different methods of text encoding.) So in general, an authority or corporation had to commit itself to a single hardware supplier, and unless it was able to write programs for itself, it would also be reliant on software suppliers licensed by that hardware supplier. And this lack of competitiveness naturally tended to maintain the high cost of processing.

Given that, as I have said, the cost of human processing power was much cheaper than the computers, the computers were only used for things they could do more quickly or cheaply than humans, and humans were left to carry on with whatever didn't fit that model.

In the next chapter, we will examine the consequences for data processing of this high-cost, efficiency-intensive, hardware-supplier-driven world.

Of course, nowadays computer processing power has become so much cheaper that we scarcely think about it; the display function alone of the smartphones in our pockets has many times the power of the biggest mainframe computers of the 1970s. Software efficiency and maximum utilisation have long ceased to be the driving forces of computing.

This change didn't happen overnight, but it did take less than a decade. It started with the emergence of the UNIX workstations, based on a new kind of processor chip, and initially developed by relatively small start-up businesses such as Apollo, Sun Microsystems and Silicon Graphics along the west coast of the USA. These machines delivered processing power at a cost an order of magnitude lower than that of the mainframes, and began to turn the machine cost : human cost ratio on its head.

Not only that, but because they ran the freely available UNIX operating system, with its integral IP networking suite, they could easily be connected in order to share data, and this provided direct competition on price, in an exact reversal of the mainframe pricing structure. Eventually the huge and seemingly impregnable mainframe manufacturers (like Honeywell, DEC, Unisys, Sperry-Univac and ICL) were swallowed by smaller companies or simply disappeared, or (like IBM) downsized and completely changed their business direction. Few of those names are familiar today.

The idea of the rdbms had been around since at least 1970 , but had not gained popularity, largely because of its relative inefficiency. The idea of any kind of computer system which could guarantee data integrity, but only at the cost of using much more computer power, was a very hard sell in those days. Ted Codd spoke of "the ten or more years in which government, industry and commerce were strongly opposed to the relational approach to database management" (Codd E.F. 1990).

But with the advent of the UNIX machines, that relative inefficiency became much less important than the enormous data management benefits which the rdbms offered, and it began to gain ground. (Here, I can't resist noting that Codd published most of his work while working for IBM Labs, and it could well be said that the rise of UNIX, which made his ideas viable, also contributed to the downfall of IBM as a mainframe manufacturer.)

So is relational a panacea?

For almost all large databases in the world, the sacrifice of performance for the sake of data integrity is absolutely worth it, but there are important exceptions:

- Where the quantity of data is small, or there are few regular users, it may just not be worth the complexities of a relational system; the job might just as well be done on spreadsheets;

- Where performance is absolutely crucial, the quantity of data is relatively small, and there may be a need for simultaneous multiple accesses; I'm thinking very much of air traffic control or military command-and-control applications;

- Where interfacing application software with a relational database is particularly problematic; I'll say more about this in Chapter 20.

Chapter 3: File based systems

Let us now look at the nature of those old, mainframe-based database systems, and how their many disadvantages explain the popularity of less efficient, relational systems, in the modern era of cheaper processing.

I characterise these old systems as "file based," because they tended to require the user to access data files directly, rather than through any database management system.

(This is a deliberate over-simplification. What I describe here as file based systems certainly existed, but they are something of an extreme case. The various mainframe manufacturers did develop systems for database management which mitigated some of the problems of file based systems, but they never achieved the full benefits of a modern rdbms. However, the comparison with those original file based systems will highlight those latter benefits.)

The main features of a file based system are as follows

- Users must know the physical structure of a data file in order to use it

  To open a file and access its data, the user has to know where that file physically exists (probably on which machine within a network, but certainly where within the logical folder or directory structure of the machine concerned, and often within the physical disk and controller structure as well), and usually the file type and block size and so on. The "user" in a file based system is almost always an application program, and so all this file location stuff will be stored in the program(s), but it clearly means the system cannot exhibit *physical data independence.* If, as is often necessary for a variety of reasons, the file has to be moved to a different physical location, all the programs which need to access that file will need to be changed, recompiled, tested and so on.

- Users must know the logical structure of a data file in order to use it

  Take this representation of part of a data record in a file-based system :

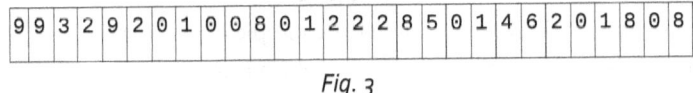

| 9 | 9 | 3 | 2 | 9 | 2 | 0 | 1 | 0 | 0 | 8 | 0 | 1 | 2 | 2 | 2 | 8 | 5 | 0 | 1 | 4 | 6 | 2 | 0 | 1 | 8 | 0 | 8 |

Fig. 3

As I said before, *data* is no use without its *context*; we cannot extract any useful information from it. Once we add that context, so,

Employee No	Location	Date joined	Salary	Line manager	Month appraisal due
9 9 3 2	9 2	0 1 0 0 8 0 1	2 2 2 8 5 0	1 4 6 2 0 1	8 0 8

Fig. 4

we see that, in order, say, to find the identifier of the line manager of employee 9932, the user has to know that the identifier of that line manager occupies positions between 15 and 18 places further along the record. So the context we've included in the header row above – let's call it the *template* of the logical structure of the file – has to be known to every application program which accesses this file.

What happens if the company expands and takes on more staff, and finds that, to store all the employee numbers, it will now need 5 places instead of 4? This will mean restructuring all the records in the file to add the necessary space, and this in turn means that the *template* changes; the line manager identity, for example, will now be between 16 and 20 places further along the record. So the template will have to be changed in all the application programs, with the attendant recompilation, testing and so on which that change will involve.

- Users must have been granted access to the file in order to use it.

  Access to files is controlled only by the operating system, so a user given access to a file has access to the whole file, and can't be restricted to certain records or parts of records

  In an ideal world, we'd store all the company's data in one place where everyone could share it. But in the example above, we can see that the employee record stores the salary, which the company may well not want to be visible to the rest of the staff. There are two approaches to this problem:

— we can write programs to control access to the various data within a record. This imposes two further levels of complexity: the program must still be granted access to the file, but in addition the user must be given permission to use the program, and then the program itself is written so as to only access the desired parts of the file. Consequently, there will have to be multiple programs, each accessing different parts of the file, so as to provide differing access for different users. And all this means more programs, and more recompilation and testing if the file structure changes.

Alternatively, we can make multiple copies of the file, some of them with and some without the sensitive data, and only give users access to the copies containing the data they are allowed to see (resulting in *duplication of data*, with considerable chance of *inconsistency* between the various copies, as updates are applied to some but maybe not all copies

- The files themselves have no mechanism for maintaining relationships or *consistency* between the data

    For example, again using the record shown above, the file itself has no means of ensuring that line manager number 0146 is even an employee within the company, to say nothing of whether he or she is of the correct level to supervise 9932; nor has it any way to ensure that the data remains consistent 9932 is given a different line manager.

So we can see that the principle disadvantages of a file-based system are that

- Application programs are not data independent, and in fact are closely tied to the logical and physical data structure, meaning that they have to be expensively changed as circumstances evolve. The system exhibits *resistance to change*.

- The limitations of the approach are often worked around by holding multiple copies of data, leading to *duplication* and potential *inconsistency*.

- A great deal of facilities which the files themselves don't provide, such as *access control* and *data integrity*, have to be expensively provided in the application programs instead, if at all.

As long as the cost of computer power remained high, and the cost of pa humans to sort out problems which could arise with the data remained relatively, this kind of system continued to be fairly effective. But as we've seen, once the pratio between computers and people began to switch around, there was botdesire and an opportunity for the advantages of database management systems.

Section II: Theoretical Solutions

We now look at three ideas, from the 1970s and 1980s, for a much better kind of information system, one which would avoid all or most of the problems outlined at the end of the previous chapter. Each of the first two of these ideas proposes, in its own way, a model for data storage, and while neither of them has been adopted in its entirety, they both underpin our modern relational database systems. The third, rather than proposing *how* a complete database management system should work, details *what* it should deliver; and it does very much describe the functionality of the systems we now have.

Chapter 4: The ANSI/SPARC 3 schema architecture

In 1975, the American National Standards Institute Standards Planning and Requirements Committee put forward a model for a database system (ANSI/SPARC 1975) finalised in more detail later (Tsichritzis 1977), which would provide full logical and physical data independence. The model provides a *database schema* which contains a definition of the logical and physical structures of the data, separate from both the data itself and the users which access it.

In turn this database schema is divided into three independent parts, as shown in the simplified diagram on the next page.

(Don't try to interpret this model in terms of some actual system which implements it: none exist. It's just a theoretical model.)

The logical schema contains a full definition of the logical structure of all the data items in the database. *Mappings*, shown by the dashed lines, relate these items in the logical schema to the definitions of their physical structure, including file types and indexes, and where they are actually physically stored, which are held in the storage schema. Other mappings relate the items in the logical schema to each of a number of external schemas.

From the diagram, it will be seen that the only contact a user can have with the database is through an external schema; in effect, this is the user's window onto the data. The user cannot see, and is therefore not concerned with, anything else about the database.

Equally, the only part of the whole system which has any contact with the actual stored data, is the storage schema, and therefore it is only this schema which needs to know anything about the physical characteristics of the data.

Because of this, when we make any change to the physical structure of the data items, such as adding an index, moving a file to a different disk or controller, or even moving the entire database system to a different machine (functions which together comprise database *re-organisation*), the only thing which needs to change is the storage schema; everything else can carry on as before. Users need know nothing about it. Thus, we have *physical data independence*.

And because the external schemas are the only part of the whole system which the users "see", they do not, as was the case in the file based system, always need to know

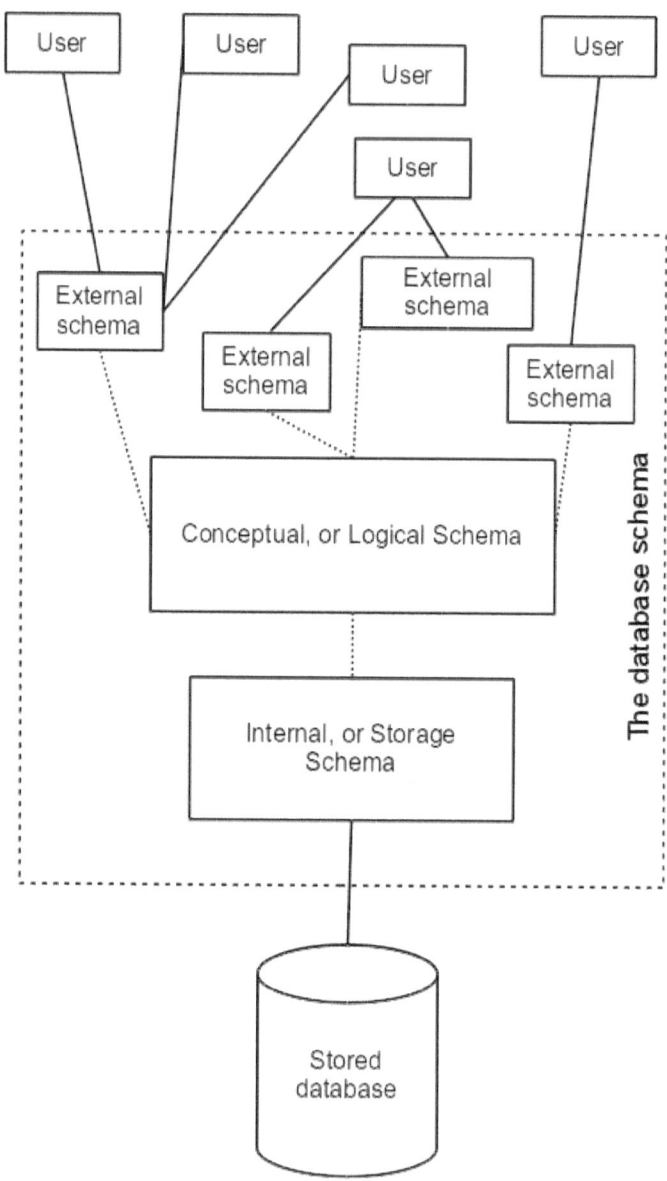

Fig 5: the ANSI/SPARC 3-schema architecture

anything about any changes in the logical structure of the data. The only things which have to change are the mappings between the external and logical schemas, and this should be managed automatically by the dbms. In our personnel database example above, the file-based system illustrated earlier would, by contrast, have to change all of its access programs if it were to become necessary, say, to additionally keep an employee's date of birth in the record.

I have been careful to say that, in the 3 schema model, the users do not *always* need to know about changes to the logical structure. After all, some users, those who need to use the additional data, *will* obviously need to know. To continue with the same example, presumably the date of birth will have been added to the record because some users needed it, and so of course those end users and their access programs will need to change to include the new item. But others who don't need the new item, won't need any change. And so we have *logical data independence*.

Chapter 5: The relational model

Although various ideas for the management of data as sets had been around for a while, Ted Codd was the first to describe a complete relational system (Codd 1970). Various other authors, notably Chris Date, as well as Codd himself, proposed additions and changes to that initial model, and it remains the case that there is no single agreed version of the model on which all the authorities would agree. The model I present in this book is intended as a synthesis of the various views.

Codd's central idea was for a system which would provide data independence and prevent inconsistency, while protecting the user from any need to know how the data was organised in the machine; but which would in fact organise the data based upon its own natural structure, without any of the kinds of additional superimposed structure which were necessary in the existing database systems of the period. And the result is nothing less than a theory of the structure of information.

1   The relation

In the model, a relation may be pictured as a kind of table, used to represent some entity or thing which has attributes of its own. (Take care, however, to remember that a relation is *not* a table. Depicting it as such seems to be the only useful way to get the idea across, but it does inevitably give the impression of ordered rows and columns, and those are emphatically not characteristics of a relation, which is an unordered set of data.)

Employee			
NatInsNo	Surname	Grade	DateJoined
DQ435721A	Johnson	Fitter	04/01/08
FV546890B	Robinson	Fitter	07/08/12
QQ525687D	Smith	Apprentice	01/10/15
UD987234A	Wilkins	Chargehand	18/06/10
VU241367D	Johnson	Receptionist	04/01/08
VF219787C	Khan	Fitter	09/07/11

Fig 6: a relation Employee, depicted as a table

In figure 6, I show a relation used to record details of some employees at a garage.

The entity or thing being represented here is Employee, and this entity has four **attributes** (each depicted as a column): National Insurance Number, Surname, Grade and Date Joined. Our example contains six **occurrences** of an Employee (Johnson, Robinson, Smith, Wilkins and Khan), each recorded as a **tuple** (depicted as a row) in this relation .

A relation has six essential properties:

1   Each value in the relation is atomic; that is, for each tuple, the value within an attribute is always one value and never a group or range of values.

2   The values within an attribute are all of the same kind in every tuple of the relation.

3   Each relation has a name, different from that of any other in the schema, e.g. Employee.

4   Each attribute of the relation has a name, different from any other in the table, by which it may be identified, e.g. Grade.

5   Each tuple is unique, meaning that it is different in some respect from each other tuple.

6   The ordering of tuples and attributes is not significant. For example, the rows need not have been printed in ascending order of NatInsNo, and NatInsNo need not have been the first column.

There is a potential, but highly disputed, further property, namely

7   Every attribute of every tuple must contain a value; i.e., there can be no missing values or nulls.

(Codd 1979) proposed that, except where specifically prohibited (see below), nulls *should* be allowed in the relational model, and since SQL happily allows nulls, the relational model described in this book does so too. Authorities such as Chris Date have however argued strongly against the idea (Date 1982), advocating instead the use of default values wherever, as is often the case in the real world, data is missing; as we'll see, though, default values are by no means a panacea.

The subject of nulls, and the many problems they can create, is one to which I will return. For the moment, I'll simply say that, in the version of the model I describe in this book, every attribute of every relation is allowed to contain nulls, unless it has been constrained to prevent that in some way. A *primary key* is automatically prevented from containing nulls, but other attributes would need a specific declaration to achieve that effect. At the end of this chapter, I'll show how, in a *relational* schema, we could define that and all the other necessary properties of each relation.

(And NB: "null value" is a term which is often used by those who should know much better; it's just nonsense. NULL means the *absence* of a value.)

The six properties are mutually consistent and explanatory, and they also explain just about everything else about the model. For example, if every relation has a unique name (property 3), every attribute has a name which is unique within a relation (property 4), and each tuple is unique (property 5), then we do not need there to be any significance in the ordering of tuples and attributes (property 6), because we can find any data item without knowing where in the database it physically is. We have reached Codd's aim of associative, rather than positional addressing. Let us now look at properties 1 and 2 in detail:

a)   **Atomic values**

The model requires that every value within any attribute shall be atomic, which means that such a value cannot be *parsed*. Some examples may help here:

1

15

15000321.008

are all atomic values, but on the other hand

9-15

and

189, 215, 4301

are not.

But while

green

and

Stonehenge

are clearly atomic values, and

green, red, blue

is not;

on the other hand

Buckingham Palace

at least as commonly understood, certainly *is* an atomic value. Which leads us to the next heading.

(Students of object oriented systems will note that this means that we cannot directly represent compound data in the relational model; or, more accurately, in Codd's words, "there is only one type of compound data: the relation" (Codd 1990)

b)   *Domains*

Property 2 requires that all the values within any given attribute must be *of the same type.* The simplest and most obvious interpretation of that phrase is that they all have to be of the *same data type,* and clearly that, at least, is a necessary restriction. After all, the following set of values for the attribute DoctorName is evidently wrong:

DoctorName
Smith
Jones
37
Hussein

But from the point of view of our relational model, "of the same type" has a meaning which goes well beyond that of simple data types; and for us the following is also wrong:

TeamName
USA
Norway
Arsenal
France

These may all be the names of teams, indeed possibly they are all football teams; but Arsenal is not, like the others, a national team.

So we are evidently talking about *meaning* here. To put it another way, all of the values within any given attribute must be *comparable*, both in strict data type and in meaning.

And this is where *domains* come in. In the relational model, every attribute must be defined on some domain, and the definition of the domain incorporates both type and meaning. We could define some domains for a relational model of a railway company database thus:

domains

```
PersonNames = string

Years = 1950 .. 2050

LocomotiveNumbers = 1000 .. 9999

WagonNumbers = 1000 .. 9999
```

Note two particular features of these definitions:

- three of the domains define not only a data type, but also a range of values. These are examples of a *constraint* within a domain (and these constraints can get a good deal more complex than the examples shown here). Defining such constraints in a domain, rather than repeatedly for each individual attribute to which they apply, brings simplicity, avoids inconsistency, and makes it easier for someone reading the schema to see where the constraints are; and

- in defining separate domains for WagonNumbers and LocomotiveNumbers, we confirm that, although these two kinds of things may have an identical range of identifying numbers, they are emphatically not "of the same type," and so cannot be compared with each other.

As we shall see, although SQL provides support for domains, it is not nearly as insistent on their use as is the relational model.

c)   *Candidate, primary and alternate keys*

Property 5 requires that "Each tuple is unique, meaning that it is different in some respect from each other tuple." The main reason we want this property is so that we can readily *identify* each tuple, so for practical purposes we want a uniform mechanism for doing so. And that mechanism is the *primary key*.

A **primary** key is an attribute, or combination of attributes, such that no two tuples in the relation can have the same value for the attribute(s) comprising the primary key. In the *relation heading*, we tend to show the primary key as the first of the listed attributes, and to underline it, thus:

Employee (NatInsNo, Surname, Grade, DateJoined)

National Insurance Number is a pretty obvious choice for the primary key here, because it's guaranteed to be unique, and every employee has to have one. Which highlights another requirement for a primary key: not only must its values be unique, but it must *contain* a value in every tuple. That's to say, the primary key attribute (or attributes, if it's made up of a combination) can't contain any nulls. (Pretty obvious, if you think about it for a bit. Given that null is not a value, we can't constrain it to be unique, and therefore if one tuple could contain a null, many could, and then the primary key would be useless for identification). So declaring that an attribute is (or is part of) a primary key, explicitly prevents it from containing a null.

But what if our relation contains more than one attribute (or combination of attributes) which is potentially unique? This is a situation which frequently arises. Consider, for example, an addition to our Employee relation:

Employee				
NatInsNo	Surname	Grade	DateJoined	DrivingLicenceNo
DQ435721A	Johnson	Fitter	04/01/08	JOHNS403196DP9JH
FV546890B	Robinson	Fitter	07/08/12	ROBIN704197PV7TB
QQ525687D	Smith	Apprentice	01/10/15	SMITH910274IB0IV
UD987234A	Wilkins	Chargehand	18/06/10	WILKI711198SS5BE
VU241367D	Johnson	Receptionist	04/01/08	
VF219787C	Khan	Fitter	09/07/11	KHANA808197CD1AS

Employee (<u>NatInsNo,</u> Surname, Grade, DateJoined, Driving LicenceNo)

Fig 7: a modified Employee relation.

We now have two attributes – National Insurance Number and Driving Licence Number – which are each guaranteed to be unique, and so might be possible choices of primary key. Unsurprisingly, we call such attributes **candidate keys**.

But as we can see in Fig. 7, while all employees have to have a National Insurance Number, they don't all have to have a driving licence, and so that attribute can contain nulls – meaning that it's no use to us as a primary key. The name we give to any candidate keys which are left over once we've chosen the primary key, is **alternate keys**, and we define them as such in the schema.

You may ask why we would even bother to do that; surely they're no further use, once we've chosen the primary key. In fact, declaring an attribute as an alternate key gives us two benefits:

> a) it has the effect of constraining values to be *unique;* in this case, it will prevent anyone mistakenly trying to enter the same licence number for two employees, and

> b) even though it can't be our primary means of identifying tuples, it is still of use for identification, because it *does* uniquely identify those tuples where it *does* contain a value. In Fig. 7, for example, we could use it to locate quickly the owner of a found driving licence. (And as we'll see in the next section, we can reference an alternate key, as well as a primary key, with a foreign key.)

We can now improve on our definitions of these keys:

A **candidate key** (of which there can be any number in any given relation) is an attribute, or combination of attributes, within a given relation, which does not contain the same values in any two tuples.

A **primary key** (of which there can be only one in any relation) is a specific candidate key which contains no NULLs.

An **alternate key** is a candidate key not being used as the primary key of its relation, but which is still constrained to hold only unique values.

I also must add, very importantly, that when we say that a candidate key must uniquely identify a tuple, it must also be *minimally unique;* and this means that *no candidate key can be part of another candidate key.* I'll explain this, next.

d)   *Uniqueness and minimality*

If we take the (modified) heading of our Employee relation:

Employee (<u>NatInsNo,</u> Surname, Grade, DateJoined, Driving LicenceNo)

we can see that there are many possibilities for *combinations* of attributes, which would be unique. For example, since NatInsNo is known to be unique, any combination of attributes which included it, such as (NatInsNo, Surname) must also be unique. But Surname is adding nothing to this uniqueness, in fact it's redundant, because NatInsNo is unique on its own.

However, there are many cases where no attribute in a relation is, on its own, unique, and then it is necessary to find some combination of attributes which we can use as a candidate, and indeed primary key. Take, for example, the following relation, BusAllocation, which records each time a bus is allocated to a driver:

BusAllocation (RegistrationNo, DriverNo, Route, Date, Time)

None of these attributes can, individually be unique within this relation (for example, choosing RegistrationNo would mean no bus could be allocated more than once). Obviously buses and drivers each have to be allocated more than once, and there will have to be many bus allocations on any given route or at any given date and time. So we'll need to combine two or more attributes as primary key. How to choose them?

If we choose RegistrationNo with DriverNo

BusAllocation (<u>RegistrationNo, DriverNo,</u> Route, Date, Time)

it will certainly work, and uniquely identify tuples; but the declaration of a primary key imposes a *constraint*. In this case, we'd be saying that any combination of a given bus with a given driver could occur, at most, **once**. That's to say, no driver could be allocated more than once to the same vehicle (which might pose a problem for the bus company!).

Counter-intuitively, the *less* attributes we combine to make a candidate key, the *more* restrictive it becomes. So, to relax the restriction that a driver could only take any given bus out once, we need to add a third attribute. Perhaps

BusAllocation (<u>RegistrationNo, DriverNo, Date</u>, Route, Time)

- this would now allow the driver to take any given bus out many times – but only *once on any given date*. To make it more realistic, we probably need

BusAllocation (<u>RegistrationNo, DriverNo, Date, Time</u>, Route)

2 Representing relationships

I have described how an entity or thing can be represented by a relation, which is able to represent its attributes and their meaning and possible data types and values, and also how each occurrence of the entity is identified.

But recording details of individual, stand-alone entities would not give us a very useful database; an essential part of any information system is the recording of how these entities relate to each other. For example, our *Employee* relation is only part of the database which is needed by our imaginary garage business. They will also need to record the work done, so they may have another relation that looks like this:

Job

RegNo	DateStart	JobDescription	Make	DateEnd	Hours
AQ12CDE	04/01/16	12,000 service	Ford	04/01/16	2.5
AQ12CDE	04/01/16	Front pads & discs	Ford	04/01/16	1.5
MN03TSK	04/01/16	Replace clutch & gbox	VW	05/01/16	6
VD09BVC	05/01/16	Replace exhaust	Renault	05/01/16	0.75
QP11ABC	05/01/16	20,000 service	Ford	05/01/16	3.5
VI14PPK	05/01/16	Timing belt	Citroen	05/01/16	4

Job(<u>RegNo, DateStart, JobDescription</u>, Make, DateEnd, Hours)

Fig 8: the Job relation

Exercise 1: Could we have chosen any other single attribute, or combination of attributes, to be the primary key of *Job*?

But clearly, the firm will need to record which employee carries out each of these jobs, so that they can monitor performance and keep track of how their resources are used. So there must be a *relationship* between Employee and Job.

In the relational model, there is just one way to record relationships between relations: the *foreign key* mechanism.

Here is a formal definition:

A ***foreign key*** is an attribute (or combination of attributes) in a relation, whose values are the same as values of a candidate key (normally the primary key) of some (not necessarily distinct) relation.

The significance of the last few words, about "not necessarily distinct," refer to the possibility of a *recursive* relationship between a relation and itself; I'll come back to that. But for the moment we'll concentrate on this method of representing a relationship by having an attribute which exists in two relations, in (at least) one of which its a candidate key, and which can have the same values in both of them. We can call this the **shared attribute** method.

Continuing the example of the garage database, this is how we would represent the information as to which employee had carried out each job:

Job						
RegNo	DateStart	JobDescription	Make	DateEnd	Hours	Employee
AQ12CDE	04/01/16	12,000 service	Ford	04/01/16	2.5	DQ435721A
AQ12CDE	04/01/16	Front pads & discs	Ford	04/01/16	1.5	DQ435721A
MN03TSK	04/01/16	Replace clutch & gbox	VW	05/01/16	6	UD987234A
VD09BVC	05/01/16	Replace exhaust	Renault			VF219787C
QP11ABC	05/01/16	20,000 service	Ford			
VI14PPK	05/01/16	Timing belt	Citroen			

Job(RegNo, DateStart, JobDescription, Make, DateEnd, Hours, **Employee**)

Fig 9: an extended Job relation

Job now has an additional attribute, *Employee,* which contains some of the same values as *NatInsNo*, the primary key of the *Employee* relation. For each tuple of the *Job* relation, we can now tell which employee carried out that job. We refer to this as the

posted attribute method; we've *posted* the primary key of Employee into Job as an additional attribute, where we declare it to be a foreign key (and I highlight this here by emboldening the name of the attribute).

As our formal definition told us, a foreign key always references a candidate key (usually a primary key), and this is, clearly, because we need to be able to *uniquely identify* the tuple to which it refers.

> **Exercise 2**: Instead of posting NatInsNo into *Job*, could we have represented the same relationship the other way round, i.e. by posting the primary key of *Job* into *Employee?*

a)   *Referential integrity*

Apart from simply representing a relationship, the declaration of a foreign key brings an enormous benefit in terms of guaranteeing data integrity. The formal definition of a foreign key tells us that its values are *the same* as (some of) the values of the candidate key it references. And in fact *they can only ever be the same*. Having declared that *NatInsNo* is a foreign key referencing the primary key of *Employee*, we automatically impose the restriction that whenever we insert a value into that foreign key, it *can only be a* value which already exists in the primary key of *Employee*. In other words, we can only allocate a job to an employee who actually exists and is recorded in our database; we can't make a typo in inputting the National Insurance Number, and we can't allocate a job to someone who's left the firm. (We'll see, shortly, what happens when we want to delete the record of an employee who has, in fact, left the firm.)

Remembering what we said earlier about domains and comparability, and that, in our relational model every attribute must be defined on some domain, it follows that a foreign key must always be defined on the *same domain* as the candidate key it references; otherwise, the system would not be able to compare a foreign key value with those of the candidate key, to ensure that a match existed.

b)   *Degree and participation*

The issue I've started to address, in the solution to Exercise 2, is that of *degree*. All relationships have two properties: degree and participation.

The degree of a relationship can be either

- one-to-many, written as 1:n, or

- one-to-one, written as 1:1, or

- many-to-many, written as m:n

Participation, on the other hand, has only two possibilities: it's either optional or mandatory. That's to say, we need to specify, in each case, whether every tuple of each relation has to be related to a tuple of the other, or whether it can exist without participating in the relationship. So while a relationship has just one degree – one of the above three bulleted possibilities – it will have two participation conditions, one at each end.

The degree of the relationship between *Employee* and *Job* is 1:n – one *Employee* carries out many *Jobs.* And as we saw, we represent that relationship with a foreign key in *Job*, which was the only place it could go. Wherever we place a foreign key, it represents, by default, a relationship of 1:n, with the foreign key at the "n", or *many* end. Equally, like every other attribute in a relation except the primary key, the foreign key can contain nulls unless we constrain it otherwise, so by default it represents an *optional* participation condition. The possibility of having nulls in a foreign key enables us to show that the tuple where it occurs is not involved in the relationship which that foreign key represents.

In Fig. 9, not all of the tuples do, in fact, have values in the foreign key *Employee*, showing that the jobs which they represent have yet to be allocated to an employee. So *Job* has optional participation in the relationship with *Employee*, meaning that jobs can be recorded before they've been allocated.

> **Exercise 3**: If, instead, we wanted *Job* to have mandatory participation in the relationship with *Employee* (meaning that no job could be recorded until it had been allocated to someone), how would we represent that in our model?

It will no doubt also be necessary to allow *Employee* to have optional participation in the relationship, otherwise the garage wouldn't be able to record to details of a new employee until they had completed at least one job. And again, this is the default position. If we need to represent *mandatory* participation at the *referenced* end of a relationship, i.e. at the opposite end to the foreign key, then in the relational model we would need to do so using relational algebra or the relational calculus, neither of which I cover in this book. In Section III, I'll show how to do that in SQL.

Now let us imagine a situation which requires a relationship with a degree of 1:1. The garage also needs to keep a record of its customers, so it will need another relation, *Customer*:

Customer			
Surname	**PostCode**	**Address**	**Phone**
Johnson	BV1 9SW	9 High St	402973
Petty	BV1 9ST	250 High St	407865
Wilson	BV7 0BB	22 The Drive	881545
Simpson	BV3 1AS	32 Forest Row	690513
Newman	BV2 1PO	42 Union St	409111
Ellis	BV3 4RT	12 Windsor Ave	690190

Customer(Surname, PostCode, Address, Phone)

Fig 10: the Customer relation

But some employees, notably the admin and sales staff, are also customers at the garage, and for any work they have done on their vehicles, they are given a discount. So for any customers who are in that category, the firm needs to keep track by recording their employee identifier and their discount level, thus:

Customer					
Surname	**PostCode**	**Address**	**Phone**	**Discount%**	**EmployeeNo**
Johnson	BV1 9SW	9 High St	402973	20	DQ435721A
Petty	BV1 9ST	250 High St	407865		
Wilson	BV7 0BB	22 The Drive	881545		
Simpson	BV3 1AS	32 Forest Row	690513		
Newman	BV2 1PO	42 Union St	409111		
Ellis	BV3 4RT	12 Windsor Ave	690190		

Customer(Surname, PostCode, Address, Phone, Discount%, **EmployeeNo**)

Fig 11: an extended Customer relation

Now, we can establish that necessary relationship between customers and employees, by making the last attribute in *Customer*, i.e. *EmployeeNo*, a foreign key referencing the primary key of Employee. But as we said, *by default* a foreign key declaration establishes a relationship of 1:n, with the foreign key at the "n" end; so in this case, that would mean that several customers could be identified as being the same single employee, which is clearly not right. What we need here, then, is a degree of 1:1: each employee could also be just one customer, and vice versa.

To understand the logic of how we prevent that, and establish the degree of 1:1, look at this version of the *Customer* relation, as it might be if we left the degree as the default 1:n:

Customer					
Surname	PostCode	Address	Phone	Discount %	EmployeeNo
Johnson	BV1 9SW	9 High St	402973	20	DQ435721A
Petty	BV1 9ST	250 High St	407865		
Wilson	BV7 0BB	22 The Drive	881545	20	DQ435721A
Simpson	BV3 1AS	32 Forest Row	690513	20	DQ435721A
Newman	BV2 1PO	42 Union St	409111		
Ellis	BV3 4RT	12 Windsor Ave	690190		

Customer(<u>Surname, PostCode</u>, Address, Phone, Discount%, **EmployeeNo**)

Fig 12: a Customer relation containing incorrect data

As we can see, three customers have all been linked to the same employee. And as a result, we have the same National Insurance Number value appearing three times in the EmployeeNo foreign key. This is perfectly valid so far as the technicalities of the relational model are concerned: except for where specifically prohibited, the values of any given attribute can be duplicated as often as needed. But it doesn't represent the valid situation we need, that a Customer can only be at most one Employee, and vice versa. What we need to do, to make the relationship 1:1, is simply to *create* such a specific prohibition: i.e., in this foreign key attribute *EmployeeNo,* there must be no duplicated values. And the way we do that, is simply to declare that it is an *alternate key* in this relation, and therefore it can contain only unique values, as in the original relation in Fig. 11.

As with the relationship between *Employee* and *Job,* the relationship between *Employee* and *Customer* is also optional at both ends; it clearly isn't necessary for a customer to be an employee, or vice versa.

> **Exercise 4**: Instead of posting the primary key of *Employee* into *Customer* to represent this relationship, could we have done it the other way round, i.e. by posting the primary key of *Customer* into *Employee*?

So now we come to consider the third possible degree of a relationship, m:n or many-to-many. In our earlier version of the *Job* relation (Fig. 9), I showed each employee being able to carry out many jobs, but each job being carried out by just one employee. In fact, this is not at all what the firm requires: many jobs require at least two employees to carry them out. So the relationship needs to be many-to-many, rather than one-to-many. How do we achieve this?

We cannot, in fact, directly represent a m:n relationship with just a simple posted foreign key. The reason for this is the same one which means we always have to put the foreign key at the "n" end of a relationship; i.e., that first property of a relation, that all values must be atomic. With a 1:n relationship, putting the foreign key at the "1" end would mean it having to hold non-atomic values; with a degree of m:n we have the same problem whichever end we put it.

So a different approach is called for: we create an additional new relation, not to represent any actual entity, but just to record instances of the *relationship*. We call this new relation an *intersection relation*. Here is the one we need, to record the relationship between *Employee* and *Job*:

Work_MN			
NatInsNo	**RegNo**	**StartDate**	**Description**
DQ435721A	AQ12CDE	04/01/16	12,000 service
DQ435721A	AQ12CDE	04/01/16	Front pads & discs
UD987234A	MN03TSK	04/01/16	Replace clutch & gbox
FV546890B	MN03TSK	04/01/16	Replace clutch & gbox
VF219787C	VD09BVC	05/01/16	Replace exhaust
QQ525687D	VD09BVC	05/01/16	Replace exhaust

Work_MN (**NatInsNo, RegNo, StartDate, Description**)

Fig 13: the intersection relation Work_MN

We are still recording the fact that each employee carries out many jobs, for example two by DQ435721A, but also that each job can have more than one person working on it, for example UD987234A and FV546890B sharing the gearbox job on MN03TSK.

This new relation exists *only* to record instances of work carried out by an employee on a job, i.e. instances of the relationship between their respective relations. It has no new attributes of its own. It sits between the two relations, with one foreign key referencing each, and in fact it contains *only* the primary key attributes I've placed here as foreign keys: *NatInsNo* referencing Employee, and (*RegNo, StartDate, Description*) referencing *Job.*

And because it only exists to record instances of the relationship, the participation represented by each of its foreign keys is always *mandatory*. We don't need to do anything further to represent that, because both the foreign keys form part of the primary key of this relation, and as we know, no part of a primary key can contain a NULL.

Note that Fig. 13 doesn't contain any tuples relating to the bottom two tuples shown in Fig. 9. This is because those two jobs have yet to be allocated to an employee, and so there is no occurrence of the relationship to be represented.

c)   *Recursive relationships*

The significance, in my formal definition of a foreign key, of the words " some (not necessarily distinct) relation", are that while a foreign key has to reference a candidate key, that candidate key could be an attribute of the same relation, in what we call a *recursive relationship*. This kind of relationship is in fact quite common.

Take, for example, the employees in our garage database. They each need to have a line manager, and that line manager will be an employee of the same company. We represent this by taking the primary key of *Employee*, and posting it into the same relation, as an additional attribute and foreign key, thus:

Employee					
NatInsNo	Surname	Grade	DateJoined	DrivingLicenceNo	Manager
DQ435721A	Johnson	Fitter	04/01/08	JOHNS403196DP9JH	UD987234A
FV546890B	Robinson	Fitter	07/08/12	ROBIN704197PV7TB	UD987234A
QQ525687D	Smith	Apprentice	01/10/15	SMITH910274IB0IV	FV546890B
UD987234A	Wilkins	Chargehand	18/06/10	WILKI711198SS5BE	
VU241367D	Johnson	Receptionist	04/01/08		
VF219787C	Khan	Fitter	09/07/11	KHANA808197CD1AS	UD987234A

Employee (NatInsNo, Surname, Grade, DateJoined, Driving LicenceNo, **Manager**)

Fig 14: a further modified Employee relation.

The new attribute *Manager* now contains values which match those in *NatInsNo*, showing the line manager of the employee concerned. (No managers are shown for either the chargehand or the receptionist; this is just because our sample relation doesn't include all of the *Employee* tuples which the complete system would need to contain, and we can assume that the managers of those two employees are among the tuples which aren't shown.)

d)   Deletions from a referenced relation

As we saw in section 5 above, referential integrity means that any value contained in a foreign key must match some actual value of the candidate key it references.

> **Exercise 5**: Isn't that the same as saying that a foreign key can only contain values which match some actual values of the candidate key it references?

And as we also saw, that prevents us from deleting any tuple which is referenced by a foreign key, because that would break referential integrity and leave us with invalid date.

But in the real world, we do sometimes need to delete data. For example, imagine that employee DQ435721A Johnson leaves the company. Fig. 13 shows that there are two tuples of relation *Work_MN* which reference Johnson's record, so deleting him without taking any other action would leave us with inconsistent data.

To handle this situation, the relational model allows us to define one of four *referential actions* for any foreign key:

RESTRICT: this is the default action when a foreign key is declared – it's simply impossible to delete any tuple referenced by that key. We could, however, first delete the referencing tuples altogether, or set their values to something else, and then delete the desired referenced tuple.

SET NULL: deleting any tuples referenced by the key, will cause all the referencing foreign key values to be set to NULL. This, of course, assumes that the foreign key is allowed to be NULL, and it also requires that such a course would make sense in the context of the database concerned.

SET DEFAULT: a foreign key can, like any other attribute, be defined with a default value, and that would enable us to use this referential action so that, when a referenced tuple was deleted, all the referencing foreign key values would be set to that default value. This requires that such a course would make sense in the context of the database concerned, but another problem is that, since foreign keys can only reference candidate keys, a candidate key would have to exist which matched the default value.

CASCADE: when a referenced tuple is deleted, all tuples containing a foreign key referencing that tuple, would themselves be automatically deleted. Again, it requires that this course of action would make sense.

The table on the next page shows whether or how we could use each of these actions, in our example database where an *Employee* is being referenced by a tuple of *Job* or *Work_MN*, and we need to delete that employee.

How relationship implemented	RESTRICT	SET NULL	SET DEFAULT	CASCADE
1:n using posted foreign key in *Job*	Before deleting the *Employee* tuple we have to do something about the foreign key. Relationship is optional, so we could manually set the foreign key value to NULL, however this results in the *Job* being shown as not carried out. Or we could simply first delete the entire *Job*.	In this case the value of the *Employee* foreign key in *Job* would automatically be set to NULL when we delete the *Employee*, but this means the *Job* is shown as not being carried out.	We would have to have defined a tuple in the *Employee* relation to represent a dummy employee, and then, by using this action, when we deleted the *Employee* tuple, any tuples of *Job* which referenced it would automatically be set to this default value. However, since the default value would have to fit in the domain of the primary key of *Employee*, it would have to look like a valid National Insurance Number, which would be confusing on any direct reading of the data; we might need an application program to automatically translate this default value for the end user, into some message such as "former employee"	Using this action, all tuples of *Job* which referenced the deleted employee, would themselves be completely deleted. Not ideal because we would then have no record of those jobs.
m:n with foreign key in intersection relation *Work_MN*	Before deleting the *Employee* tuple we have to do something about the foreign key. In this case its part of the primary key of *Work_MN*, so it could not be set to NULL. Or we could set it to a default value, but see comments on SET DEFAULT. Or we could delete the entire *Work_MN* tuple; if the job concerned had been carried out by this one employee then it would end up being shown as not performed; if it had been shared by one or more others then they would end up being shown as the only workers concerned.	Not possible; the foreign key is part of the primary key of *Work_MN*.	We would have to have defined a tuple in the *Employee* relation to represent a dummy employee, and then, by using this action, when we deleted the *Employee* tuple, any tuples of *Work_MN* which referenced it would automatically be set to this default value. However, since the default value would have to fit in the domain of the primary key of *Employee*, it would have to look like a valid National Insurance Number, which would be confusing on any direct reading of the data; we might need an application program to automatically translate this default value for the end user into some message such as "former employee"	Using this action, all tuples of *Work_MN* which referenced the deleted employee, would themselves be completely deleted. If the job concerned had been carried out by this one employee then it would end up being shown as not performed; if it had been shared by one or more others then they would end up being shown as the only workers concerned.

Table 1: the effects of the referential actions

3   A relational schema

Let us now pull together what we've said so far about the definition of our relations, and show how we might put all of it together in a single schema, showing all the attributes and their domains, and all of the foreign key, alternate key and not null constraints.

Schema GARAGE

Domains

      NatInsNos = AA000000A .. ZZ999999Z

      Names = string

      Grades = (Fitter, Apprentice, Chargehand, Receptionist)

      Dates = Date

      DLNos = AAAAA000000AA0AA .. ZZZZZ999999ZZ9ZZ

      PostCodes = string

      Addresses = string

      PhoneNos = string

      Discounts = 0 .. 50

      RegNos = AA00AAA .. ZZ99ZZZ

      Descriptions = string

relation Employee

      NatInsNo: NatInsNos

      Surname: Names

      Grade: Grades

      DateJoined: Dates

      DrivingLicenceNo: DLNos

      Manager: NatInsNos

      Primary key NatInsNo

      Foreign key Manager **references** Employee

relation Customer

      Surname: Names

      PostCode: PostCodes

      Address: Addresses

      Phone: PhoneNos

      Discount: Discounts

      EmployeeNo: NatInsNos

Primary key (Surname, PostCode)
Alternate key EmployeeNo
Foreign key EmployeeNo **references** Employee

relation Job

RegNo: RegNos
DateStart: Dates
JobDescription: Descriptions
Make: Makes
DateEnd: Dates
Hours: Hours
Primary key (RegNo, DateStart, JobDescription)

relation Work_MN

NatInsNo: NatInsNos
RegNo: RegNos
StartDate: StartDates
Description: Descriptions
Primary key (NatInsNo, RegNo, StartDate, Description)
Foreign key NatInsNo **references** Employee
Foreign key (RegNo, StartDate, Description) **references** Job

Fig. 15: a relational schema for the Garage database

4   Relation-for-relationship, and some issues around NULL

One of the main reasons that Chris Date, and others, have had such a problem with null, is that it causes considerable problems with logical and arithmetical manipulation. We'll take a look at this in Chapter 12, where I discuss how it's handled by SQL.

But the other reason is that its meaning can be ambiguous. Does it mean that the attribute concerned is not applicable, or that the value is just (for the moment, perhaps) unknown?

For example, in Fig. 9, one Job has been allocated to an employee, but there is no value (i.e. null) for the date on which it was completed. Does this mean it is are still ongoing, or just that we have yet to get around to entering the date? And in that same relation, there are two other jobs which apparently have a start date but no employee shown: again, does this mean they haven't really been started yet, or that we just haven't got around to entering details of the employee carrying out the work?

In the first case (the apparently uncompleted job), a simple solution would be to create some default value for DateCompleted which indicates that the job is ongoing. However, because in this case *Employee* is a foreign key, we need a different approach; and it is an issue only for optional relationships.

To avoid the occurrence of nulls where a foreign key would represent an optional relationship, we can use an additional relation instead of a posted foreign key. Notice that this is what we've already done, in Fig. 13, where we decided that the relationship between *Job* and *Employee* was really m:n; i.e., an *Employee* can work on many *Jobs*, and a *Job* can be carried out by many *Employees*. And so we used the additional intersection relation *Work_MN* to represent it. In that case, it was simply because in the relational model, remember, it is the only way to represent a relationship of m:n. Having done so, the issue of a foreign key containing nulls doesn't arise, even though the relationship may be optional. If a given employee has never worked on any job, or (more likely) if a job had yet to be allocated anyone to work on it, there simply won't be any tuples of the intersection relation linking to them.

But with a degree of 1:n (Fig. 9) or 1:1 (Fig. 11), we've so far only shown the optional relationships being represented by a posted foreign key; and as a consequence, we can see that in both cases, the foreign key attributes contains nulls.

So here, first, is a relation to represent the relationship between *Customer* and *Employee*:

CustomerEmployee			
Surname	**PostCode**	**Discount%**	**EmployeeNo**
Johnson	BV1 9SW	20	DQ435721A

Customer(Surname, PostCode, Discount, EmployeeNo)

Fig 16: an intersection relation to represent the Customer – Employee relationship

It's important to note the choice of primary key here. The attributes (Surname, PostCode) and EmployeeNo will be declared as foreign keys referencing, respectively, *Customer* and *Employee*. This far, that is similar to what we did with the m:n intersection relation, *Work_MN*.

But with *Work_MN,* we combined the two foreign keys to form the primary key of the new relation. Remember, a combination of attributes in a primary key only enforces the uniqueness of *any combination* of values across all those attributes; each of the attributes can still, individually, contain values which are repeated many times. So, in *Work_MN,* each of those two foreign keys could contain repeated values, so they each represented the "n" end of a 1:n relationship; so overall, the new relation gave us a degree of m:n.

The Customer – Employee relationship, however, is 1:1, so we don't want *either* of the foreign keys in the intersection relation to be able to contain duplicate values. So, in Fig 16, we've declared the primary key to be (Surname, PostCode), i.e., the foreign key referencing *Customer.* So the new relation has a 1:n relationship with *Customer.* The other half of the puzzle is to make the attribute EmployeeNo an *alternate key* – so then, the new relation will also have a 1:1 relationship with *Employee* – and overall we have the 1:1 relationship we want.

There's one further thing to do. An intersection relation can, itself, only have mandatory relationships, whatever the participation conditions of the relationship is used to represent. It exists only to record instances of the relationship and it would make no sense to have, for example, an occurrence of the CustomerEmployee relation which was linked to a *Customer* but not to any *Employee.* The (Surname, PostCode) side is taken care of: its the primary key and so cannot be NULL. But in the relational schema, we will need to explicitly declare that the EmployeeNo attribute is itself not allowed to be null.

In fact, in this symmetric 1:1 scenario, we could equally well have chosen to use just the Employee attribute (i.e. the foreign key referencing *Employee*) as the primary key of the intersection relation. We would then have made (Surname, PostCode) an alternate key, and have explicitly declared it not null. Everything works just as well that way round.

The solution is, however, slightly less easy to understand if we come to use the relation-for-relationship method to represent a 1:n relationship, such as that between *Job* and *Employee* depicted in Fig. 9. With that asymmetric degree, there is no choice about the primary key.

Work_1N			
NatInsNo	RegNo	StartDate	Description
DQ435721A	AQ12CDE	04/01/16	12,000 service
DQ435721A	AQ12CDE	04/01/16	Front pads & discs
UD987234A	MN03TSK	04/01/16	Replace clutch & gbox
FV546890B	MN03TSK	04/01/16	Replace clutch & gbox
VF219787C	VD09BVC	05/01/16	Replace exhaust

*Work_1N (**RegNo, StartDate, Description,** NatInsNo)*

Fig 17: the intersection relation Work_1N

When we use an intersection relation to represent a 1:n relationship, the primary key has to be the foreign key referencing the relation (in this case *Job*) which was on the "n" side of the original relationship, because we need to ensure that values of that foreign key attribute cannot be duplicated. This is perhaps counter-intuitive: we are thus creating a 1:1 relationship between our intersection relation and the relation which was originally "n". However, thinking it through makes it clearer. We leave the foreign key attribute NatInsNo, referencing *Employee*, as the default duplicates-allowed (as in Fig 17 above); so this means that each employee can be related to many occurrences of *Work_1N*, each of which is, in turn, related to exactly one occurrence of *Job*; giving us our original overall degree of 1:n.

What we do share with the 1:1 situation, is that we still have to declare the non-primary key foreign key (in this case NatInsNo) as not allowed null, in order to maintain the all-mandatory-participation required for an intersection relation.

The **benefits** of this relation-for-relationship method are:

- it avoids using nulls

- it treats all relationships in the same way, i.e. they are all represented by a relation rather than m:n with a relation and others with a posted key, and so

- it makes the schema easier to read.

As we will see, however, it also makes the schema more complex.

5   A relational schema using relation-for-relationship

Here now is a revised version of Fig. 15, using the method described in section 10 above:

Schema GARAGE

Domains

      NatInsNos = AA000000A .. ZZ9999999Z
      Names = string
      Grades = (Fitter, Apprentice, Chargehand, Receptionist)
      Dates = Date
      DLNos = AAAAA000000AA0AA .. ZZZZZ999999ZZ9ZZ
      PostCodes = string
      Addresses = string
      PhoneNos = string
      Discounts = 0 .. 50
      RegNos = AA00AAA .. ZZ99ZZZ
      Descriptions = string
      Makes = string
      Hours = 00.0

relation Employee

      NatInsNo: NatInsNos
      Surname: Names
      Grade: Grades
      DateJoined: Dates
      DrivingLicenceNo: DLNos
      Manager: NatInsNos
      Primary key NatInsNo

relation ManagedBy

      NatInsNo: NatInsNos **not allowed null**
      Manager: NatInsNos
      Primary key (Manager)
      Foreign key NatInsNo **references** Employee
      Foreign key Manager **references** Employee

*relation **Customer***

> Surname: Names
> PostCode: PostCodes
> Address: Addresses
> Phone: PhoneNos
> Discount: Discounts
> EmployeeNo: NatInsNos
> **Primary key** (Surname, PostCode)

*relation **CustomerIsEmployee***

> Surname: Names
> PostCode: PostCodes
> NatInsNo: NatInsNos **not allowed null**
> **Primary key** (Surname, PostCode)
> **Alternate key** NatInsNo
> **Foreign key** (Surname, PostCode) **references** Customer
> **Foreign key** NatInsNo **references** Employee

*relation **Job***

> RegNo: RegNos
> DateStart: Dates
> JobDescription: Descriptions
> Make: Makes
> DateEnd: Dates
> Hours: Hours
> **Primary key** (RegNo, DateStart, JobDescription)

*relation **Work_MN***

> NatInsNo: NatInsNos
> RegNo: RegNos
> StartDate: Dates
> Description: Descriptions
> **Primary key** (NatInsNo, RegNo, StartDate, Description)
> **Foreign key** NatInsNo **references** Employee
> **Foreign key** (RegNo, StartDate, Description) **references** Job

Fig. 18: a relational schema for the Garage database using relation-for-relationship

Chapter 6: Codd's eight functions of a dbms

Codd (1982) summarised the functions which he thought a "full-scale dbms should provide." (Codd was here concerned entirely with relational systems; but we may consider that these rules should apply equally to any kind of self-respecting database system.)

- data storage, retrieval, and update;

- a user-accessible catalogue for data description;

- transaction support to ensure that all or none of a sequence of database changes are reflected in the pertinent databases ;

- recovery services in case of failure (system, media, or program);

- concurrency control services to ensure that concurrent transactions behave the same way as if run in some sequential order;

- authorisation services to ensure that all access to and manipulation of data be in accordance with specified constraints on users and programs ;

- integration with support for data communication;

- integrity services to ensure that database states and changes of state conform to specified rules.

To these we can add three further functions which would today be taken for granted:

- restructuring, or the ability to change the logical structure (Navathe & Fry 1979)

- re-organisation, or the ability to change the physical structure (Yao, Das & Teorey 1976), and

- data manipulation

All of these are features which enable a user to *define*, in each case, the required functionality, which will then be implemented automatically by the dbms.

The first of the 11 is self-explanatory, but we may consider the other ten in more detail.

A user-accessible catalogue for data description

The most important aspect of having the dbms contain the definitions of all the data structures, is that it will avoid the worst of the problems of file-based systems which we looked at in Chapter 3; that is, the need for every user (human or program) to hold its own copy of those definitions, in order to be able to make any use of the data, and the resultant need to change all those copies of the definitions whenever the definitions change. So in this respect, the catalogue for data description performs part of the function of the *logical schema*, which we discussed in Chapter 4.

As we saw there, logical data independence in the three schema architecture relies upon the logical schema being hidden from users through the use of external schemas. In using the words "user-accessible catalog," Codd is not advocating that the whole thing should be thrown open; rather that a series of what we nowadays call *system tables* should automatically record the structure of all the data, without the need to examine each relation or table individually. In other words, this is the function of *data definition*, which gives us *logical data independence*.

In Chapter 5, we saw how the relational model enables such a central data definition to give access to required data items without any need to know where or how they are stored. As Codd explained (Codd 1982), it relies on replacing the positional addressing which was necessary in the file-based approach, by totally associative addressing.

The SQL data definition language provides the mechanisms for defining the structure of the actual data containers, or tables, much along the lines of the relational schemas shown in Chapter 5; and in Chapter 12 we will look at how it does that. It does not, however, fully define Codd's "user-accessible catalog," or meta-structure, to provide a dictionary of data definitions; it is left to individual SQL implementations to do that, through what are variously called the Data Dictionary, Directory, System Tables, or, in the case of Codd's original IBM RM system (Codd 1990), unsurprisingly, the Catalog.

Transaction support

To simplify Codd's language a little, we may say

A **transaction** is a series of operations which either fails completely or succeeds completely.

What we need is for the dbms to allow us to *define* some series of operations in just that way. A complete success of all the operations is, of course, what we desire, but our second preference will be just that the whole thing fails cleanly, leaving the database in its unaltered state prior to our attempt at changing it.

Take, for example, a simple operation in internet banking, such as transferring a sum of money from a savings account to a chequeing account. This will consist of a debit from the first account, and a credit of the same sum to the second. Depending on whether we are the customer or the bank, we might well be quite happy for one of these two operations to succeed and the other to fail; but in the interests of a successful banking system it's probably best if the two are defined as a transaction!

But a transaction could be much larger than that simple example; in fact (subject to any physical limitations of the host system) there should be no limit to the number of individual operations which could be defined as a transaction. So this could include a major restructuring of the database, say, or the loading of a large volume of back data from an external source, while the database is off line overnight. Such large sequential operations carry the risk of failure at some intermediate point, leaving the database in an uncertain or unusable state, requiring it to be restored to some previously backed up point with consequent loss of service and loss of data. Without transaction support in the dbms, the only way we can ensure that this doesn't happen is by laboriously coding checkpoints into the program code; something which, in the days of file-based systems, wasn't always assiduously done, often resulting in unwelcome news when the staff returned to work the following morning.

In Chapter 17 we'll see how SQL implements this facility through the COMMIT and ROLLBACK commands.

Recovery services

This function enables the organisation to determine, effectively, the amount of data it can afford to lose in the event of a system failure, and to configure the dbms so that it will ensure that no more than that would ever be lost. Obviously, in an ideal world we'd never lose any data at all, but the problem here is that this kind of security always comes at a cost.

In a stand-alone system, recovery requires that we take complete copies of the database at some pre-determined interval. We may want to keep more than one, and store them at a separate location, in case these back-up copies fail, as well as the operational system itself. We may even want to keep records of every *transaction* applied to the database since the last copy was taken (a process known as *journalling)*, so that, as well as re-installing the last complete backup, we can re-apply to it all the more recent (completed) transactions, so that the system is virtually back where it was at the instant the failure occurred.

However, the process of taking backup copies, and indeed of journalling, takes processing effort and may reduce availability, and of course the resultant copies take up storage space. This is the reason why each organisation needs to balance just how much data it can, in the worst case, afford to lose, against the money and resource costs of each step towards increased security.

All modern dbm systems provide recovery facilities. However, the recovery facility is entirely concerned with the safety of the physical data store, and as such it relates, in the three schema architecture, to the storage schema. As SQL doesn't provide facilities for storage schema definition or manipulation (it's left to each rdbms implementation to provide its own), I don't cover the configuration of recovery in this book.

Concurrency Control

When I talk of concurrent access, in this context, I am essentially talking about data updating, and not simply data retrieval. Allowing multiple users to *read* the same data simultaneously is really only a matter of providing suitable hardware. Allowing them to *change* the *same* data *at the same time* is far more problematic, and we certainly do need to be able to manage a situation where such a requirement seems to exist.

Take, for example, an office where an organisation's client data is maintained by a number of employees. One of these employees opens the morning's mail, and finds a notification of the change of address of a client. He opens that client's database record, and starts typing in the new address. Meanwhile, another employee picks up a telephone call from that same client, notifying the number of his new phone, which has just been connected. So she, too, opens the same client record (which at this point still contains the old address), and types in the new phone number. Typing done, both employees try to save their copies of the record. What is the result?

a) old address, new phone number

b) new address, old phone number, or

c) both updates fail

It's a good question! Having concurrency services in the dbms will allow such updates to be written to the database only (in Codds words) "as if run in some sequential order" - where that order is chosen by the dba. In Chapter 17, we'll see how a SQL enables that choice to be made, using the ISOLATION LEVEL feature.

Authorisation

As we saw earlier, this book assumes that a database is a shared resource; ideally a single copy, shared by the entire organisation to which it belongs, so that we avoid all the problems of inconsistency which arise from holding multiple copies of the same data.

As we also saw in Chapter 3, the problem with that idea is the very one which, in the past often led to those multiple copies being kept: simply that the organisation probably doesn't want everyone who has access to the data to have access to *all* of the data. So the dbms needs to provide a facility for defining and identifying users, and for restricting or permitting their respective levels of access. And SQL does so, through the GRANT and associated commands, and also through the CREATE VIEW statement, which I cover in Chapters 14 & 15.

Integration with support for data communication

It is interesting that Codd included this function, at a time when he could surely only have been thinking in terms of the limited data communications available within the proprietary computing environment I described in Chapter 2. However, even within that limited world, a database system would have been of little use if it could only have been accessed interactively through a terminal on the machine where it resided; at the very least it would need to be open to communications from remote user terminals and from application programs.

SQL does not define these necessary communication methods, but today a plethora of them is available, ranging from the basic ODBC (Open Database Connect) drivers provided with every implementation, through various middleware to more modern ways of connecting applications such as JDBC and SQLJ (see Chapter 20).

Integrity services

Imagine the database of a railway operating company. It stores details of all the employees, from cleaners to directors, and of all their locomotives, rolling stock, and train operations. In the case of locomotive drivers, it records the types of locomotives they're qualified to drive, those to which they've actually been allocated, and the identities of their line managers. Maintaining the integrity of the database would require that:

a) wherever a driver is shown as having a line manager, both employees actually exist (i.e. haven't quit or been fired, or had their identities mis-typed), and are each of the correct grade to be in that relationship with each other, and

b) wherever a driver is allocated to drive a locomotive, they, too both exist, and also the driver is qualified to drive that locomotive;

and that this integrity would be maintained whenever any change was made to the data.

In that old file-based world, we'd either have had to laboriously code all those conditions into all of the application programs that could apply changes to the data – or bear the unfortunate consequences. In the world of the dbms, we want to be able to define those conditions once, in each case, for the entire database, and let the system do the rest for us, automatically.

SQL supports integrity services through a wide range of commands for defining integrity constraints, including CHECK constraints, triggers, definable functions and procedures, as well as the definition of primary, alternate and foreign keys, which mirror the way those keys are provided in the relational model.

Restructuring

The single central data definition is held in Codd's "user-accessible catalogue for data description," or in terms of the three-schema architecture, in the logical schema, and we are thinking here in terms of the logical data structure. We want this definition to be able to change as requirements evolve, as in the example I gave in Chapter 3 above, where we needed 5 places instead of 4, to store all the employee numbers. These changes to the logical definition almost always arise as a result of *changes to the data requirement*.

In order to facilitate such changes, while at the same time maintaining data independence, users should still be able to access their data items through the same associative addressing. And for *that* to happen, we need to be able to change the definitions from *within* the dbms; hence the need for the dbms to have this restructuring function.

In Chapter 12, we'll see how SQL provides this functionality through a number of commands including CREATE, CREATE . . INSERT, DROP, and ALTER TABLE.

Re-organisation

While restructuring is a question of changes to the logical definition of the data, re-organisation concerns changes to its *physical* definition, and so, in terms of the three-schema architecture, is an activity which would take place within the storage schema. For example, we will need to add or maintain an index on a given data item, or move files to a different disk structure, or even to a different computer on a network. This kind of change is almost always undertaken in order to *improve performance*.

This kind of facility is essential to any fully formed dbms, but because SQL does not provide any equivalent of the storage schema, it is left to each individual rdbms implementation to arrange it in its own way, as with the recovery facility. For that reason, I don't address it in this book.

Data manipulation

With the information systems which preceded the relational dbms, getting any answers out of a database required that either an application program had already been written, to access the data and return the required answers, or that a new program be written to ask a specific new question (known as an "ad hoc query"). Such work was not lightly undertaken and many IT departments were decorated with this famous period cartoon.

YOU WANT IT WHEN ?!

Later developments, in particular the development of the IBM RM system (Codd 1990), led to the appearance of what we now take for granted: a specific, near-common-language query facility, able to formulate and execute *any* valid query of the data. And in terms of an rdbms, we are of course thinking of the SQL data manipulation language (DML), which we will look at in Chapter 9.

Section III:
Real world relational database management systems

The only real world dbms implementations of the relational model use the SQL (Structured Query Language) data definition and data manipulation languages (DDL and DML). In this section, I start by comparing SQL with the relational model, and with the three schema architecture. Then, from Chapter 9 onwards, I will show you how to use the SQL query facilities, how to analyse a data requirement and then to use it to create a new database.

You should now refer to Appendix 4, and install SQL Anywhere and the Garage database, which you will need in order to carry out the practical work in this section.

Chapter 7: SQL and the relational model

There has been a series of ANSI standards which define SQL. All current commercial implementations comply, to a greater or lesser extent, with these standards; the implementations differ from each other both in the standard features they leave out, and in the non-standard ones they include. The standards were initially created after various manufacturers had already created their own implementations, and so they support several different ways of doing things; for example, the DDL allows three different kinds of syntax for defining a foreign key. In addition, the manufacturers try to improve and add to their products in order to gain competitive edge, so that each implementation tends to contain features which are not (or not yet) part of the standards.

Even the SQL standards themselves do not fully implement the relational model, although they go a long way towards doing so. The following table gives a comparison.

Relational model	SQL
Entities are represented by relations, consisting of tuples and attributes	Entities are represented by tables, consisting of rows and columns
Each relation has a name, unique within the schema	Each table has a name, unique within the schema*
Each tuple represents an occurrence of the entity and is unique within its relation	Each row represents an occurrence of the entity. A table can contain duplicate rows
Each attribute represents an attribute of the entity and has a name which is unique within the relation	Each column represents an attribute of the entity and has a name which is unique within the table
The ordering of tuples and attributes is not significant	The ordering of rows and columns is not significant
Every value in the relation is atomic	Every value in a table is atomic
The values within each attribute are all of the same kind (in that they must share the same meaning as well as data type)	The values within each column are all of the same kind (in that they must share only the same data type)
Domains must exist which specify (at least) a data type, and optionally a range or set of values, for all attributes defined on them. Every attribute must be defined on some domain	Domains which specify (at least) a data type, and optionally a range or set of values, may exist. Where they do exist, columns can be defined on them, but this is also optional.

Relational model	SQL
Every relation has exactly one primary key, comprised of one attribute or a combination of two or more attributes. It cannot contain any nulls, and can contain only a value (or combination of values) unique within that primary key	A table does not require a primary key but cannot have more than one. Where the key exists, it will be comprised of one column or a combination of two or more columns. It cannot contain any nulls and can contain only a value (or combination of values) unique within that primary key
In addition to the primary key, one or more alternate keys can be defined in a relation, each consisting of one attribute or a combination of attributes. They may contain nulls but any values (or combinations of values) they contain must be unique within each alternate key.	In addition to the primary key, one or more unique indices can be defined in a relation, each consisting of one column or a combination of columns. They may contain nulls but any values (or combinations of values) they contain must be unique within each index.
By default, every attribute of every tuple may contain nulls, but this is prevented either by defining an attribute as part of the primary key of the relation, or by a specific "not null" declaration	By default, every column of every row may contain nulls, but this is prevented either by defining an attribute as part of a primary key of the table, or by a specific "not null" declaration
Relationships between two relations A and B are represented by declaring an attribute (or combination of attributes) of relation A, defined on the same domain(s) as the primary or alternate key of relation B, to be a foreign key in relation A referencing relation B	Relationships between two tables A and B are represented by declaring a column (or combination of columns) of table A, defined on the same or compatible data type(s) as the primary or alternate key of table B, to be a foreign key in table A referencing table B

Table 2: a comparison of the relational model with SQL

* (NOTE: SQL allows for each user of a database to have their own set of tables, or **user schema**, and the names of tables only need to be unique to each user schema; I will discuss this further in Chapter 14.)

Chapter 8: SQL and the 3-schema architecture

You'll recall that the ANSI-SPARC 3-schema architecture provides logical and physical data independence. SQL only partly supports that architecture.

1   The logical schema

In the 3-schema architecture, the central data definition is contained in the logical schema. This is largely represented, in an SQL database, by the *database schema*. This contains two kinds of tables: *user tables*, which contain the actual data, and *system tables*, which contain the necessary information on how the data is structured and accessed, such as the properties of each user table, rights of ownership and access, and display characteristics.

2   The external schema

Logical data independence is provided, in the 3-schema architecture, by the external schemas, which map to data items in the logical schema. Users have no access to the logical schema, and therefore can access data items only through an external schema. Because mappings from the external schemas to the logical schema remain consistent when changes are made to the logical schema, or can be changed so as to maintain consistency, users can be protected from the effects of those changes.

SQL does not provide an external schema as such. Users can be given direct access to the data tables (known as *base tables*). They will not be affected by changes to the tables so long as the data items they themselves use retain the same names and data types, but if those things change there is no facility to re-map, and user programs would have to be changed.

SQL does, however, provide for the definition of *views*. Views have the same format as a base table and can be queried in exactly the same way as a base table; indeed, in SQL, the term "table" can refer to either a view or a base table. But views do not contain any data; they map to one or more tables, and are only called into existence when they themselves are queried.

So views can provide a kind of external schema, but their use is entirely optional. It would be possible to create a database in which views were created for all users, with users only being given access to those views; this would effectively give the same data independence benefits as the external schema in the 3-schema architecture. However, as we will see in Chapter 15, the creation of views brings an administrative overhead, and views can be problematic when it comes to updating data.

3   The storage schema

In the 3-schema architecture, physical data independence is assured by the storage schema, which is the only interface between the physically stored data and the rest of the dbms, and therefore the only part which needs to know anything about where the data items physically exist. Consequently, it would be possible to move the physical data around and re-organise it, without any effect on any users.

SQL does not, however, provide the facility to define a storage schema. But however much the database approach frees us from the file-based need for every user to know the physical location of every data item, it's still necessary to somehow link the data items which are logically defined in the database schema, with their actual physical existence. Since SQL doesn't cover it, how this is done is left to each implementation. In many cases suppliers provide commands for defining storage which look very much like SQL operators.

The way it's done varies widely, and for that reason this book does not cover the details of how individual implementations do it. I will however look briefly here at the available methods and their possible advantages and disadvantages.

As I mentioned when talking about the file-based approach, data is ultimately stored in files, controlled by the computer's operating system, and normally stored on hard disks. Within the disks, data is stored in the form of blocks of a fixed size, e.g. 4 kilobytes, and the dbms stores and retrieves data in the form of these numbered blocks. It also stores additional information to enable it to link the rows of a table with the block(s) where they are stored.

At the most primitive level, disk operations are carried out by the operating system's *disk manager*, which knows the physical disk address of each numbered block. Higher level operations are carried out by the *file manager*, which is concerned with the location of rows within a block or blocks. It knows the number of each block, and organises data within blocks, but for the physical location of the blocks it relies on the disk manager.

In many cases, dbms implementations simply use the file manager provided by the underlying operating system, to manage the internal structure of the files. While this has the probable advantage of making the best use of the operating system design, it limits the storage options available.

An alternative approach is for the dbms to provide its own file manager, so as to build its own storage and retrieval capabilities.

These differences naturally affect the storage choices which are available, and should be taken into consideration when choosing a dbms, since different kinds of file organisation have implications for storage and retrieval operations. In the simplest examples, the only real choice will be the ability to define indexes on columns.

The differences also have implications when it comes to transferring data from one database to another. As long as the transfer involves two databases with the same dbms, the transfer is fairly straightforward, from one table direct to another. But if there are two different kinds of system, it will be necessary to use the first system's *export* facility, to write the data out to a flat file with some commonly understood format such as .csv, and then to use the second system's *import* facility (see Chapter 19).

Chapter 9: The SQL data manipulation language (DML)

At the start of this Section, I briefly described how the first SQL standards were developed at a time when dbms suppliers were already each producing relational database management systems of their own.

The first international standard for SQL was published by the American National Standards Institution (ANSI) in 1987, and is referred to as SQL:1987. In order to allow as many as possible of the existing implementations to conform to it, it could include only their very basic core elements; hence, for example, it does not include even primary and foreign key constraints.

A revision, referred to as SQL:1989, was published in 1989, which specified the constraint definitions that could be used; this was a new development which was subsequently included in most implementations.

In 1992 a new version, referred to as SQL:1992, was published, which included domains and many other new capabilities.

A major new version, SQL:1999, included a number of entirely new features, including triggers, which I cover in Section 4(h) of Chapter 12, but also such things as structured types and binary objects, which go entirely beyond the scope of the relational model. I cover some of these latter features in the final chapters of this book.

In this chapter I cover all the basic facilities of the SQL DML, and by the time you have successfully completed the practical activities you will be able to:

- use SQL to retrieve data from a database,

- update a database, and

- describe the processing model for a given SQL statement,

To demonstrate the use of the DML, I have created an SQL database called *garage*, which is as far as possible an implementation of the relational schema of the same name in Figure 15 of Chapter 5. Refer to Appendix 4 for a guide to installing this database and running the practical exercises with it.

Note that the format of some results you get from my prepared SQL queries, particularly date and time values, may vary from that of those on the page, generally because of the default settings in your system.

1 Simple SQL queries for retrieval

The five most commonly used SQL retrieval operators are

```
SELECT {column name(s)}
FROM {table name(s)}
        WHERE {search condition}
              GROUP BY {grouping column(s)}
              HAVING {search condition}
```

As a minimum, a query must include a SELECT and a FROM clause. WHERE and GROUP BY are optional, and a HAVING clause can only be used when preceded by a GROUP BY. But the syntax requires that the clauses, where present, are used in the order shown above.

a)   SELECT and FROM

Open Interactive SQL. Complete both the *User ID* and *Password* as dba. Under Action, select "Start and connect to a database on this computer." Press the *Browse* button alongside the "Database file" box, navigate to where you stored the *garage* database file (it will be called *garage.db*), press *Open*, and then press *Connect*.

For Interactive SQL operations, you can either type the query into the upper box (headed *SQL Statements*) and press the Execute button (the black triangle in the toolbar), or you can select *File – Open* , navigate to your SQLPackage folder, select the query in question (in this case *query1.sql*) and press *Open*, and then press the Execute button.

Either way, execute the following query:

```
SELECT * FROM employee;
```
[1]

Where a * is used for the column list, as above, all columns in the named table(s) are produced; so in this case, we get the complete contents of the Employee table, thus:

---

[1] the termination character (which by default is the semi-colon ;) must be added to the end of any command in a script, but can in fact be omitted for single commands within Interactive SQL

nat_ins_no	surname	grade	date_joined	dl_no	manager
UD987234A	Wilkins	Chargehand	2010-06-18	WILKI711198SS5BE	(NULL)
DQ435721A	Johnson	Fitter	2008-01-04	JOHNS403196DP9JH	UD987234A
FV546890B	Robinson	Fitter	2012-08-07	ROBIN704197PV7TB	UD987234A
QQ525687D	Smith	Apprentice	2015-10-01	SMITH910274IB0IV	FV546890B
VF219787C	Khan	Fitter	2011-07-09	KHANA808197CD1AS	UD987234A
VU241367D	Johnson	Receptionist	2008-04-01	(NULL)	(NULL)

Query 1: `select *`

However, instead of using *, we can specify any subset of the columns in the named tables by listing their names e.g.

```
SELECT surname, dl_no FROM employee;
```

surname	dl_no
Wilkins	WILKI711198SS5BE
Johnson	JOHNS403196DP9JH
Robinson	ROBIN704197PV7TB
Smith	SMITH910274IB0IV
Khan	KHANA808197CD1AS
Johnson	(NULL)

Query 2: select {column_names}

Notice that the primary key column of Employee is missing; this is allowed; as I mentioned in Chapter 7, an SQL table does not need to contain a primary key. As a result, an SQL table can contain duplicate rows, as in the table resulting from the query:

```
SELECT reg_no
FROM work_mn;
```

reg_no
AQ12CDE
AQ12CDE
MN03TSK
MN03TSK
VD09BVC
VD09BVC

Query 3: select from

However, duplicate column values can be avoided by adding the DISTINCT operator to the SELECT clause, thus:

```
SELECT DISTINCT reg_no
FROM work_mn;
```

reg_no
AQ12CDE
MN03TSK
VD09BVC

Query 4: select distinct

Exercise 6: In English, what request is answered by the above query?

b)   The WHERE clause

The addition of a WHERE clause enables us to search for specific rows:

```
SELECT surname, dl_no FROM employee
WHERE surname = 'Johnson';
```

(The SQL standard requires that, in a query, a text value must be enclosed in quotation marks, as shown above; however, many implementations will process a query correctly without them.)

68

surname	dl_no
Johnson	JOHNS403196DP9JH
Johnson	(NULL)

Query 5: select from where

c)   *Queries using NULL*

What if we need, in a query, to test for whether a column contains a NULL? Since NULL is not a value, we cannot say

> WHERE dl_no = NULL (or, for that matter, <> NULL)

Instead, SQL provides us with the logical operators IS NULL and IS NOT NULL.

So, for example, if we wanted to list the employees who have driving licences, we would use the query

```
SELECT surname FROM employee
WHERE dl_no IS NOT NULL;
```

surname
Wilkins
Smith
Robinson
Khan
Johnson

Query 6: query using NULL

d)   *Value expressions, data types and built-in functions*

SQL also enables us to manipulate the raw data retrieved with a query, by including functions or value expressions in the SELECT clause:

```
SELECT surname,grade,YEAR(date_joined)
FROM employee
```

surname	grade	YEAR(employee.date_joined)
Wilkins	Chargehand	2010
Johnson	Fitter	2008
Robinson	Fitter	2012
Smith	Apprentice	2015
Khan	Fitter	2011
Johnson	Receptionist	2008

Query 7: select *function*

YEAR is a built-in SQL function which extracts the year from a date value (similarly *DAY* and *MONTH* are available). We can also re-name the output columns within a SELECT clause, to make them more clearly understood, using the AS operator:

```
SELECT surname,grade,YEAR(date_joined) AS
'Year joined'
FROM employee;
```

surname	grade	Year joined
Wilkins	Chargehand	2010
Johnson	Fitter	2008
Robinson	Fitter	2012
Smith	Apprentice	2015
Khan	Fitter	2011
Johnson	Receptionist	2008

Query 8: re-naming a column

And the arithmetical operators (+ - * and /) allow us to do such things as, for example, calculate an employee's length of completed service up to 2018:

```
SELECT surname,grade,2018-YEAR(date_joined) AS
"Years of service"
FROM employee;
```

surname	grade	Years of service
Wilkins	Chargehand	8
Johnson	Fitter	6
Robinson	Fitter	10
Smith	Apprentice	3
Khan	Fitter	7
Johnson	Receptionist	10

Query 9: using arithmetic

The data type of each column determines which operators and functions can be used. The YEAR function, for example, can only work here because the *date_joined* column of the Employee table is defined as a DATE type. And the subtract operator in our last expression works because the value 2018 and the output of the YEAR function are both integers.

Some numerical data types can validly be combined in an arithmetical operation, for purely logical reasons; for example, an INTEGER type can be multiplied or divided by a DECIMAL type.

Scalar functions transform a single value. For example, the UPPER function

```
SELECT DISTINCT UPPER(grade)
FROM employee;
```

changes the string values in the *grade* column to all upper case:

UPPER(employee.grade)
CHARGEHAND
FITTER
APPRENTICE
RECEPTIONIST

Query 10: UPPER

The CAST function

```
SELECT surname, 'Discount ' ||CAST(discount AS
CHAR(2)) ||  ' per cent' AS level
FROM customer
WHERE discount IS NOT NULL;
```

transforms a value into another data type – in this case the integer column *discount* into a character type, so that it can be concatenated using the || operator to give a meaningful message:

surname	level
Johnson	Discount 20 per cent

Query 11: CAST

Aggregate functions give a single value which is some kind of aggregate of all the values in a column or other set of values.

For example

```
SELECT COUNT(nat_ins_no) AS "Number of staff"
FROM employee;
```

gives the number of individual employees recorded in our database

Number of staff
6

Query 12: COUNT

- while

```
SELECT CAST(AVG(hours) AS DECIMAL(2,1)) AS
'Average hours per job'
FROM job;
```

gives the hours allocated to the average job

Average hours per job
2.5

Query 13: AVG

Aggregate functions are more commonly used with the GROUP BY operator, which we look at shortly.

Note that the presence of NULLs in a table may have an unexpected effect on the outcome of an aggregate function. Take for example the *customer* table, which contains a number of rows for customers who, not being employees, have no discount figure shown:

surname	postcode	address	phone	discount	employee
Johnson	BV1 9SW	9 High St	402973	20	DQ435721A
Petty	BV1 9ST	250 High St	407865	(NULL)	(NULL)
Wilson	BV7 0BB	22 The Drive	881545	(NULL)	(NULL)
Simpson	BV3 1AS	32 Forest Row	690513	(NULL)	(NULL)
Newman	BV2 1PO	42 Union St	409111	(NULL)	(NULL)
Ellis	BV3 4RT	12 Windsor Ave	690190	(NULL)	(NULL)

Fig. 18a: a table with NULLs

If we COUNT the number of customers with discount levels

SELECT COUNT(discount) FROM customer;

we quite correctly find that there is only one:

COUNT(customer.discount)
1

Query 15: COUNT with NULLs

However, if we calculate an average value for the same column

```
SELECT AVG(discount) FROM customer;
```

we get an average, not of the discount levels for all customers, but only for the one who has a discount level recorded, i.e. ignoring all the rows where the discount level is NULL:

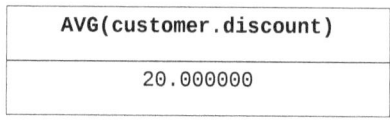

AVG(customer.discount)
20.000000

Query 16: AVG with NULLs

This would have been avoided had we shown the discount for the other customers as zero instead of leaving it as NULL, and of course Date and others would argue that it could have been prevented altogether by forbidding NULLs in the database.

Text functions enable us to manipulate text, whether in the SELECT, WHERE or HAVING clause.

The concatenate operator '||' joins two or more text strings together:

```
SELECT surname, 'Date joined '|| date_joined
AS Details
FROM employee
WHERE grade = 'Fitter';
```

surname	Details
Robinson	Date joined 2012-08-07
Johnson	Date joined 2008-04-01
Khan	Date joined 2011-07-09

Query 17: concatenate

The pattern symbols '_' , which stands for any single character, and '%' which stands for any number of unknown characters, can be used with the LIKE operator to permit wildcard searching of text strings:

"Find details of any customers who live in the first part of High Street (remembering that Street might have been abbreviated)"

```
SELECT *
FROM customer
WHERE address LIKE '__High_S%t';
```

surname	postcode	address	phone	discount	employee
Johnson	BV1 9SW	9 High St	402973	20	DQ435721A

Query 18: wildcards

Lists of SQL data types and operators can be found respectively at Appendices 1, and 2. However SQL implementations vary considerably in the extent to which they implement the standard facilities, so for completeness you should always refer to the documentation for the particular dbms you are using.

e)   *The logical processing model*

So far, we have looked at some fairly simple queries, where the logic behind them is fairly obvious. But the SQL standards define a logical processing model which dictates quite specifically what the outcome of any query will be, by describing its *logical* effect.

(That is to say, the standards do not specifically insist that a dbms must *physically* execute a query in a particular way, but only that it must always do so *so that the outcome is the same* as if it had actually been processed according to the model; which is not quite the same thing. It allows a supplier to find a more efficient way of processing a query, as long as the outcome is the same.)

The logical processing model is very useful to dbms users, both in understanding what a fairly complex query may be doing, and in writing queries of their own, because it permits the query to be looked at as a series of discrete steps.

The FROM clause is always present in any query, and it is always processed first.

If there is a WHERE clause, it is processed next.

And if there are no GROUP BY or HAVING clauses, the SELECT comes next.

So, in the simple example query I gave in section 2 above

```
SELECT surname, dl_no
FROM employee
```

```
WHERE surname = Johnson
```

the FROM clause first identifies the table to be used, and it copies this into a temporary intermediate table in memory.

Next, the WHERE clause processes that first intermediate table, from which it takes all the complete rows which have Johnson as the value in the *surname* column, and writes them to a second intermediate table, which would look like this:

nat_ins_no	surname	grade	date_joined	dl_no	manager
DQ435721A	Johnson	Fitter	2008-01-04	JOHNS403196DP9JH	UD987234A
VU241367D	Johnson	Receptionist	2008-04-01	(NULL)	(NULL)

Finally, the SELECT clause takes as its input that second intermediate table, and writes just the requested columns into the output table:

surname	dl_no
Johnson	JOHNS403196DP9JH
Johnson	(NULL)

f) The GROUP BY clause

As the name suggests, the GROUP BY clause allows us to group rows by their value for a given column or columns, thus:

```
SELECT manager, surname
FROM employee
WHERE manager IS NOT NULL
GROUP BY manager, surname;
```

manager	surname
FV546890B	Smith
UD987234A	Khan
UD987234A	Johnson
UD987234A	Robinson

Query 19: GROUP BY

In general, the GROUP BY clause is most often used in conjunction with an aggregate function, because it enables us to calculate values for a group of rows which all have the same value.

For example,

```
SELECT manager, COUNT(nat_ins_no) AS Employees
FROM employee
WHERE manager IS NOT NULL
GROUP BY manager;
```

gives us the number of staff each manager is responsible for

manager	Employees
FV546890B	1
UD987234A	3

Query 20: GROUP BY with COUNT

- while

```
SELECT make, CAST(AVG(hours) AS DECIMAL(2,1))
FROM job
WHERE hours IS NOT NULL
GROUP BY make;
```

gives the average hours for recorded jobs on each make

make	AVG(job.hours)
VW	4.0
Ford	1.8

Query 21: GROUP BY with AVG

I need to emphasise that, where a GROUP BY is used, the query produces just one row for each value present in the grouping column(s), whether or not an aggregate function is used as well. In this respect is has the same effect as a SELECT DISTINCT.

```
SELECT date_start
FROM job;
```

date_start
2016-01-04
2016-01-04
2016-01-04
2016-01-05
2016-01-05
2016-01-05

Query 22: output of multiple duplicate rows

```
SELECT date_start
FROM job
GROUP BY date_start;
```

date_start
2016-01-04
2016-01-05

Query 23: multiple rows eliminated using GROUP BY

This is important because it has an effect on the formulation of queries. *Where a GROUP BY is used, the SELECT clause can contain only columns named in the GROUP BY clause, and aggregate functions.* This is quite simply because of the effect I just described, that the GROUP BY produces just a single row for each value in the grouping columns. Any non-grouped columns could, and probably would, contain a range of different values, and since only atomic values are permitted, that would require the creation of multiple rows in the output, which could not be combined with a single row from the grouping.

g)   The HAVING clause

The HAVING clause can be described as a kind of WHERE clause for groups: while the WHERE clause selects rows based on a given test or value, the HAVING does the same for the output of a GROUP BY clause.

```
SELECT manager, COUNT(nat_ins_no) AS Employees
FROM employee
WHERE manager IS NOT NULL
GROUP BY manager;
```

manager	Employees
FV546890B	1
UD987234A	3

Query 24: GROUP BY

```
SELECT manager, COUNT(nat_ins_no) AS Employees
FROM employee
WHERE manager IS NOT NULL
GROUP BY manager
HAVING Employees >2;
```

manager	Employees
UD987234A	3

Query 25:GROUP BY with HAVING

h) The logical processing model when using GROUP BY and HAVING

A GROUP BY clause is processed after the WHERE clause (if there is one, otherwise after the FROM), and it is followed by the HAVING (if there is one) and then the SELECT.

So, in our last example query above:

The FROM is processed first, producing an intermediate table which is a full copy of the *Employee* table

Next, the WHERE clause takes the rows of that first intermediate table where the *manager* column is not null, and writes them to a second intermediate table.

The GROUP BY then creates a third intermediate table, and writes into it a single row for each distinct value of the *manager* column in the second intermediate table.

The HAVING clause creates a fourth intermediate table, and writes into it just the rows in the previous table where the value of *manager* is greater than 2.

And finally the SELECT clause writes all the rows from the fourth intermediate table to the output table, at the same time calculating the result of the aggregate function for each one.

i)   *The ORDER BY clause*

I now mention the last clause permitted in an SQL query, the ORDER BY. This is purely a display function, used to re-order the final output from the query, and so it is always processed last in the logical processing model.

```
SELECT surname,grade,date_joined
FROM employee;
```

surname	grade	date_joined
Wilkins	Chargehand	2010-06-18
Johnson	Fitter	2008-01-04
Robinson	Fitter	2012-08-07
Smith	Apprentice	2015-10-01
Khan	Fitter	2011-07-09
Johnson	Receptionist	2008-04-01

Query 26: ORDER BY *(1)*

```
SELECT surname,grade,date_joined
FROM employee
ORDER BY surname;
```

80

surname	grade	date_joined
Johnson	Fitter	2008-01-04
Johnson	Receptionist	2008-04-01
Khan	Fitter	2011-07-09
Robinson	Fitter	2012-08-07
Smith	Apprentice	2015-10-01
Wilkins	Chargehand	2010-06-18

Query 27: ORDER BY (2)

The default for ORDER BY is order by ascending values; this can be changed to descending by using ORDER BY {column name} DESC

ORDER BY can be used to order on multiple columns; in that case rows are ordered first by their value for the first column in the list and then by the second, and so on.

```
SELECT grade, surname, date_joined
FROM employee
ORDER BY grade, surname;
```

grade	surname	date_joined
Apprentice	Smith	2015-10-01
Chargehand	Wilkins	2010-06-18
Fitter	Johnson	2008-01-04
Fitter	Khan	2011-07-09
Fitter	Robinson	2012-08-07
Receptionist	Johnson	2008-04-01

Query 28: multiple ORDER BY

j) The two clause sequences: composing and processing

The DDL syntax requires that simple queries be composed with the clauses in a fixed order, while the logical processing model handles them in a different order.

Query sequence	Logical processing sequence
SELECT	FROM
FROM	(WHERE)
(WHERE)	(GROUP BY)
(GROUP BY)	(HAVING)
(HAVING)	SELECT
(ORDER BY)	(ORDER BY)

Table 3: Query sequence compared with logical processing sequence

2   Using joins

Until now, we have looked only at queries which use a single table. More information can however be extracted from a database when a query uses two or more tables, and the simplest way to do this is to join them in the FROM clause.

A join of tables occurs when the rows of one table have the same value in one or more columns as comparable columns of another table. Note that, for all the many kinds of join, the joining columns must be of the same data type.

Take for instance the tables *customer* and *employee*

Customer					
surname	postcode	address	phone	discount	employee
Johnson	BV1 9SW	9 High St	402973	20	DQ435721A
Petty	BV1 9ST	250 High St	407865	(NULL)	(NULL)
Wilson	BV7 0BB	22 The Drive	881545	(NULL)	(NULL)
Simpson	BV3 1AS	32 Forest Row	690513	(NULL)	(NULL)
Newman	BV2 1PO	42 Union St	409111	(NULL)	(NULL)
Ellis	BV3 4RT	12 Windsor Ave	690190	(NULL)	(NULL)

Employee					
nat_ins_no	surname	grade	date_joined	dl_no	manager
UD987234A	Wilkins	Chargehand	2010-06-18	WILKI711198SS5BE	(NULL)
DQ435721A	Johnson	Fitter	2008-01-04	JOHNS403196DP9JH	UD987234A
FV546890B	Robinson	Fitter	2012-08-07	ROBIN704197PV7TB	UD987234A
QQ525687D	Smith	Apprentice	2015-10-01	SMITH910274IB0IV	FV546890B
VF219787C	Khan	Fitter	2011-07-09	KHANA808197CD1AS	UD987234A
VU241367D	Johnson	Receptionist	2008-04-01	(NULL)	(NULL)

Fig. 19: customer *and* employee *tables*

There is only one row of *customer* which has a column value matching a value in *employee*: the *employee* column for the customer named Johnson. And we know that the relationship between these two tables is 1:1, so only one row of *employee* will have that same value; which means that the table which results from the join should, itself, have only a single row.

surname	postcode	address	phone	discount	employee	nat_ins_no	surname	grade	date_joined	dl_no	manager
Johnson	BV1 9SW	9 High St	402973	20	DQ435721A	DQ435721A	Johnson	Fitter	2008-01-04	JOHNS403196DP9JH	UD987234A

Fig. 20: the one row which should result from a join of customer *and* employee

On the other hand, the relationship between *job* and *work_mn* is 1:n, so there can be several rows of *work_mn* which have values matching those in job, and the table resulting from a join of those two will necessarily have more rows:

reg_no	date_start	job_description	make	date_end	hours	surname	postcode	nat_ins_no	reg_no	start_date	description
AQ12CDE	2016-01-04	12 000 service	Ford	2016-01-04	2	Ellis	BV3 4RT	DQ435721A	AQ12CDE	2016-01-04	12 000 service
AQ12CDE	2016-01-04	Front pads & discs	Ford	2016-01-04	1.5	Ellis	BV3 4RT	DQ435721A	AQ12CDE	2016-01-04	Front pads & discs
MN03TSK	2016-01-04	Replace clutch & gbox	Vw	2016-01-05	4	Newman	BV2 1P0	UD987234A	MN03TSK	2016-01-04	Replace clutch & gbox
MN03TSK	2016-01-04	Replace clutch & gbox	Vw	2016-01-05	4	Newman	BV2 1P0	FV546890B	MN03TSK	2016-01-04	Replace clutch & gbox
VD09BVC	2016-01-05	Replace exhaust	Renault	(NULL)	(NULL)	Petty	BV1 9ST	VF219787C	VD09BVC	2016-01-05	Replace exhaust
VD09BVC	2016-01-05	Replace exhaust	Renault	(NULL)	(NULL)	Petty	BV1 9ST	QQ525687D	VD09BVC	2016-01-05	Replace exhaust

Fig. 21: rows resulting from a join of job *and* work_mn

There are two rows each for vehicles MN03TSK and VD09BVC, even though only one job has been carried out on each of them; this is because in each case two employees are allocated to that single job.

The joining of the table gives us information not available from the two tables separately – we can see which employees were allocated to each job.

SQL supports several different methods for joining tables, as we see next (although not all of them are supported in all SQL implementations).

a)　　　　　　　*Implicit joins using FROM*

We can join two tables simply by naming them in the FROM clause:

```
SELECT *
FROM customer, employee;
```

Query 29: implicit join with no join condition

The logical processing model, remember, says that the FROM clause is to be processed first of all. When there is just one table named in the FROM clause, we saw that it simply takes a complete copy of that table to create an intermediate table. So what is it to do in this situation, with no information other than the names of two tables?

The answer is that it joins each row of the first-named table to every row of the second-named. We call this a *Cartesian product*, because the number of rows in the intermediate table it creates will be the *product* of the number of rows in each of the two original tables; in this case, 6 x 6 = 36.

Clearly such a table contains very little useful information. In order to create the joined table we looked at at the start of this section, and thus find out the details of the employees who are also customers, we need to tell the system *how* to join the two tables, in other words on *which* column or columns it is to look for matching values. And we do this by adding a WHERE clause to the query; we call this a *join condition*.

```
SELECT *
FROM customer, employee
WHERE employee = nat_ins_no;
```

Query 30: join condition added

This gets us what we want:

surname	postcode	address	phone	discount	employee	nat_ins_no	surname	grade	date_joined	dl_no	manager
Johnson	BV1 9SW	9 High St	402973	20	DQ43572 1A	DQ4357 21A	Johnson	Fitter	2008-01-04	JOHNS40 3196DP9 JH	UD98723 4A

Fig. 23: result of adding a join condition

The logical processing model has proceeded in this case just as before: the FROM clause has indeed, again, created an intermediate table which is the Cartesian product of *customer* and *employee.* But the WHERE clause has then been executed, and this has searched that first intermediate table for rows where the value of *employee* from the *customer* table matched that of *nat_ins_no* from the *employee* table, and written just that single row to the second intermediate table. That second table is then processed by the SELECT clause, which, since in this case it is SELECT *, simply goes on to write the whole row to the output table.

This may not seem to be a very efficient method of processing; even with the very small tables in our demonstration database, a table of 36 rows has been created, occupying space in memory, when only one of those rows was actually wanted by the request. As I have already mentioned, vendors are allowed to physically process queries any way they like, as long as the outcome is always *logically* the same as that prescribed by the logical processing model, and there are opportunities to do so with stored queries; but in the case of a an interactive query entered in real time by a human user, the logical processing model will usually be followed.

The implicit join can potentially be used with any number of tables, e.g.

```
SELECT *
FROM table_1, table_2, table_3 . . .
```
- but this will require several join conditions, in the WHERE clause, one between each table and the next one named; and this brings us on to the next topic.

b)   Qualified names, and aliases

In the join of the *customer* and *employee* tables, we used the join condition

```
WHERE employee = nat_ins_no
```

and this worked successfully because there was no ambiguity. We already know that

86

column names have to be unique only within each table – they can be used again in two or more tables – but in this case, between both tables involved there is only one column named *employee* and one name *nat_ins_no*.

It would be a different story if we wanted, for example, to join the *employee* and *work_mn* tables, to find the name of each employee who had worked on each car, because a column named *nat_ins_no* exists in both tables. We would need to specify which of the two columns we were referring to, by *qualifying* it with the name of its table ; and so the successful query would look like this

```
SELECT reg_no, surname
FROM employee, work_mn
WHERE employee.nat_ins_no = work_mn.nat_ins_no
GROUP BY surname, reg_no;
```

reg_no	surname
AQ12CDE	Johnson
VD09BVC	Khan
VD09BVC	Smith
MN03TSK	Robinson
MN03TSK	Wilkins

Query 31: qualified column names

We can save a lot of typing by creating short *aliases* for the tables. We do this in the FROM clause:

```
FROM employee e, work_mn w
```

Once aliases like this have been declared, they have to be used throughout the query, because after the FROM clause has been processed, the system no longer recognises the original table names. (*Note that I am here describing ANSI standard SQL; if you run Query 32 in SQL Anywhere, it will ignore the invalid syntax and complete successfully.*)

```
SELECT reg_no, surname
FROM employee e, work_mn w
WHERE e.nat_ins_no = w.nat_ins_no
GROUP BY surname, reg_no;
```
Query 32: invalid query omitting aliases

The use of aliases to save typing becomes more apparent when we are joining more than one table and there is more than one repeated column name requiring qualification. Take, for example, a join of the tables *employee, work_mn* and *job*, to find which employees were allocated to uncompleted jobs:

```
SELECT work_mn.reg_no, employee.surname,
date_end
FROM employee, work_mn, job
WHERE date_end IS NULL
AND employee.nat_ins_no = work_mn.nat_ins_no
AND work_mn.reg_no = job.reg_no
AND start_date = date_start
AND description = job_description
GROUP BY date_end, employee.surname,
work_mn.reg_no;
```
Query 33: long query without aliases

By using aliases, we can reduce this to

```
SELECT w.reg_no, e.surname, date_end
FROM employee e, work_mn w, job j
WHERE date_end IS NULL
AND e.nat_ins_no = w.nat_ins_no
AND w.reg_no = j.reg_no
AND start_date = date_start
AND description = job_description
GROUP BY date_end, e.surname, w.reg_no;
```
Query 34: query shortened using aliases

with the same result

reg_no	surname	date_end
VD09BVC	Khan	(NULL)
VD09BVC	Smith	(NULL)

c)   Self joins

Aliases are essential when joining a table to itself. We might want to do it, for example, to find out the full details of employees and their managers. Since of course in this case *all* the columns have the same names in both the tables involved, we have to qualify them all; and in order for the query to distinguish between two identically named tables, we have to give them aliases

```
SELECT emp.surname AS "Employee name",
       emp.grade AS "Employee grade",
       emp.date_joined AS "Employee joined",
       man.surname AS "Manager name",
       man.grade AS "Manager grade",
       man.date_joined AS "Manager joined"
FROM employee emp, employee man
WHERE emp.manager = man.nat_ins_no
ORDER BY emp.surname;
```

Employee name	Employee grade	Employee joined	Manager name	Manager grade	Manager joined
Johnson	Fitter	2008-01-04	Wilkins	Chargehand	2010-06-18
Khan	Fitter	2011-07-09	Wilkins	Chargehand	2010-06-18
Robinson	Fitter	2012-08-07	Wilkins	Chargehand	2010-06-18
Smith	Apprentice	2015-10-01	Robinson	Fitter	2012-08-07

Query 35: a self join

Notice that we did not need to include an IS NOT NULL condition, to exclude those employees for whom no manager is shown. The join condition

```
WHERE emp.manager = man.nat_ins_no
```

requires the two columns to have equal values and so any rows of either table which contain a NULL in those columns, must be excluded. Had we wanted to include employees with no manager, we would need an outer join, which we discuss shortly.

d)   Explicit joins using JOIN . . ON

An alternative method of joining tables is the JOIN . . ON

```
SELECT *
FROM customer JOIN employee
ON employee = nat_ins_no
```

performs exactly the same function as

```
SELECT *
```

```
FROM customer, employee
WHERE employee = nat_ins_no
```

and the logical processing model is the same, with the join condition in the ON clause being processed after the FROM, in place of the WHERE.

e)   The natural join (don't try this at work!)

It's possible, but in no way recommended, to save a little typing by letting the system work out the join condition for itself.

Where the tables are to be joined with columns which not only have the same values and data type but also the same name, the system can assume that these are meant to be the joining columns; so

```
SELECT reg_no, surname
FROM employee e NATURAL JOIN work_mn w
GROUP BY surname, reg_no
```

has exactly the same effect as

```
SELECT reg_no, surname
FROM employee e, work_mn w
WHERE e.nat_ins_no = w.nat_ins_no
GROUP BY surname, reg_no
```

without the bother of having to type a WHERE clause.

The problem comes when at some later point the table is restructured and, say, someone decides to change the name of one of the joining columns. The natural join query will stop working and it will take quite a bit of work to find out why, and possibly even how the join was supposed to work in the first place. (One would hope that it would all have been properly set down in the documentation, but it seems to me rather unlikely that anyone lazy enough to use a natural join would bother to do decent documentation.) Avoid it.

f)   Outer joins

In subsection c) I mentioned the need to use an outer join when, for the sake of completeness, we want to include rows where one or other of the joining columns contained nulls; for example to find details of all employees and their managers, but include those who don't have one. This does it:

```
SELECT emp.surname AS "Employee name" ,
       emp.grade AS "Employee grade",
       emp.date_joined AS "Employee joined",
       man.surname AS "Manager name",
       man.grade AS "Manager grade",
       man.date_joined AS "Manager joined"
FROM employee emp LEFT OUTER JOIN employee man
ON emp.manager = man.nat_ins_no
ORDER BY emp.surname;
```

Employee name	Employee grade	Employee joined	Manager name	Manager grade	Manager joined
Johnson	Receptionist	2008-04-01	(NULL)	(NULL)	(NULL)
Johnson	Fitter	2008-01-04	Wilkins	Chargehand	2010-06-18
Khan	Fitter	2011-07-09	Wilkins	Chargehand	2010-06-18
Robinson	Fitter	2012-08-07	Wilkins	Chargehand	2010-06-18
Smith	Apprentice	2015-10-01	Robinson	Fitter	2012-08-07
Wilkins	Chargehand	2010-06-18	(NULL)	(NULL)	(NULL)

Query 36: LEFT OUTER JOIN

The significance of the word LEFT in LEFT OUTER JOIN, is that it is the table which is named first in the FROM clause (i.e. the one to the *left* of the OUTER JOIN command) is the one which will have its rows included even when its joining column contains NULLs.

A RIGHT OUTER JOIN does things the other way around, that is, the table named last in the FROM clause is the one which will have its rows included even when its joining column contains NULLs.

A FULL OUTER JOIN is also available; as you might guess, this will include rows from either of the tables whose joining column contains NULLs.

In all cases, and as you can see from the example table above, when a row appears from one table which can't be joined to any row of the other table because its joining column contains a NULL, the remainder of the row in the results table will contain NULLs for the columns of the other table.

3. Composite queries

Because the output from any valid SELECT query is always a table, quite complex queries can be built up by using that output as the input to another SELECT query. There are three main methods for doing this:

- combining two or more complete output tables with the UNION operator

- embedding a complete SELECT query, known as a subquery, as part of a search condition within a WHERE or HAVING clause

- using the output table from a complete SELECT query as a virtual table named in a FROM clause

We will look at these one by one.

a) The UNION operator

The join of two or more tables, using any of the three methods covered in section 2 above, can be thought of as a *horizontal* join – it joins together some or all of the *rows* of two or more existing tables. In a logical sense, it can be thought of as an AND operation. For example, the query

```
SELECT *
FROM customer, employee
WHERE employee = nat_ins_no
```
could be thought of as answering the request

"give all details of any people who are both customer AND employee of the garage".

By contrast, the UNION operator joins two or more tables *vertically*: it pasts together their *columns*. So, logically, it is an OR operation. For example, the query

```
SELECT *
FROM employee
WHERE grade = 'Fitter'
UNION
SELECT *
FROM employee
WHERE grade = 'Apprentice';
```
answers the request

"give all details of employees whose grade is either Fitter OR Apprentice".

Of course, this simple example could have just as well been formulated by using an actual OR operator within a WHERE clause, i.e.

```
SELECT *
FROM employee
WHERE grade = Fitter
OR grade = Apprentice;
```

they both produce the same result:

nat_ins_no	surname	grade	date_joined	dl_no	manager
DQ435721A	Johnson	Fitter	2008-01-04	JOHNS403196DP9JH	UD987234A
FV546890B	Robinson	Fitter	2012-08-07	ROBIN704197PV7TB	UD987234A
QQ525687D	Smith	Apprentice	2015-10-01	SMITH910274IB0IV	FV546890B
VF219787C	Khan	Fitter	2011-07-09	KHANA808197CD1AS	UD987234A

Query 37: UNION

The tables which are combined with UNION must be compatible – that is to say, they must both have the same number of columns, and, reading from left to right, the first column of the first table must have the same data type as that of the first column of the second table, the second column of the first table must have the same data type as the second column of the second table, and so on. Given that the columns are effectively pasted together top to bottom, it could not work any other way.

For example, the query

```
SELECT surname, phone
FROM customer
UNION
SELECT surname, grade
FROM employee
```

is valid, and produces valid output, even if it makes no sense (we end up with a second column that contains both telephone numbers and the names of grades), because the two input tables are compatible.

On the other hand, the query

```
SELECT surname, discount
```

```
FROM customer
UNION
SELECT surname, grade
FROM employee
```

is invalid because the *discount* column of *customer* is an integer data type, whereas the *grade* column of *employee* is a character type.

The ORDER BY clause cannot appear in either of the SELECT queries used as input to the UNION, because ORDER BY is just a display operation and makes no difference to the actual output.

ORDER BY can, however be used on the final output from a UNION operation, but it gives us a problem: we normally ORDER BY the name of one or more columns, but the original names of the columns joined together top-to-bottom may not be the same (e.g. *phone* and *grade*, in the first example above). So they have to be referred to by the position in which they occur in output, left to right (notice how, in this case, SQL ignores the relational principle that ordering of columns is not significant!)

```
SELECT surname, phone
FROM customer
UNION
SELECT surname, grade
FROM employee
ORDER BY 1;
```

surname	phone
Ellis	690190
Johnson	402973
Johnson	Fitter
Johnson	Receptionist
Khan	Fitter
Newman	409111
Petty	407865
Robinson	Fitter
Simpson	690513

Smith	Apprentice
Wilkins	Chargehand
Wilson	881545

Query 38: ORDER BY with UNION

A final comment on this operator. Because UNION is effectively an OR operation, it seems possible that, if a row were present in both the tables being joined, both occurrences could end up in the output of the UNION.

For example, in our *employee* table there are three rows where the employee in question has the grade *fitter* and a manager with identifier *UD987234A*, meaning that those three rows will occur in the output of both these queries:

```
SELECT * FROM employee
WHERE grade = 'fitter'

SELECT * FROM employee
WHERE manager = 'UD987234A'
```

So we might expect that this query

```
SELECT * FROM employee
WHERE grade = 'fitter'
UNION
SELECT * FROM employee
WHERE manager = 'UD987234A';
```

would produce six rows, with each of those original three appearing twice.

But it doesn't; SQL automatically gets rid of the duplicates:

nat_ins_no	surname	grade	date_joined	dl_no	manager
FV546890B	Robinson	Fitter	2012-08-07	ROBIN704197 PV7TB	UD987234A
DQ435721A	Johnson	Fitter	2008-04-01	JOHNS403196 DP9JH	UD987234A
VF219787C	Khan	Fitter	2011-07-09	KHANA808197 CD1AS	UD987234A

Query 39: UNION removing duplicates

If we really want to include all the possible rows, we have to use UNION ALL:

```
SELECT * FROM employee
WHERE grade = 'fitter'
UNION ALL
SELECT * FROM employee
WHERE manager = 'UD987234A';
```

nat_ins_no	surname	grade	date_joined	dl_no	manager
FV546890B	Robinson	Fitter	2012-08-07	ROBIN704197 PV7TB	UD987234A
DQ435721A	Johnson	Fitter	2008-04-01	JOHNS403196 DP9JH	UD987234A
VF219787C	Khan	Fitter	2011-07-09	KHANA808197 CD1AS	UD987234A
FV546890B	Robinson	Fitter	2012-08-07	ROBIN704197 PV7TB	UD987234A
DQ435721A	Johnson	Fitter	2008-04-01	JOHNS403196 DP9JH	UD987234A
VF219787C	Khan	Fitter	2011-07-09	KHANA808197 CD1AS	UD987234A

Query 40: UNION ALL

b)   Subqueries within a WHERE or HAVING clause

A subquery is included in a WHERE clause of a query in order to compare the values in its output table with those in the table in the FROM clause of the main (or *outer* query).

The query

```
SELECT j.make, job_description, date_start
FROM work_mn w, job j
WHERE w.reg_no = j.reg_no
AND start_date = date_start
AND description = job_description;
```

joins the *work_mn* and *job* tables, to give us the makes of cars on which any jobs have been booked in and to which employees have been allocated, with the description of the job and the start date in each case.

make	job_description	date_start
Ford	12000 service	2016-01-04
Ford	Front pads & discs	2016-01-04
VW	Replace clutch & gbox	2016-01-04
VW	Replace clutch & gbox	2016-01-04
Renault	Replace exhaust	2016-01-05
Renault	Replace exhaust	2016-01-05

Query 41: jobs allocated to employees

The short query

```
SELECT nat_ins_no
FROM employee
WHERE grade = 'Apprentice';
```

gives the identifiers of all employees who are apprentices.

nat_ins_no
QQ525687D

Query 42: apprentices

Since the identifiers of employees who have been allocated to jobs are contained in a column of the *work_mn* table, we can compare them with the identifiers contained in the short query above, to answer the request

"give the make of vehicle, description of job and start date of any jobs to which an apprentice has been allocated"

```
SELECT j.make, job_description, date_start
FROM work_mn w, job j
WHERE w.reg_no = j.reg_no
```

```
AND start_date = date_start
AND description = job_description
AND nat_ins_no IN
    (SELECT nat_ins_no
    FROM employee
    WHERE grade = 'Apprentice');
```

make	job_description	date_start
Renault	Replace exhaust	2016-01-05

Query 43: Subquery within a WHERE clause - jobs allocated to apprentices

Note the use of the IN operator in the query above. The output of a subquery is normally a set of data and so any comparison needs to treat it as such (see also next subsection)

The subquery examples we have looked at so far were both *simple* subqueries, and they can be recognised as such because it would be, as we have shown, validly possible to execute just the subquery – the part in brackets – on its own.

The logical processing model for this type of subquery is straightforward: the subquery is processed first in its entirety, using the normal FROM, WHERE, (GROUP BY), (HAVING), SELECT sequence; and then the outer query is processed in its entirety in the same way, using the output table from the subquery as part of the condition tested in its WHERE clause.

It is also possible to include, in a very similar way, a subquery within a HAVING clause, for example, to find the identifier(s) of the employee(s) who have worked on the highest number of jobs:

```
SELECT nat_ins_no
FROM work_mn
GROUP BY nat_ins_no
HAVING COUNT(*) >= ALL
    (SELECT COUNT(*)
    FROM work_mn
    GROUP BY nat_ins_no);
```

nat_ins_no
DQ435721A

Query 44: Subquery within a HAVING clause – employee(s) with the most jobs

Again, note the use of the ALL operator.

A more complex type of subquery is the *correlated subquery*. In this case, it is not possible to run the subquery on its own, because it involves a *correlation* between a value in the table being processed by the subquery with a value in the table being processed by the outer query.

Suppose, for each day, we want to find the job which took the most hours. The following query answers that request:

```
SELECT date_start, J1.reg_no,
J1.job_description, J1.hours
FROM job J1
WHERE hours >= ALL
        (SELECT J2.hours
         FROM job J2
         WHERE J1.date_start = J2.date_start);
```

date_start	reg_no	job_description	hours
2016-01-04	MN03TSK	Replace clutch & gbox	4.0

Query 45: Correlated subquery – job(s) that took the most hours

In this example, the subquery could not be executed separately. If we tried, processing would start with the FROM clause, which would create only a copy of the *job* table aliased as J2. The WHERE clause would then be asked to compare the values of *date_start* from this table with matching column values from another table J1 – of which it knows nothing.

This reference to table J1 is an example of what we call an *outer reference*; it refers to a table named in the FROM clause of the outer query, and for this reason the subquery cannot proceed on its own.

In fact the logical processing model for a correlated subquery is quite involved and perhaps somewhat surprising:

Processing starts with the FROM clause of the outer query, which creates a first intermediate table which is a copy of the *job* table, aliased as J1.

The WHERE clause is then asked to carry out a comparison, which invokes the subquery. To do this, it pauses at the first row of that first intermediate table.

The FROM clause of the **subquery** now creates a second intermediate table, is which another copy of the *job* table, aliased as J2.

The WHERE clause of the subquery now processes that second intermediate table row by row, comparing the each value of the *date_start* column with that in the row of the first intermediate table, which is being held by the WHERE clause of the outer query. If those dates match, then that row of the second intermediate table is written to a third intermediate table. When the WHERE clause reaches the last row of the second intermediate table, processing is handed to the SELECT clause of the subquery, which takes just the *hours* column of the third intermediate table and writes it to a fourth table. Processing now passes back to the outer query.

The WHERE clause of the outer query is now able to complete its comparison: is the value of the *hours* column in the row it's holding greater than any of those in the table returned by the subquery? If so, the row it's holding is written to a fifth intermediate table.

Next, the WHERE clause of the outer query moves down to the next row of the first intermediate table, and again invokes the subquery, which again processes the entire second intermediate table against the date in the row being held by the outer query; and this process is repeated in full for every row in the first intermediate table. When the WHERE clause of the outer query finally reaches the end of that table, processing passes to the SELECT clause of the outer query.

This SELECT clause then takes just the *date_start, reg_no, job_description* and *hours* columns from the fifth intermediate table and writes them to output.

As you may well imagine, this is all very processing intensive, even for such a simple query, particularly if there were large tables involved instead of our very small samples, and for that reason correlated subqueries should be avoided if at all possible.

c)   *Comparisons with the output of a subquery*

i   *Subqueries which return a set of data*

As noted above, a WHERE or HAVING clause which contains a subquery is used to compare a single value with the output of that subquery, which is by contrast normally a set of data; and this places a restriction on the kinds of comparison which can be used. Clearly, = < and > would not be logically valid. On the other hand, any logical operator which assumes that there will be a single value on the left hand side of the equation but multiple values on the right hand side, such as IN, NOT IN, = ANY, > ALL, are acceptable.

We also have EXISTS and NOT EXISTS, specifically for use in this situation. These operators test whether the subquery returns any data at all. The nature of these operators is such that the subquery will normally be a correlated one. For example, to answer the request "What are the identifiers and names of any employees who have worked on vehicle VD09BVC?"

```
SELECT nat_ins_no, surname
FROM employee e
WHERE EXISTS
        (SELECT *
        FROM work_mn w
        WHERE e.nat_ins_no = w.nat_ins_no
        AND reg_no = 'VD09BVC');
```

nat_ins_no	surname
QQ525687D	Smith
VF219787C	Khan

Query 46: Subquery using EXISTS

Or, to answer the request, "What are the identifiers and names of any fitters who have never worked on a gearbox?"

```
SELECT e.nat_ins_no, e.surname
FROM employee e
WHERE grade = 'Fitter'
AND NOT EXISTS
        (SELECT *
        FROM work_mn w
        WHERE e.nat_ins_no = w.nat_ins_no
        AND description LIKE '%box%')
```

nat_ins_no	surname
DQ435721A	Johnson
VF219787C	Khan

Query 47: Subquery using NOT EXISTS

The comparative operators =, >, < etc can, however be used to link with a subquery when the subquery can only return a single value (or an empty set), as is the case with an aggregate function:

```
SELECT make, job_description, date_start,
hours
FROM job
WHERE hours =
    (SELECT MAX(hours)
    FROM job);
```

make	job_description	date_start	hours
VW	Replace clutch & gbox	2016-01-04	4.0

Query 48: Subquery using =

d) Joins v. subqueries

Many requests can be answered with either a join or a subquery. For example, the request, "give the names of any employees who manage others" can be satisfied with either:

```
SELECT DISTINCT s.surname
FROM employee f, employee s
WHERE f.manager = s.nat_ins_no;
```

Query 49: employees who manage others, using a join

or

```
SELECT DISTINCT surname
FROM employee
WHERE nat_ins_no IN
    (SELECT manager
    FROM employee)
```

surname
Wilkins
Robinson

Query 50: employees who manage others, using a subquery

In choosing which method to use, efficiency of processing needs to be considered. Because the join method involves a cartesian product, generating a quite large intermediate table most of which is of no use, it can take up a considerable amount of dynamic memory, if only for a few instants; although with a very large database there is the possibility of the intermediate tables exceeding dynamic memory and so causing paging to disk. The subquery avoids this memory problem, but at the cost of more intensive processing, particularly with a correlated query; so both methods have the potential to cause problems for other processes.

In any case, there are logical limits to the extent of the choice:

- where it is necessary to make a comparison with the result of an aggregate function on the second table (as in our second subquery example above), the only possible approach is to use a subquery;

- but where we need the final output to include data from both tables, we have to use a join.

e)   *Subqueries within a FROM clause*

Another way of using a subquery is to embed it within a FROM clause. This has the very useful benefit that, since the output of the subquery is inevitably a new table, it can be treated as such and used in a join with another table. So, using this technique, we can add the employee's name to the result of our subquery-within-a-HAVING-clause example, by embedding that entire query in a join using FROM :

```
SELECT surname, e.nat_ins_no
FROM employee e,
        (SELECT nat_ins_no
        FROM work_mn
        GROUP BY nat_ins_no
        HAVING COUNT(*) >= ALL
                (SELECT COUNT(*)
                FROM work_mn
                GROUP BY nat_ins_no))
    AS numbers
WHERE e.nat_ins_no = numbers.nat_ins_no
```

surname	nat_ins_no
Johnson	DQ435721A

Query 51: subquery within a FROM clause

Notice that, if it's necessary (as here) to qualify the names of columns within the temporary table created by the subquery, we first have to give it a name using AS.

Chapter 10: Database development

1   System development methodologies

An information system which includes a database to store persistent data will always include application programs as well. The relative importance of the two can range from the system where the database is at the centre, with the programs providing a user interface to facilitate access to and updating of data, to that where the database seems almost an afterthought, simply providing a useful receptacle for data created by the programs. Indeed there are many cases today, such as the WordPress blogging system, where an SQL database is generated automatically to support the user's functional requirements.

Most modern day information systems lie somewhere between these two extremes, and in many cases it would be difficult to say whether the programs or the database form the more important component. But when it comes to system development, a choice has to be made. We can design the programs first and accept that the design of the database will be to at least some extent dictated by the requirements of those programs, which might might mean that the database will be less efficient than it might have been if the design work had started there. Or we can start with the database, with the result that, when we come to design the software, we will have to live with the existing table structures.

Of course, a somewhat iterative approach is also possible; we might start with a database design and then return to revise it somewhat if we find that it poses real difficulties for the software; but this does not alter the fact that we have to start at one end or the other.

Since this book is about databases, it should be no surprise that I deal almost entirely with what is known as the *classical database development methodology*: I start with the *data requirement*, and from that I design and implement the database. In the next few sections, I'll use the same Garage scenario which I used to demonstrate the relational model, to specify and create an SQL database.

2   Specifying and analysing a data requirement

a)   The requirement

As with any computer system, it's essential from the very outset to specify, and where necessary agree on the requirements; and moreover to do so in such a way as to remove any possible ambiguity. Failure to do so can result in disputes between client and supplier, leading to disappointment on the part of the client, additional unexpected work on the part of the supplier, and all too often with some large projects, to a legal dispute. An agreed requirement at the start forestalls such problems (and remember that in all but the tiniest projects, there is always a client and a supplier, even if they are separated only by the departmental structure of the same organisation).

We start by writing down, in common language, a clear description of the data items which the database needs to store, including how they are related to each other and any restrictions on them.

In the early days, most new systems were developed to replace work which had previously been done manually on paper, and the work started with someone called a *systems analyst*. Their job was first of all to interview people and record their stated requirements in writing, and then to *analyse* those requirements so as to produce a model of them which could be computerised. Nowadays, almost all new developments involve replacing or integrating existing computer systems, and all too often what is analysed is simply a description of what the existing system does, without sufficient consideration of whether the actual requirement has changed, or whether it had ever been correctly recorded in the first place.

So here, let's go back to basics, by imagining that we are among those systems analysts. The SQL database for the garage featured in our earlier examples is as yet just an idea, and we've been round the premises, collecting requirements for the proposed new system. Here is the description of their existing manual system, which we have produced:

Garage

The garage company has a number of employees. Every employee must have a National Insurance Number, consisting of two letters followed by six numerals and one letter, and this number uniquely identifies them. If known, their driving licence number is also recorded, and this consists of five letters followed by six numerals, two letters, one numeral and two letters. For each employee we also record their surname, which can have up to twenty letters or spaces, their grade which is either Fitter, Chargehand, Apprentice or Receptionist, and the date they started with the company.

Some employees are managed by another company employee. An Apprentice can be managed by a Fitter or a Chargehand, but a Fitter can only be managed by a Chargehand. Each Fitter and Chargehand can manage zero or more employees, but a Fitter can only manage Apprentices.

An employee can also be a customer of the company, and vice versa. Details of customers are recorded, including their surname and post code which together form the unique customer identifier, their address which can have up to thirty letters or spaces, and their phone number which can have up to fifteen numerals. Where a customer is also an employee of the company, we record the level of discount (between 1 and 99) which they are allowed.

Jobs of work done by the garage are recorded. Each job is identified by a unique combination of the registration number of the vehicle concerned (consisting of two letters followed by two numerals and three letters), the date on which it was started and a description of the job (consisting of up to thirty letters and spaces). The make of vehicle is also recorded, and, once the job is completed, the date of completion and the time (in hours and tenths of an hour) taken. Each employee of grades Chargehand, Fitter or Apprentice can be recorded as working on zero or more jobs, and each job can be worked on by zero or more employees of those same grades. Each job is done for a customer. A customer can have zero or more jobs done for them.

Fig. 24: the requirement for the Garage system

b)   *The sample data*

At the same time as compiling the data requirement from what s/he is told by the company employees, the analyst will collect samples of actual data which exist in whatever system the company is using at present; it could be in the form of a card index, or an accounts book, or a register, if the system in use at present is manual.

For our purposes here, we'll use the same basic data we used as examples when we created the Garage relational model in Chapter 5 - basically Fig.s 7, 9 and 10. Here, for ease of reference, is the same data again:

Employee				
NatInsNo	Surname	Grade	DateJoined	DrivingLicenceNo
DQ435721A	Johnson	Fitter	04/01/08	JOHNS403196DP9JH
FV546890B	Robinson	Fitter	07/08/12	ROBIN704197PV7TB
QQ525687D	Smith	Apprentice	01/10/15	SMITH910274IB0IV
UD987234A	Wilkins	Chargehand	18/06/10	WILKI711198SS5BE
VU241367D	Johnson	Receptionist	04/01/08	
VF219787C	Khan	Fitter	09/07/11	KHANA808197CD1AS

Fig. 25: sample employee data

Job							
reg_no	date_start	job_description	make	date_end	hours	surname	postcode
AQ12CDE	2016-01-04	12 000 service	Ford	2016-01-04	2.0	Ellis	BV3 4RT
AQ12CDE	2016-01-04	Front pads & discs	Ford	2016-01-04	1.5	Ellis	BV3 4RT
MN03TSK	2016-01-04	Replace clutch & gbox	VW	2016-01-05	4.0	Newman	BV2 1PO
VD09BVC	2016-01-05	Replace exhaust	Renault	(NULL)	(NULL)	Petty	BV1 9ST
QP11ABC	2016-01-05	20,000 service	Ford	(NULL)	(NULL)	Simpson	BV3 1AS
VI14PPK	2016-01-05	Timing belt	Citroen	(NULL)	(NULL)	Wilson	BV7 0BB

Fig. 26: sample job data

Customer				
Surname	PostCode	Address	Phone	Discount
Johnson	BV1 9SW	9 High St	402973	20
Petty	BV1 9ST	250 High St	407865	
Wilson	BV7 0BB	22 The Drive	881545	
Simpson	BV3 1AS	32 Forest Row	690513	
Newman	BV2 1PO	42 Union St	409111	
Ellis	BV3 4RT	12 Windsor Ave	690190	

Fig. 27: sample customer data

c)   Analysing a requirement: producing a conceptual data model

As it stands, our common language statement of requirement, Fig 24 above, is intelligible to a human but not to a computer. We need to create from it a formal model which could be directly converted to a database design: a *conceptual data model*, which is produced by analysing a requirement. This model serves several purposes:

- a text statement of requirement can be subject to all the possible ambiguities of common language, but a computerised version can have no such ambiguities: each entity has just these attributes and no others, participation is just either optional or mandatory, relationships can only have one of the three possible degrees – and so on. The conceptual data model must therefore convert the text into a formalised version which eliminates any ambiguity or uncertainty;

- it is there to *help in deciding* on a design for the possible future system, so it must make no assumptions at all about what that solution is to be;

- so that both the users for whom the system is being created and the software engineers who are creating it fully understand each other, the model needs to be in such a form that they can all understand it;

- and finally, in the event that there are any disagreements about whether the system that was eventually delivered met the customers' requirements, the model (modified, if necessary, by mutual agreement as time goes on) remains as a definitive statement of what was agreed.

I have already mentioned many of the definitive aspects of a data requirement which need to be included in any model, but here is a comprehensive list.

The model needs to include:

a) a record of each **entity** or thing;

b) details of all the **attributes** of each entity, including in each case their data type, whether or not they are identifying attributes, and any restrictions on their possible values or size;

c) all the **relationships** between entities, including in each case all of their **degrees** and **participation conditions**;

d) any additional **constraints** on the data which are not already included in the other parts of the model;

e) any **assumptions** which had to be made in analysing the written requirement.

There exist many different conventions for the diagrammatic part of a conceptual data model. The Entity-Relationship convention, which I have chosen to use in this book, represents the degree and participation conditions of a relationship by combinations of the symbols at each end of a line representing that relationship:

d)   Analysing a requirement – the Garage example

Let's look at how this works for the Garage requirement, starting by showing how we represent the words, "The garage company has a number of employees . . An employee can also be a customer of the company, and vice versa."

Employees and customers are clearly kinds of entity, and we represent each entity with a box. And a relationship is represented by a line between boxes.

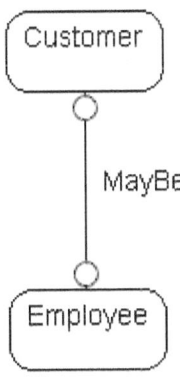

Fig 28: simple E-R diagram of
Customer and Employee

So, we have a box for each entity, Customer and Employee, and a line for the relationship between them, to which we give a meaningful name, "MayBe."

The small discs at each end of the line show both the participation conditions of the relationship. In this case both discs are white, showing optional participation by each entity (mandatory participation is shown by a black disc ●).

The line itself shows us the degree of the relationship. In this case it's a simple straight line, telling us that the degree is 1:1. (A degree of "n" is represented by the "crow's foot" symbol ➤ .)

Well, I have created these two entities and shown how they are related, but I haven't represented the *attributes* of these entities. Again, the written requirement tells us what's needed, and we record the attributes with what are called *entity types*, like this:

Entity Types

Employee(<u>NINumber</u>,Surname,Grade,DateStarted,DrivingLicenceNo)

Customer(<u>Surname,PostCode</u>,Address,Phone)

You should notice two things about these entity types:

• the identifying attribute or attributes, which were itemised in the written requirement, are underlined; for each entity type, the underlined attributes represent its *identifier*

- they only tell us the names of the attributes, and nothing about their possible values which were included in the written statement of requirements; we'll come to those details shortly, and most importantly

- the only attributes included are those in the written statement of requirements; there's nothing there to tell us about the relationship between the entities, because in the diagram this is already represented by the line between the boxes. You may remember that, back when we discussed the relational schema, we added an attribute to the Customer relation, a *posted foreign key*, to represent the relationship. But that is a specifically *relational* device, and while this book may well be about relational databases, remember also what I just said: the conceptual model *must make no assumptions at all about what the solution is to be.*

Let's move on, and look at how we represent the words, "Some employees are managed by another company employee."

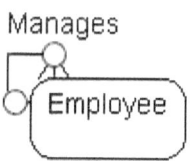

Fig. 29: E-R diagram of the recursive Manages relationship

This is a recursive relationship, so the line representing it comes out of the entity box and returns to the same box. The end of the line at the left hand side of the Employee box represents an employee managing others; the white circle shows that the managing activity is optional, while the crow's foot at the other end of the line shows that many employees can be managed.

Starting from the other end of the line – the top side of the box – this represents an employee being managed. Again, the white circle shows that it's optional to be managed, while the single line at the other end shows that, if an employee is managed, they are managed by just one other employee.

We know all this because "Some employees are managed by another company employee. An Apprentice can be managed by a Fitter or a Chargehand, but a Fitter can only be managed by a Chargehand. Each Fitter and Chargehand can manage zero or more employees, but a Fitter can only manage Apprentices." But we have more work to do yet, in representing all of the information in those words.

And again, note that we don't make any change to the entity type for Employee, to represent the relationship; it's represented just by the line between the boxes.

So now, we need to complete the diagram and entity types, by representing the relationships between Employee and Job, and between Job and Customer.

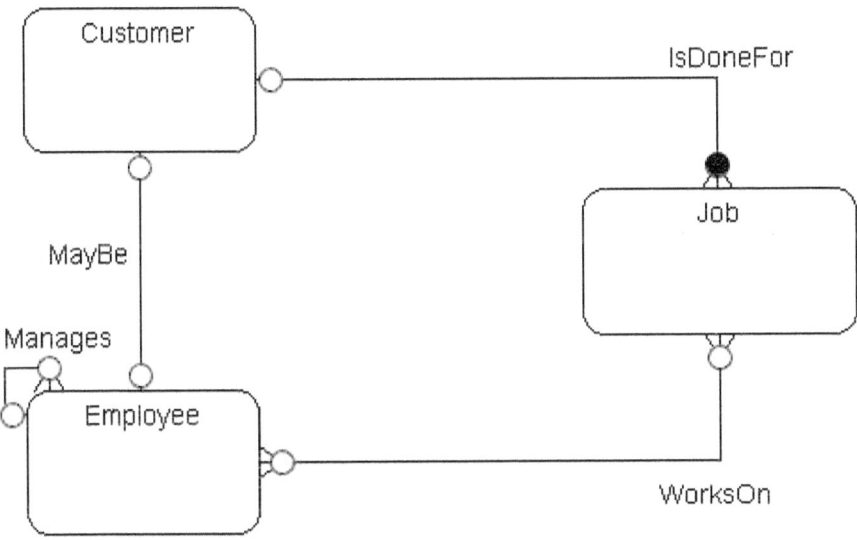

Fig 30: complete E-R diagram for the Garage requirement

(As a reminder of how to read the symbols representing degree and participation, look at the IsDoneFor relationship. For any entity in a relationship, the disc *nearest* that entity represents its participation condition –

whether or not it has to participate in the relationship – and the end of the line nearest the *other* entity represents *how many* of that other entity may be involved.

So, if we ask how many Customers a Job is done for, the black disk next to Job tells us that it's mandatory for Job; that is, a Job has to be done for *at least one* Customer. And the single ending to the line at the other end tells us that it *can't be more than one* Customer. So, a Job is done for *exactly one* Customer.

If, instead, we ask how many Jobs can be done for each Customer, the white disc next to Customer tells us it's optional for Customer, i.e. a Customer *need not have any Jobs* done. But the crow's foot at the other end tells us that it can be *more than one.* So, a Customer can have *zero, one or many* Jobs done.)

Entity Types

Employee(<u>NINumber</u>,Surname,Grade,DateStarted,DrivingLicenceNo)

Customer(<u>Surname,PostCode</u>,Address,Phone,Discount)

Job(<u>RegNo,DateStart,JobDescription</u>,Make,DateEnd,Hours)

If you remember much about how the relational schema for the Garage was written, back in Chapter 5, you will note something very different here: there are only three entities, where in the schema we had four relations. This is because, as we explained back there, the relational model cannot directly represent a relationship of m:n; and that is precisely the nature of the relationship between Employee and Job. So we had to create a special *intersection relation*, to do the job.

But because the conceptual model has to be independent of any possible solution, it has no need to be constrained by the limits of a relational system, and it's just fine to represent the m:n relationship with a line between boxes – with, of course, the appropriate degree and participation shown.

And, as with the recursive relationship in Employee, the relationship between Job and Customer is represented just by the line between the boxes, not by any additional attributes.

We now need to deal with all the other things which were detailed in the written requirement, but which were beyond the scope of the E-R diagram and the entity types.

Firstly, we need to add a section called Additional Constraints. They are *additional* because the diagram and entity types have *already* represented many constraints, for example every employee must have a unique national insurance number, a customer can be identical to at most one employee – and so on. So it's important to remember that a fact is recorded in this section only if it couldn't be represented in the diagram or the entity types.

Additional Constraints

c1   A National Insurance Number consists of two letters followed by six numerals and one letter

c2   A driving licence number consists of five letters followed by six numerals, two letters, one numeral and two letters.

c3   A surname can have up to twenty letters or spaces

c4   A grade is either Fitter, Chargehand, Apprentice or Receptionist

c5   An Apprentice can be managed by a Fitter or a Chargehand

c6   A Fitter can only be managed by a Chargehand

c7   A Fitter can only manage Apprentices

c8   Only employees of grades Chargehand, Fitter or Apprentice can work on jobs

c9   Only customers who are also employees can have a discount level recorded

c10   An address and a job description can each have up to thirty letters or spaces

c11   A phone number which can have up to fifteen numerals.

c12   A level of discount can be between 1 and 99

c13   Time is recorded in hours and tenths of an hour.

c14   A registration number consists of two letters followed by two numerals and three letters

Finally, we need a section to contain, by contrast, facts which *absolutely have already been represented in the diagram or entity types,* and we call this section the Assumptions. Remembering that everything in the diagram and entity types is definitive (an entity has just these attributes, a participation condition is just either optional or mandatory, and so on), it's possible that when we come to draw up the model we'll find that we haven't collected the definite information to make a choice about, say, a participation condition, yet we have to take a stab at it, in order to complete the model; so we mention that under Assumptions.

Equally, we may well have recorded in our written requirement something we were definitely told by users, but when we come to represent it in the model, we are left wondering if the users actually understood the implications of that choice; so this again goes in the Assumptions, for the purpose of drawing attention to it.

Assumptions

a1   A job cannot be recorded without a start date *(the consequence of including DateStart in the identifier of Job)*

a2   An employee is not necessarily supervised by anyone *(the consequence of optional participation at the "1" end of Manages)*

So to sum up, a conceptual data model consists of four parts:

- a diagram, which represents the entities and the relationships between them;

- a list of entity types, which lists the attributes for each entity including whether they are identifying or not;

- an Additional Constraints section, which details all the necessary constraints on the data which could not be represented by the diagram or the entity types;

and an Assumptions section, which details any facts already represented in the preceding three sections, for the purpose of drawing attention to their effect.

e)   Analysing a requirement – the process

I moved rather quickly from the written Garage requirement to its representation as a conceptual data model, somewhat side-stepping some of the decisions involved in doing so. It's easy enough to see how to find things like the degrees of relationships and the permitted ranges of values, but the starting point when looking at a written statement of requirements is to identify the *entities* and their *attributes*, and they may not always be obvious from the text.

In a statement of requirements, a noun can be used to identify an entity, the attribute of an entity, or sometimes the value of an entity.

"Employee" is a noun, and we decided that it was an entity; but then "Apprentice" is also a noun, but we didn't make that an entity. So what are the rules for picking out the entities and their attributes?

First of all, make a list of all the nouns in the requirement, in this case the list will be:

employee

National Insurance Number

Driving licence number

surname

grade

Fitter

Chargehand

Apprentice

Receptionist

date

customer

post code

address

phone number

discount

job

registration number

description

make

Next, separate off from this list those nouns which describe things which have a relationship with one or more other things. This give us a list of possible entities:

employee (manages / is managed by other employees, works on jobs)

Fitter (manages apprentices)

Chargehand (manages fitters or apprentices)

Apprentice (is managed)

Receptionist (as an employee, is managed or can manage, no more details given) customer (may be employee, job is done for)

job (worked on by employees, is done for a customer)

And this leaves us with the list of remaining nouns:

National Insurance Number

Driving licence number

surname

grade

date

post code

address

phone number

discount

registration number

description

make

If any of the nouns in this list describes something for which *values* are recorded, then it is definitely an attribute of some entity. And this is in fact the case for all the nouns in this list; indeed in most cases we are told the permitted length or even the actual values permitted.

But this gives a slight problem: four of the nouns in our list of possible entities (Fitter, Chargehand, Apprentice and Receptionist) are in fact permitted *values* for one of the nouns (grade) in our list of attributes. Yet they do all seem to have relationships, making them probable entities. So which is correct?

In our model above, we have opted for the simplest solution; there is just one employee entity, with an attribute of grade. The restrictions on who can manage whom are dealt with in our Additional Constraints section.

But even in a simple scenario like our Garage, there is often more than one possible valid way to model it. Having completed a first version of a data model, an analyst always needs to check back to see if by reading it, he or she could re-construct exactly the written statement of requirements it was meant to represent; if not, it will be necessary to iterate back and make changes.

However, I will now show you a possible alternative approach to modelling this requirement.

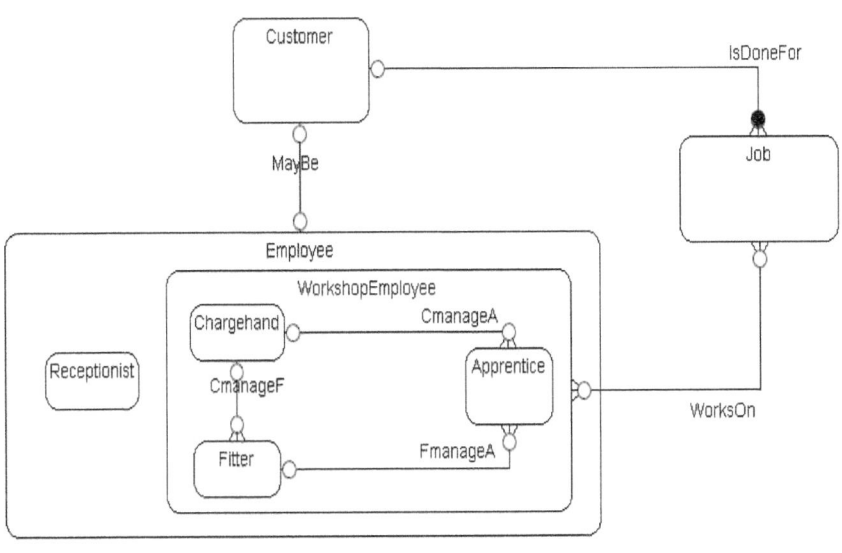

Fig. 31 an E-R diagram using subtypes

f)   Analysing a requirement – using entity sub types

Here, we've recognised that, as we noted above, Fitter, Chargehand, Apprentice and Receptionist can be viewed as possible entities themselves, as well as values of an attribute of the Employee entity; and they do each have distinct versions of the Manages relationship, e.g. only a Chargehand can manage a Fitter. And only those three grades were allowed to work on jobs. In our first version of the E-R model, where they were all represented as a single Employee entity, we had to manage those differences via some Additional Constraint entries.

But as we see here, the E-R model gives us the possibility of directly representing different forms of an entity: *entity subytpes*.

The notation for the entity types is slightly different when we use subtypes:

Entity Types

Employee(<u>NINumber</u>,Surname,DateStarted,DrivingLicenceNo)

    WorkshopEmployee()

        Fitter()

        Chargehand()

        Apprentice()

    Receptionist()

Customer(<u>Surname,PostCode</u>,Address,Phone,Discount)

Job(<u>RegNo,DateStart,JobDescription</u>,Make,DateEnd,Hours)

Here, the *entity supertype* – Employee – is given all the attributes which are common to all the subtypes. In this case it's all the same attributes given to our original single Employee entity; but as a minimum, a supertype will always have the *identifier* for the whole entity.

And the subtypes are given just the individual attributes which apply only to them (in this case, none) – and they *inherit* the shared attributes from the supertype. Likewise, if the subtype WorkshopEmployee had any attributes of its own, they would be inherited by the sub-subtypes Fitter, Chargehand and Apprentice. This is shown by the indented listing of all the subtypes.

This approach reduces our list of additional constraints somewhat, because we no longer need c_5, c_6 or c_7, which related to who-can-manage-whom, or c_8, which allowed only certain grades to work on jobs. It also removes the need for a *Grade* attribute in Employee, because the grades are now identified through the subtypes.

But it does instead call for an additional constraint, because our diagram now shows an Apprentice being possibly managed by both a Fitter and a Chargehand, when we know no-one can be managed by more than one other employee. Fortunately, the diagram convention enables us to represent this *exclusive relationship* – i.e. an Apprentice may be managed by a Chargehand OR a Fitter but not both – by an arc in the diagram instead of by an Additional Constraint. So now here is the complete Garage model, using subtypes, and showing that exclusivity:

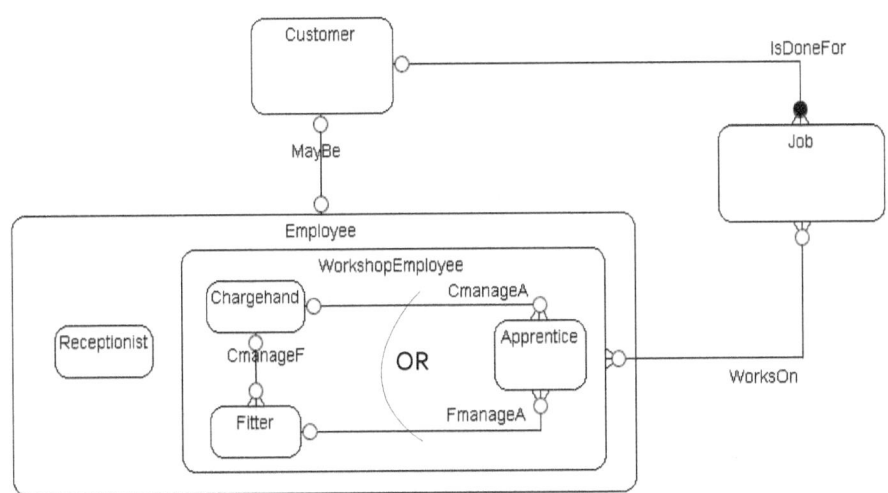

Entity Types

Employee(<u>NINumber</u>,Surname,DateStarted,DrivingLicenceNo)

   WorkshopEmployee()

      Fitter()

      Chargehand()

      Apprentice()

   Receptionist()

Customer(<u>Surname,PostCode,</u>Address,Phone)

Job(<u>RegNo,DateStart,JobDescription,</u>Make,DateEnd,Hours)

Additional Constraints

C1   A National Insurance Number consists of two letters followed by six numerals and one letter

C2   A driving licence number consists of five letters followed by six numerals, two letters, one numeral and two letters.

C3   A surname can have up to twenty letters or spaces

c4   A grade is either Fitter, Chargehand, Apprentice or Receptionist

c5   Only customers who are also employees can have a discount level recorded

c6   An address and a job description can each have up to thirty letters or spaces

c7   A phone number which can have up to fifteen numerals.

c8   A level of discount can be between 1 and 99

c9   Time is recorded in hours and tenths of an hour.

c10   A registration number consists of two letters followed by two numerals
and three letters

Fig. 32 a complete E-R model for Garage, using subtypes

g)   *Validating an E-R model*

The model we first create, by using the nouns and descriptive phrases in the written requirement to derive entities, attributes and relationships, may not always be a perfect representation of that requirement. We need to carry out two kinds of tests to check this.

Firstly, as I already mentioned, a valid model must be clear and unambiguous, so we ought to be able to intepret it, to "read it back", as it were, in order to try and reconstitute a version of the written requirement which we can compare with the original.

Secondly, we can look at the samples of actual data which we have collected from the organisation, and see whether they could be correctly represented in our model.

If our model passes both those tests, then it is correct, and we could then go on to use it to create a database design which would correctly satisfy the data requirements of the enterprise. If not then we will need to look at where our reconstituted requirement differs from the original, or where the sample data is not a good fit, so as to identify the ways in which the model needs to be changed; we can then repeat the reconstitution exercise until we have a perfect match.

So let's start by looking at our first version of the E-R model for the Garage requirement:

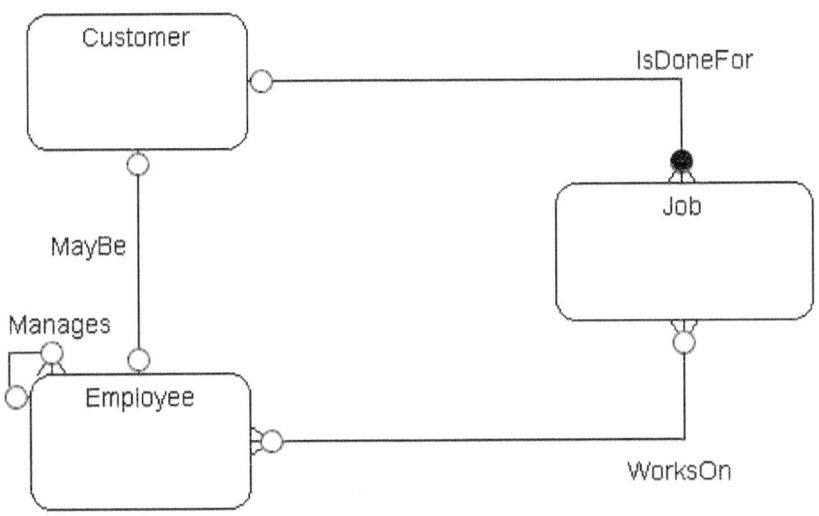

Entity Types

Employee(<u>NINumber</u>,Surname,Grade,DateStarted,DrivingLicenceNo)
Customer(<u>Surname,PostCode</u>,Address,Phone,Discount)
Job(<u>RegNo,DateStart,JobDescription</u>,Make,DateEnd,Hours)

Additional Constraints

c1   A National Insurance Number consists of two letters followed by six numerals and one letter

c2   A driving licence number consists of five letters followed by six numerals, two letters, one numeral and two letters.

c3   A surname can have up to twenty letters or spaces

c4   A grade is either Fitter, Chargehand, Apprentice or Receptionist

c5   An Apprentice can be managed by a Fitter or a Chargehand

c6   A Fitter can only be managed by a Chargehand

c7   A Fitter can only manage Apprentices

c8   Only employees of grades Chargehand, Fitter or Apprentice can work on jobs

c9   Only customers who are also employees can have a discount level recorded

c10   An address and a job description can each have up to thirty letters or spaces

c11   A phone number which can have up to fifteen numerals.

c12   A level of discount can be between 1 and 99

c13   Time is recorded in hours and tenths of an hour.

c14   A registration number consists of two letters followed by two numerals and three letters

Assumptions

a1   A job cannot be recorded without a start date

a2   An employee is not necessarily supervised by anyone

Fig. 33: the initial E-R model for Garage

h)   Interpreting the model

Employee is an entity (from the E-R diagram), hence a number of employees can be recorded. Each employee (from the entity headings) must be identified by their national insurance number, which (from Constraint c1) consists of two letters followed by six numerals and one letter. They may also have a driving licence number recorded, which (from Constraint c2) consists of five letters followed by six numerals, two letters, one numeral and two letters. And their surname (up to twenty letters or spaces, Constraint c3), grade (which must be either Fitter, Chargehand, Apprentice or Receptionist, Constraint c4) and the date they started with the company, are all also recorded.

The recursive relationship *Manages* (shown in the diagram, 1:n and optional at both ends) tells us that some employees can manage one or more other employees, or be managed by just one other; but from Constraints c5, 6, and 7 we know that an Apprentice can be managed by a Fitter or a Chargehand, but a Fitter can only be managed by a Chargehand and can in turn only manage Apprentices.

The diagram also shows the entity Customer, which means a number of customers can be recorded; and the 1:1 optional relationship MayBe shows that the same person may be both customer and employee. The entity heading tells us that a customer is identified by their surname and post code, and that their address (consisting of up to thirty letters or spaces, Constraint c10) and phone number (consisting of up to fifteen numerals, Constraint c11) are also recorded. Only if the customer is also an employee (Constraint c9) can we record their discount level, which is between 1 and 99 (Constraint c12).

The final entity in the diagram, Job, tells us that many jobs can be recorded, and the m:n relationship WorksOn shows that each employee can work on many jobs and each job can be worked on by many employees. However Constraint c8 shows that only those employees who are Chargehands, Fitters or Apprentices can work on jobs. The 1:n relationship IsDoneFor means that each job is done for some single customer, and that each customer can have none or many jobs done for them.

Meanwhile the entity headings tell us that a job is identified by a combination of the vehicle registration (consisting of two letters, two numerals and three letters, Constraint c14), the date it was started and a description of the job (consisting of up to thirty letters, Constraint c10); and that we also record the make of the vehicle, and, when it has been completed, the date of completion and the time taken (in hours and tenths of an hour, Constraint C13).

Comparing the paragraphs we have just written with the requirement for the Garage system (Fig 24), we can see that they each contain exactly the same information and restrictions; so the model is a valid representation of the requirement.

i) Checking the model against the sample data

So now we look at the data which our system will need to record (figs 25 – 27), to see whether the model can correctly represent it too.

For this, we simply need to examine the entity headings and additional constraints in our model, and compare them with the attributes and attribute values listed in the sample data. And in this case we can see that the data can indeed be correctly represented in our model.

Exercise 7

Now, here is another statement of requirements and sample data – this time for a train operating company.

Wyvern Trains

Wyvern Trains operates passenger services within its small network of 21 stations. Some stations have shorter platforms than others, and can only accommodate trains with a maximum of six coaches. Each train, which is identified by a three digit running number, is made up of either one or two sets of five coaches and an electric locomotive. Each set of coaches is identified by a serial number and weighs a total of 250 tonnes when fully laden. The locomotives are each identified by a serial number and are of various types with varying pulling power; a locomotive allocated to a train must be able to pull at least the weight of that train. Wyvern employs a number of drivers, each identified by their serial number, who need to be qualified in order to drive any given type of locomotive; the drivers' surnames are also recorded. A driver is not allowed to be on duty driving a train for more than a total of 6 hours in any day.

Wyvern wishes to install a database system to replace its existing manual records, which will enable it to allocate drivers, locomotives and carriages to trains, and to produce timetables.

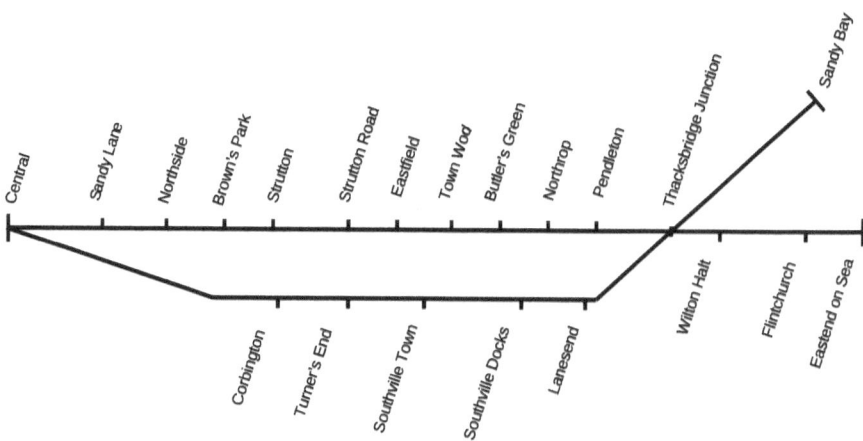

Fig. 34: the Wyvern Trains network

Station Name	Platform Length
Brown's Park	Short
Butler's Green	Short
Central	Long

Station Name	Platform Length
Corbington	Long
Eastend on Sea	Long
Eastfield	Short
Flintchurch	Long
Lanesend	Long
Northrop	Short
Northside	Short
Pendleton	Long
Sandy Bay	Long
Sandy Lane	Short
Southville Docks	Long
Southville Town	Long
Strutton	Short
Strutton Road	Short
Thacksbridge Junction	Long
Town Wood	Short
Turner's End	Long
Wilton Halt	Short

Fig. 35: stations and platform lengths

Monday to Friday		Central to Sandy Bay or Eastend on Sea					
Service number		711	811	311	813	815	
Central	d	0725	0740	-	0900	0945	
Corbington	d	-	0745	-	0905	0950	
Turner's End	d	-	0750	-	0910	0955	
Southville Town	d	-	0755	-	0915	1000	
Southville Docks	d	-	0800	-	0920	1005	
Lanesend	d	-	0805	-	0925	1010	
Sandy Lane	d	0730	-	-			
Northside	d	0735	-	-			
Brown's Park	d	0740	-	-			
Strutton	d	0745	-	-			
Strutton Road	d	0750	-	-			
Eastfield	d	0755	-	-			
Town Wood	d	0800	-	-			
Butler's Green	d	0805	-	-			
Northrop	d	0810	-	-			
Pendleton	d	0815	-	-			
Thacksbridge Jcn	d	0820	0810	0815	0930	1015	
Wilton Halt	d	0825	-	-			
Flintchurch	d	0830	-	0820			
Eastend on Sea	a	0835	-	0830			
Sandy Bay	a	-	0815	-	0935	1020	

Monday to Friday	Sandy Bay or Eastend on Sea to Central			
Service number		801	802	701
Sandy Bay	d	0650	0730	-
Eastend on Sea	d	-	-	0755
Flintchurch	d	-	-	0800
Wilton Halt	d	-	-	0805
Thacksbridge Jcn	d	0655	0735	0810
Pendleton	d	-	-	0815
Northrop	d	-	-	0820
Butler's Green	d	-	-	0825
Town Wood	d	-	-	0830
Eastfield	d	-	-	0835
Strutton Road	d	-	-	0840
Strutton	d	-	-	0845
Brown's Park	d	-	-	0850
Northside	d	-	-	0855
Sandy Lane	d	-	-	0900
Lanesend	d	0700	0740	-
Southville Docks	d	0705	0745	-
Southville	d	0710	0750	-
Turner's End	d	0715	0755	-
Corbington	d	0720	0800	-
Central	a	0725	0805	0905

Fig. 36: extracts from timetables

129

NatInsNo	Surname	Qualifications
DQ435721A	Johnson	Type 15, Type 12
FV546890B	Robinson	Type 15
QQ525687D	Smith	Type 12, Type 22
UD987234A	Wilkins	Type 12, Type 15, Type 22
VU241367D	Johnson	Type 15
VF219787C	Khan	Type 12, Type 15

Fig. 37: extract from list of drivers

Serial number	Type	Max towing weight
120560	12	400 tonnes
120562	12	400 tonnes
120563	12	400 tonnes
153450	15	600 tonnes
153467	15	600 tonnes
159901	15	600 tonnes
220030	22	750 tonnes
220443	22	750 tonnes
220444	22	750 tonnes

Fig. 38: extract from list of locomotives

Serial Number
153340
153341
153342
159901
159902
159903
158790
158793
158794
157777
157678
156789
156799
156800

Fig. 39: extract from list of carriage sets

Using what we've covered so far, analyse the Wyvern Trains requirement and create an E-R model to represent it, including diagram, entity types, additional constraints and assumptions. In this scenario, parts of the requirement are implied by the information in Figures 34-39, as well as in the written statement of requirements.

Bear in mind that, in addition to any constraints explicitly mentioned in the requirement, in a computer system further constraints may be needed for consistency, e.g. a train can't arrive before it's departed, a driver can't be in two places at once, etc. Do not use entity subtypes.

Chapter 11: Data model to database design

1   Basic mapping from a model to an SQL schema

This process can be described by the following simple mapping, which largely follows the principles of the *relational* schema:

> - an entity becomes a table

> - an entity subtype can either become a table in its own right, or be subsumed into a table with other subtypes of the same entity (we will discuss this choice later)

> - an attribute becomes a column, where

>> - the identifier becomes the primary key

>> - a defined value set can be defined in a domain or in a check constraint

>> - compound data can be represented with columns or with additional tables

> - relationships are represented by a foreign key or keys

>> - degrees of 1:1 and 1:n by a single foreign key or by relation-for-relationship

>> - degrees of m:n by relation-for-relationship only

> - constraints are represented by check constraints or by triggers.

As a simple example, let us compare the entity Employee, in the initial E-R model for the Garage requirement (Fig. 33 above), with its implementation in the Garage relational schema (Fig. 15 above) and in the Garage SQL database which you have:

E-R model
Employee(<u>NINumber</u>,Surname,Grade,DateStarted,DrivingLicenceNo)

Relational model
relation Employee
>   NatInsNo: NatInsNos
>   Surname: Names
>   Grade: Grades
>   DateJoined: Dates
>   DrivingLicenceNo: DLNos

Manager: NatInsNos
Primary key NatInsNo
Foreign key Manager **references** Employee

SQL schema
        CREATE TABLE employee (
                nat_ins_no nat_ins_nos,
                surname names,
                grade grades,
                date_joined dates,
                dl_no dl_nos,
                manager nat_ins_nos,
                PRIMARY KEY (nat_ins_no),
                FOREIGN KEY (manager) REFERENCES employee
*(Don't for the moment worry about the structure of the SQL CREATE TABLE statement,
which I will explain in full in the next chapter.)*

In this comparison, you will note that I have chosen to represent the allowed value
sets for each column by using defined domains (nat_ins_nos, names, grades, etc.) as
in the relational model. Unlike the relational model, however, SQL does not insist
upon the use of domains, and I could instead have written individual constraints for
each column. However, for example, both the employee and the manager columns
need to have the allowable values for national insurance numbers constrained by the
same rules, so including them in a single place in a domain (with its own value set
constraint, which we'll discuss later), avoids tiresome repetition and ensures
consistency.

You will also note the declaration of the single foreign key *manager*, again as in the
relational model, to represent the recursive 1:n relationship *is managed by*.

2   *Compound data*

Compound data can be said to occur where an attribute consists of a possibly
unknown number of values, and this can be a problem for relational databases,
because a relation can only have a fixed number of attributes (its degree), and all
values are atomic (see Chapter 5 Section 1). We have two potential solutions: multiple
attributes or separate entities.

A good example of compound data is given by postal addresses, and this is where the multiple attribute approach is usually taken. In the Customer relation of the Garage schema (Figure 10), I chose, for the sake of simplicity, to record the customer addresses in two attributes, PostCode and Address.

Customer

Surname	PostCode	Address	Phone
Johnson	BV1 9SW	9 High St	402973
Petty	BV1 9ST	250 High St	407865
Wilson	BV7 0BB	22 The Drive	881545
Simpson	BV3 1AS	32 Forest Row	690513
Newman	BV2 1PO	42 Union St	409111
Ellis	BV3 4RT	12 Windsor Ave	690190

In fact, within the UK, in theory a postal address needs only a street number (or, where there is no street number, a building name) to guarantee correct addressing, so we could neatly satisfy that requirement by changing just one column and removing the street names altogether:

Customer

Surname	PostCode	StreetNumber	BuildingName	Phone
Johnson	BV1 9SW	9		402973
Petty	BV1 9ST	250		407865
Wilson	BV7 0BB	22		881545
Simpson	BV3 1AS	32		690513
Newman	BV2 1PO	42		409111
Ellis	BV3 4RT	12		690190

This data could then be linked to a copy of the UK postcode database to produce, if necessary, to full address details in each case, including locality, town, county etc, and indeed this is the approach taken with many operational databases.

However, this already gives us at least a small issue, in that we now have two columns, StreetNumber and BuildingName, one of which will always be empty for every tuple, and we will need a constraint of some kind to ensure that this is always the case.

And this won't work for most addresses in other countries; even for our garage database we might have to allow for one of our customers having a principle address in another country. Postal codes in many countries can define quite large areas, too, so additional details will always be needed to give a unique address. Obviously the most common situation where the full details are needed is in the printing of an address label, and that can only be done correctly if each separate line of an address is stored as a separate value, and that means a separate attribute for each of those lines. The number of lines in an address can vary widely, but to cater for all eventualities we would need to provide maybe as many as six or seven attributes – several of which would remain empty for the majority of addresses which are shorter.

The only alternative to this arrangement, in a relational database, is to store the multiple values in a separate entity. Since, in our example, each customer has many address lines, and most of the address lines (street name, town, etc) will relate to many customers, we are necessarily talking about a relationship with a degree of m:n:

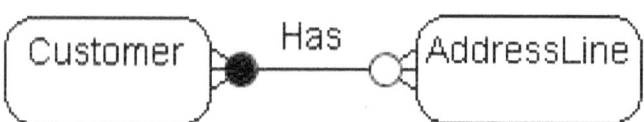

Figure 40 - an initial representation of compound data using separate entities

However, this is too simple. When we come on to create an SQL schema we will of course need an intersection relation to represent the relationship, but even in the E-R model we need an intersection entity, because in order to print out an address we must know in what order the address lines should appear, so:

Entity Types

Customer(<u>Surname,Phone</u>)

Has(<u>Surname,Phone,LineRef</u>,SequenceNo)

AddressLine(<u>LineRef</u>,Data)

Figure 41 – a better representation of compound data using separate entities

As you can see this is a rather complex solution, and the simpler multiple attribute approach is probably more likely to be used for address data, despite its drawbacks. The separate entity approach is more applicable where the potential number of attributes is much larger, for example where it is necessary to record the individual components of some mechanical assembly, which might run into the hundreds, and where it would be very undesirable to store such a large number of potentially empty attributes.

3   *Entity subtypes*

In Figure 31, above, I showed an alternative, and arguably more accurate way of representing the Employee entity of the Garage database, using two subtypes, Receptionist and WorkshopEmployee, and in turn three subtypes of WorkshopEmployee: Fitter, Chargehand and Apprentice. Rather like the separate entity approach to compound data which we just discussed, this avoided unnecessary empty attributes, but at the cost of added complexity.

However, we cannot directly represent entity subtypes in a relational database. A relation has just a fixed number of attributes and a variable number of tuples; it doesn't have subtypes.

(At this point, you might well ask why, then, in a book about relational databases, should we have even mentioned entity subtypes? The answer is that, as we said earlier, the data analysis activity should always properly be undertaken in the absence of any decision about a solution. A case might arise, for example, where we thought the direct representation of entity subtypes was so important that we would decide on a different, non-relational solution.)

As with compound data, there are just two possible approaches to representing entity subtypes: we can use a single relation for all the subtypes, with additional, possibly empty, attributes, to distinguish between them; or we can use a separate relation for each subtype.

You will have seen that, in the actual SQL implementation of the Garage database which we used in Chapter 9, I chose the single relation approach. Receptionists, Chargehands, Fitters and Apprentices were all recorded in the same way in a single relation, with a attribute of Grade to distinguish between them. The E-R diagram in Figure 30 shows much of the way that would have to work. From the relationships shown, all those employees could apparently manage other employees, and work on jobs. So where we use a single relation, we need additional constraints to ensure, for example, that a Receptionist couldn't work on Jobs, and that an Apprentice couldn't manage other employees.

We could, alternatively, have used the separate relation approach; four in all, one for each of the Employee subtypes in Figure 31. This would obviate the need for most of those additional constraints, because the relationships are separated out in such a way that, for example, a Receptionist could never be involved in carrying out a Job, and only Chargehands and Fitters could be involved in management of others.

So far so good; but because of the inability to represent supertypes and subtypes, we have no way, in this separate relation approach, to directly show that Chargehands, Fitters, Apprentices and Receptionists are even Employees, so their possible connections to Customers and Jobs would have to be shown by a series of separate relationships, with accompanying constraints.

An additional issue in this approach concerns the uniqueness of primary keys. Since all of these employees would have to be identified by keys (in this case national insurnace numbers) taken from the same domain, the potential arises for the same national insurance number value to occur for, say, both a Receptionist and a Fitter, meaning duplication of what must remain a value which is unique to an individual. So we would need a constraint in each of the new relations, to prevent any such duplication.

Chapter 12: The SQL Data Definition Language (DDL)

If you haven't already done so, you will need to refer to Appendix 4, to find how to install SQL Anywhere and create databases, in order to carry out the practical work in this chapter.

1   *A word about* base tables *and* views

In Chapter 8, I touched briefly on the difference between base tables and views; it's time now to go into more detail.

- a **base table** is what we usually mean when we carelessly use the word "table"; it's the direct representation of a relation, and, like a relation, we would create it as an empty container to hold data; together, the base tables comprise the "real" database

- but SQL also provides for something called a **view**, which is effectively a stored query, having the exact structure of a base table, but the data it appears to contain is actually drawn from parts or the whole of one or more actual base tables; it doesn't itself actually contain any physical data. The usefulness of views will become apparent later.

We are quite correct to use the term "table" to include both base tables and views, because from the point of view of the DML, they can be queried and manipulated together as if they were the same thing (subject to some restrictions, which we'll come to later); for example, a base table can be JOINed to a view.

But for now, we'll be concerned with just the base tables.

2   *Creating and removing tables*

As we saw briefly in Section 1 of the last chapter, the syntax of the command for creating an SQL base table is very similar to that for creating a relation, basically just

```
CREATE TABLE <table name> (
      <column definition list>,
      PRIMARY KEY (<column name list>) )
```

However, defining columns requires that they each be given a defined data type, e.g.

```
CREATE TABLE bus (
        regno CHAR(7),
        maker CHAR(10),
        type CHAR(20),
        seats SMALLINT,
        PRIMARY KEY (regno) )
```
Query 52: the initial Bus table

(A list of standard SQL data types is given in Appendix 1.)

Let's create a new database, wyvernbuses, to try out the DDL. In Appendix 4, you will find instructions for doing that. Then close SQL Central.

Next, open Interactive SQL, enter the User Id and Password, select the Action "Start and connect to a database on this computer." Browse to the location where you stored the database file for wyvernbuses (which will be *wyvernbuses.db*, press *Open* and then *Connect*. Now run Query 52 above.

(Note that Interactive SQL responds to any successful query, other than the retrieval of data, with the slightly disconcerting message "(No Results)" - this is normal.)

Check that the table has been created, by running

```
SELECT *
FROM bus
```
You will find that an empty table has been created, with the four columns in the CREATE TABLE statement.

Open SQL Central, double click on the *wyvernbuses* line in the main window. This will display all the information headings relating to the new database. Double click on the *Tables* entry at the top, and then on the single entry *bus*. You will now see full details of your new table, showing that the four columns have exactly the data types you specified.

You will also note the column *Null*, which contains check boxes showing whether occurrences of each column are allowed to be null. The box for the primary key is unchecked, because (as we know from the relational model), primary keys are never allowed to contain nulls.

However the other two columns are checked, because by default, all non-primary-key columns in an SQL database *are* allowed to contains nulls. Shortly, we'll look at how to prevent a non-primary-key column from containing nulls.

In Interactive SQL, run

```
DROP TABLE bus
```

In SQL Central, select View – Refresh All. You will find that the new database now contains no tables.

3 *Inserting and updating data*

The INSERT statement is used to populate a table with data.

First, run Query 52 again, to re-create the *bus* table, and then run the following queries. Notice that values for a string data type must (according to the standard) be enclosed in quotes, although some dbms implementations do not insist on this.

```
INSERT INTO bus(regno,maker,type,seats)
       VALUES ('AQ12CDE','Volvo','B7TL',68);
INSERT INTO bus(regno,maker,type,seats)
       VALUES ('MN03TSK','Volvo','B5LH',90);
INSERT INTO bus(regno,maker,type,seats)
       VALUES
('VD09BVD','Iveco','Europolis',23);
INSERT INTO bus(regno,maker,type,seats)
       VALUES
('VD09BVE','Iveco','Europolis',23);
INSERT INTO bus(regno,maker,type,seats)
       VALUES
('VD09BVF','Iveco','Europolis',23);
INSERT INTO bus(regno,maker,type,seats)
       VALUES ('QP11ABC','VDL','CLE',70);
INSERT INTO bus(regno,maker,type,seats)
       VALUES
('VI14PPK','Optare','CityPacer',25);
INSERT INTO bus(regno,maker,type,seats)
       VALUES ('VI17LFK','Ford','Tourneo','8');
```
                    Query 53: data for the Bus table

Now run

```
SELECT *
FROM bus
```

to check that your data has been correctly inserted.

Now try the following, which should all fail

```
INSERT INTO bus(regno,maker,seats)
        VALUES ('MN03TSK','Iveco',30)
```
Query 53a: duplicate primary key

(the primary key value already exists – the dbms gives a correct error message)

```
INSERT INTO bus(regno,maker,seats)
        VALUES (NULL,'Iveco',30)
```
Query 53b: null in primary key

(a primary key cannot be NULL – the dbms gives a correct error message)

```
INSERT INTO bus(regno,maker,seats)
        VALUES ('MN03TSL',Iveco,30)
```
Query 53c: quote marks missing

(the value for *maker* is not enclosed in quotes so the dbms attempts to match it with a column name)

```
INSERT INTO bus(regno,maker,seats)
        VALUES ('MN03TSL','Leyland DAF
Vehicles',30)
```
Query 53d: value outside range

(the value for *maker* is too long for the column as defined)

```
INSERT INTO bus
        VALUES ('MN03TSL',30,'Iveco')
```
Query 53e: values not matched to columns

(it is perfectly possible to use an INSERT statement without specifying column names, but in that case the value set must exactly match the defined column structure, i.e. all the columns must be given values or NULLs, and they must be in the right order. In this case the columns are out of order, so the dbms is trying to read 'Iveco' as an integer).

The DELETE FROM statement is used to delete rows from a table

```
DELETE FROM bus
        WHERE regno = 'VI14PPK'
```
After running this, you can check using SELECT * or via SQL Central, that only the first seven rows you inserted now remain in the table.

The simple statement

```
DELETE FROM bus
```
would delete all the rows in the table.

The UPDATE statement is used to change data in existing rows

```
UPDATE bus
      SET seats = 70
      WHERE regno = 'AQ12CDE'
```

Let's now create another table, to record bus drivers, and populate it with some data, in order to look at some other aspects.

```
CREATE TABLE driver (
      nat_ins_no CHAR(9),
      name CHAR(20),
      dob DATE,
      PRIMARY KEY (nat_ins_no) )
```
Query 54: the initial Driver table
```
INSERT INTO driver(nat_ins_no,name,dob)
      VALUES
('UD987234A','Khan','1997/06/18');
INSERT INTO driver(nat_ins_no,name,dob)
      VALUES
('DQ435721A','Wilson','1990/01/07');
INSERT INTO driver(nat_ins_no,name,dob)
      VALUES
('FV546890B','Smith','1991/08/20');
INSERT INTO driver(nat_ins_no,name,dob)
      VALUES
('QQ525687D','Robinson','1980/12/10');
INSERT INTO driver(nat_ins_no,name,dob)
      VALUES
('VF219787C','Desai','1972/06/12');
INSERT INTO driver(nat_ins_no,name,dob)
      VALUES
('VU241367D','Winston','1983/02/07');
```
Query 55: values for the Driver table

4   Constraints

In our new Wyvernbuses database, we have already created several constraints, just by defining the tables, as we saw when entering data into the Bus table:

- a primary key cannot contain duplicate values

- a primary key cannot contain a NULL

- a column can only contain values matching its defined data type

- a column can only contain values within its defined data length

Let us now look at further constraints which can be defined, to implement those in a data requirement.

a)   Referential constraints, and relationship degrees

As we saw when looking at the relational model in Section 7 of Chapter 5, the single method of representing a relationship is the foreign key, which imposes a *referential constraint*. In SQL as in the relational model, the definition of a foreign key on a table constrains the table to which the key refers:

- by default, a foreign key confers the ON DELETE RESTRICT referential action, which means the referenced row cannot be deleted unless all referencing rows in the foreign key are first deleted or amended;

- optionally, a foreign key can be defined as

  ○ ON DELETE SET NULL, where if a referenced row is deleted all referencing foreign key values will be automatically set to NULL – provided their column definition allows this;

  ○ ON DELETE SET DEFAULT, where if a referenced row is deleted all referencing foreign key values will be automatically set to a pre-defined default value; or

  ○ ON DELETE CASCADE, where if a referenced row is deleted all referencing rows will be deleted too.

To start with, let's assume that we need to define a foreign key on the Driver table, showing that a Driver can be assigned to a Bus. This would implement the following E-R model:

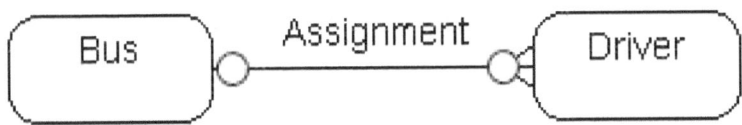

Entity types

Bus(regno,maker,seats)

Driver(nat ins no,name,dob)

Assumptions

a1   Only a driver's current assignment is shown (because this model only allows a driver to be assigned to a single bus

Figure 42 – an initial data model for Wyvern Buses

To create the foreign key necessary to represent the Assignment relationship, we first use the ALTER TABLE statement, to add a column to the Driver table.

The new column has to be defined with the same data type and length as the column it will be referencing, in this case the primary key of the Bus table, i.e. *regno*, which is CHAR(7). And we then make it a foreign key:

```
ALTER TABLE driver
      ADD bus CHAR(7);
ALTER TABLE driver
      ADD CONSTRAINT assignment
          FOREIGN KEY (bus) REFERENCES bus
```
Query 55a: foreign key in *driver*

Two points to note here about this statement:

- a constraint, other than a primary key or a column definition, can optionally be given a name – in this case we follow a common principle of naming a foreign key for the relationship it represents, *assignment*

- in fact this adds the possibility of a simple way to remove a constraint, if necessary, by using its name, i.e. DROP CONSTRAINT <constraint-name>

- by default, a foreign key references the primary key of the table it is referencing, so the referenced column does not need to be included in the foreign key definition; as we saw in the relational model, though, a foreign key could reference an *alternate key*, and in that case the referenced column would have to be named.

The foreign key we have now created correctly represents the *assignment* relationship shown in Figure 42: it's an optional 1:n relationship, with the "n" end in Driver. To give a foreign key mandatory participation, as in the relational model, we define its column as NOT ALLOWED NULL. However, it would be impossible to do this using ALTER TABLE on a table which, as in this case, already contains data, because it would mean that all the drivers we've already inserted would instantly have to have valid foreign key values, before we've inserted any values in that column; so for the moment we can only leave it as optional anyway.

The other aspect which needs attention is the degree of the Assignment relationship. Given our Assumption that only a driver's current assignment is recorded, the degree of 1:n must surely be wrong: it means that many different drivers could be assigned to the same bus. So we need to amend the data model, to make the relationship 1:1:

Wyvern Buses

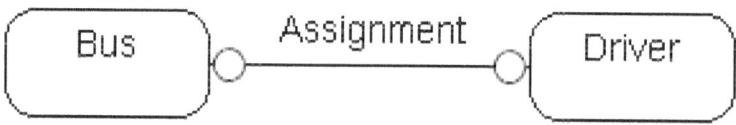

Entity types

Bus(regno,maker,seats)

Driver(nat_ins_no,name,dob)

Assumptions

a1   Only a driver's current assignment is shown (because this model only allows a driver to be assigned to a single bus

Figure 43 – an amended data model for Wyvern Buses

To make a foreign key "1" instead of "n", as with the relational model, we need to define it as having unique values; what, in the relational world, is known as an *alternate key*. SQL doesn't use that term, instead we define a column as UNIQUE:

```
ALTER TABLE driver
        ADD CONSTRAINT one_driver_per_bus
            UNIQUE (bus)
```

While this statement should work in standard SQL, SQLAnywhere does not allow a column defined as unique in this way to contain NULLs; it would make the relationship mandatory for *driver*, and this is not what is required by Figure 43.

Instead, we have to create a *unique index*, in this way:

```
CREATE UNIQUE INDEX one_driver_per_bus
on driver (bus)
```

We can now add actual driver assignments:

```
UPDATE driver
        SET bus = 'AQ12CDE'
        WHERE nat_ins_no = 'DQ435721A';
UPDATE driver
        SET bus = 'MN03TSK'
        WHERE nat_ins_no = 'FV546890B';
UPDATE driver
        SET bus = 'QP11ABC'
        WHERE nat_ins_no = 'QQ525687D';
UPDATE driver
        SET bus = 'VD09BVF'
        WHERE nat_ins_no = 'VF219787C';
```
Query 56: bus assignments for the initial Driver table

You can use SQL Central, or just SELECT * FROM driver, to confirm that the data is all in the *driver* table, with four of the drivers uniquely assigned to buses.

However, it is unlikely that Figure 43 actually represents a likely bus company scenario. The company probably does at least some forward planning to ensure it has enough vehicles and drivers available for the days ahead, and the drivers would probably like to know their next assignment.

This means allowing for drivers to be assigned, over time, to different buses, and for buses to be assigned to different drivers. And that means the Assignment relationship would become m:n

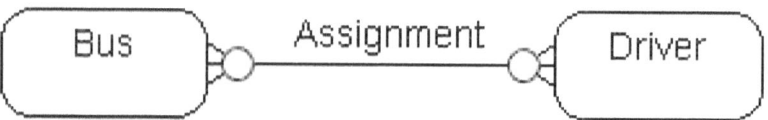

But even this doesn't really do a satisfactory job; it shows that a bus can have many drivers and a driver many buses, but there's nothing to stop that all happening at the same time.

If this is ringing bells in your memory, it should, because this is very much the same scenario we discussed in the context of uniqueness and minimality, in Section 3 of Chapter 5.

We know that we can't, in a relational database, directly represent a relationship of m:n with a simple foreign key, because there is no "right end" to place it. We have to create an intersection relation (or "link table", as it's sometimes called in an SQL context), to represent the relationship; and since that will store individual *instances* of the relationship, i.e. each time one driver is assigned to one bus, that's the right place to store data about each such assignment. So the model ought to look instead like this:

Wyvern Buses

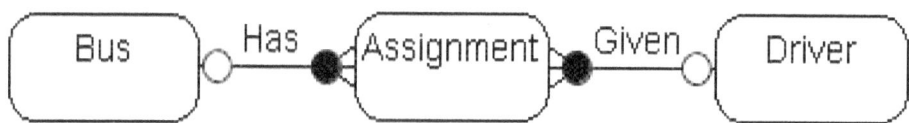

Entity types

Bus(regno,maker,seats)

Driver(nat_ins_no,name,dob)

Assignment(regno,nat_ins_no,time,date,route)

Figure 44 – a further amended data model for Wyvern Buses

Now let's remove the existing Driver table, complete with its data and 1:1 foreign key, and replace it, adding the new Assignment table complete with the necessary foreign keys:

```
DROP TABLE driver;
CREATE TABLE driver (
      nat_ins_no CHAR(9),
      name CHAR(20),
      dob DATE,
      PRIMARY KEY (nat_ins_no) );
CREATE TABLE assignment (
      nat_ins_no CHAR(9),
      regno CHAR(7),
      timedate DATETIME,
      route SMALLINT,
      PRIMARY KEY (nat_ins_no,regno,timedate),
      FOREIGN KEY has (regno) REFERENCES bus,
      FOREIGN KEY given (nat_ins_no)
REFERENCES driver)
```
Query 57: a new Driver table with new link table Assignment

Note that SQLAnywhere does not implement a DATE data type, but instead uses DATETIME, which is in fact implemented as a TIMESTAMP type. For that reason I've chosen to implement the *date* and *time* attributes as a single *timedate* column (note also that "time" and "date" cannot be used as column names because they are reserved names).

> **Exercise 8**: how does Query 57 represent participation of Assignment in both the Has and Given relationships as mandatory?

We need to re-populate the re-created Driver table (we can just use Query 55 again):

```
INSERT INTO driver(nat_ins_no,name,dob)
      VALUES
('UD987234A','Khan','1997/06/18');
INSERT INTO driver(nat_ins_no,name,dob)
      VALUES
('DQ435721A','Wilson','1990/01/07');
```

```
INSERT INTO driver(nat_ins_no,name,dob)
     VALUES
('FV546890B','Smith','1991/08/20');
INSERT INTO driver(nat_ins_no,name,dob)
     VALUES
('QQ525687D','Robinson','1980/12/10');
INSERT INTO driver(nat_ins_no,name,dob)
     VALUES
('VF219787C','Desai','1972/06/12');
INSERT INTO driver(nat_ins_no,name,dob)
     VALUES
('VU241367D','Winston','1983/02/07');
```
Query 55: values for the Driver table

Let us now just assign one driver to one bus, to show that it works:

```
INSERT INTO assignment
(nat_ins_no,regno,timedate,route)
VALUES ('QQ525687D','AQ12CDE','2019-11-08
07:00',23
          )
```
Query 58: values for one row of Assignment

```
SELECT * FROM assignment
```

b)   Participation constraints

We just saw how having a foreign key which is also part of a primary key, means that such a foreign key can only represent mandatory participation. However, we may well need to represent mandatory participation in other circumstances.

To show this, let's add to the Wyvern Buses model.

Wyvern Buses

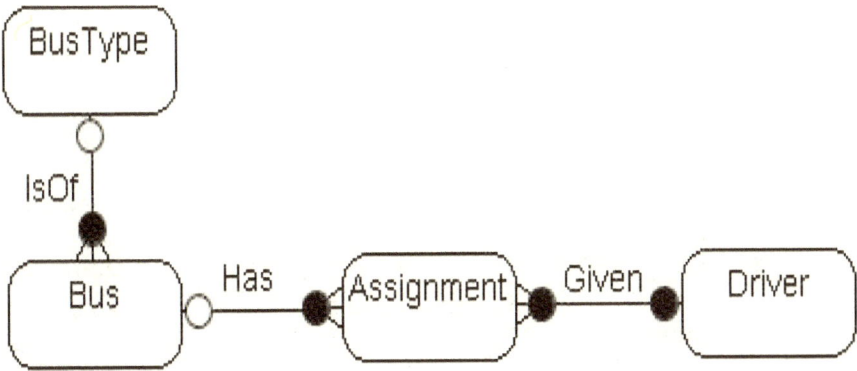

Entity types

Bus(regno,type)

BusType(type,maker,seats)

Driver(nat ins no,name,dob)

Assignment(regno,nat ins no,time,date,route)

Assumptions

None

Figure 45 – a final data model for Wyvern Buses

We will need to remove all our existing Wyvern Buses tables, before re-creating them.

```
DROP TABLE assignment;
DROP TABLE bus;
DROP TABLE driver
```

Note the order of those three statements: referential integrity would prevent the removal of either the *bus* or the *driver* table without first removing *assignment*.

Referential constraints also determine the order in which we create the new tables. Since in Figure 45 *BusType* is referenced from *Bus*, we have to create *BusType* first, so that *Bus* has something to reference. Similarly, both *Driver* and *Bus* have to be created before *Assignment*.

```
CREATE TABLE bustype (
        type CHAR(20),
        maker CHAR(10),
        seats SMALLINT,
        PRIMARY KEY (type)
    );
CREATE TABLE bus (
        regno CHAR(7),
        type CHAR(20) NOT NULL,
        PRIMARY KEY (regno),
        FOREIGN KEY isof (type) REFERENCES
bustype
        )
```

Query 59: creating the *bustype* table and a new version of *bus*

In our new *bus* table, we have a foreign key – the new *type* column – which references *bus*. According to Figure 45, *bus* has mandatory participation in the *IsOf* relationship which this foreign key represents. This has been achieved by defining the *type* column as NOT NULL. Hence every row in this table must contain a value for that foreign key – so every bus must be of some bus type.

When we need to insert data into these tables, we will have to observe the same issue which determined the order in which we created them. We cannot insert a row into *bus* until we have first inserted a row into *bustype,* which the *bus* row will refer to.

So, making a relationship mandatory at the foreign key end is a simple matter of ensuring that the foreign key column(s) cannot be NULL. If those columns form part of the primary key, the job is already done; otherwise, they must be explicitly declared NOT NULL.

However, making a relationship mandatory at the non-foreign-key end – the "1" end – is not such a simple matter.

According to Figure 45, the *Given* relationship is now mandatory for both *assignment* and *driver*. In common language, the effect of this is that we cannot record a driver unless s/he is given at least one bus assignment. We know that the requirement for every row of *assignment* to relate to some driver is already assured, because the relevant foreign key in *assignment* is part of the primary key of that table.

To achieve mandatory participation by *driver*, we have to ensure that every row of the *driver* table has at least one row of *assignment* which refers to it. For this, we need a CHECK constraint in the *driver* table:

```
CHECK (
        nat_ins_no IN
                (SELECT nat_ins_no
                FROM assignment)
        )
```

The subquery lists out the foreign key values of all the drivers being referenced from the *assignment* table, and the CHECK constraint ensures that the primary key value of every row of the *driver* table is in that list.

We can't, however, include this constraint in the initial creation of the *driver* table. We know that we have to create the *driver* and *bus* tables before *assignment*, in order that the foreign keys of assignment have something to refer to. When *driver* is first created, the *assignment* table won't exist, and the above CHECK constraint would not be valid. The sequence must be

- create *driver* table

- create *assignment* table

- add CHECK constraint to *driver* table

```
CREATE TABLE driver (
        nat_ins_no CHAR(9),
        name CHAR(20),
        dob DATE,
        PRIMARY KEY (nat_ins_no) );
CREATE TABLE assignment (
        nat_ins_no CHAR(9),
        regno CHAR(7),
        timedate DATETIME,
        route SMALLINT,
        PRIMARY KEY (nat_ins_no,regno,timedate),
        FOREIGN KEY has (regno) REFERENCES bus,
        FOREIGN KEY given (nat_ins_no)
REFERENCES driver);
ALTER TABLE DRIVER
        ADD CONSTRAINT
driver_must_have_assignment
```

```
CHECK (
nat_ins_no IN
        (SELECT nat_ins_no
        FROM assignment)
)
```
Query 60: new Driver and Assignment tables, with participation constraint on Driver

We have now correctly represented the *given* relationship, as shown in Figure 45: it's mandatory for both the tables involved. However, we haven't yet attempted to insert any data in either *assignment* or *driver.*

> **Exercise 9**: What problems might arise, when inserting data in the *assignment* and *driver* tables?

Fortunately, several options exist to overcome these problems.

> a. We could defer the creation of the mandatory participation by one table until we had filled it with data, and then add the constraint. This can work reasonably well where one of the tables doesn't change very much, and we would choose that one to do this with. In this case the *driver* table is the only option anyway, since the fact that the relevant foreign key of *assignment* is part of the primary key means we have no opportunity to relax mandatory participation there. And as long as the list of drivers we employ doesn't change too much, it could work. So in this case the sequence would be:
>
> > - create *driver* table without participation constraint
> >
> > - insert rows for all our drivers
> >
> > - populate the *assignment* table by giving at least one assignment to each driver
> >
> > - and then add the constraint to the *driver* table.

> b. We could omit one of the constraints permanently, and use an SQL procedure (described in Chapter 16) as the sole means of updating the two tables. In this case the procedure could insert a row in each table, check to see that mandatory participation on both sides was being observed, and if not roll back the update and issue an error message. We could prevent any

inconsistent update from taking place outside of the procedure, because as we will see later, it's possible to give a procedure permission, denied to everyone else, to update a table.

c. We could do the same thing as in (b) using an external application program, rather than an SQL procedure, to carry out the updates. This is however a less satisfactory option from a data consistency point of view, as we would not have the same facilities to prevent an inconsistent update taking place outside of the program.

d. Provided it is supported by the dbms implementation (and as we will see later, SQL Anywhere does partly support it), we could use *deferred constraint checking*. This gives the possibility of defining mandatory participation in both tables from the outset, and then using this option to insert rows in both tables before checking the constraints.

c) *Inclusivity and exclusivity*

In addition to restricting the participation and degree of relationships, it is sometimes necessary to ensure

- that in order to participate in one relationship, a row of a table must also participate in some second or further relationship(s) (inclusivity), or

- that a row of a table may not participate in more than one of two or more relationships (exclusivity).

We saw an example of exclusivity in Chapter 10, when we modelled the Garage requirement using entity subtypes (Figure 32). As we saw in Section 3 of Chapter 11, representing subtypes in an SQL database means making a choice between representing them in one single table representing the supertype, or with a separate table for each subtype.

Figure 32 shows us that an Apprentice can be managed by *either* a Chargehand *or* a Fitter. If, in an SQL implementation of that requirement, we chose to represent the subtypes (Apprentice, Chargehand an Fitter) using separate tables, we would need to represent that exclusivity constraint using an SQL constraint, and this could be done using CHECK:

```
CREATE TABLE apprentice (
        nat_ins_no nat_ins_nos,
        surname names,
```

```
        date_joined dates,
        dl_no dl_nos,
        c_manager nat_ins_nos,
        f_manager nat_ins_nos,
        PRIMARY KEY (nat_ins_no),
        FOREIGN KEY (c_manager) REFERENCES
chargehand,
        FOREIGN KEY (f_manager) REFERENCES
fitter,
        CHECK (
        (c_manager IS NULL AND f_manager IS NOT
NULL)
        OR
        (c_manager IS NOT NULL AND f_manager IS
NULL))
        )
```

Exercise 10

What assumption about the participation of an Apprentice in the two relationships is implicit in the above CHECK statement?

Had we wished instead to allow for the possibility that an Apprentice could be managed by no-one at all, but not by both a Fitter and a Chargehand, the constraint would have been simpler:

```
        CHECK (c_manager IS NULL OR f_manager IS NULL)
```

For an example of an **in**clusive relationship, look at this fragment of an E-R model for a hospital:

Hospital

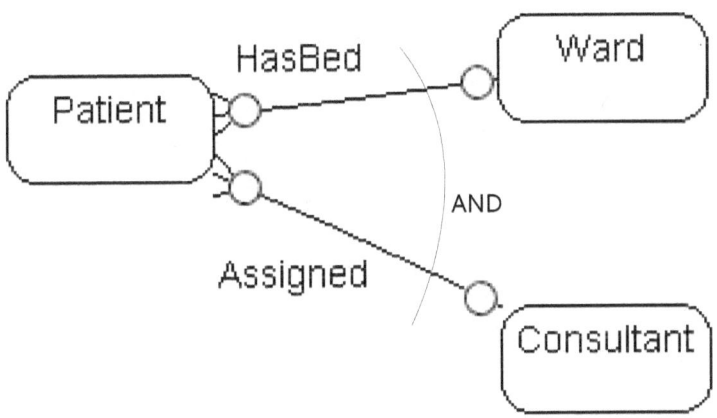

Entity types

Patient(<u>patient_no</u>,first_name,surname)

Ward(<u>name</u>,beds)

Consultant(<u>doctor_no</u>,first_name,surname,specialism)

Figure 46 – a partial data model for a hospital

If we needed to represent an Additional Constraint in this model, as follows

     "c1.   If a patient has a bed in a ward, s/he must also be assigned to a consultant"

then the Patient table in an SQL database implementing the model would have to look like this:

```
CREATE TABLE patient (
        patient_no CHAR(12),
        first_name CHAR(20),
        surname CHAR(20),
        consultant CHAR(10),
        ward CHAR(10),
        PRIMARY KEY (patient_no),
```

```
            FOREIGN KEY (consultant) REFERENCES
      consultant,
            FOREIGN KEY (ward) REFERENCES ward,
            CHECK (
                  (consultant IS NULL AND ward IS
      NULL)
                  OR
                  (consultant IS NOT NULL AND ward
      IS NOT NULL)
                  )
      )
```

Exercise 11.

In the CHECK constraint in the above definition of the *ward* table, one or other of the statements linked by the OR must be true; either a row of the *patient* table participates in both the relationship with *ward* and that with *consultant*, or in neither. What kind of constraint would be needed if every row of *patient* had to participate in **both** relationships?

d)   *The SQL three-valued logic*

An issue with logic arises as a consequence of SQL allowing columns to contain NULLs, which was another reason why Chris Date (see Section 1 of Chapter 5) objected to the practice.

In classical logic, a proposition must either be TRUE or FALSE. The basic principle of logic is that a proposition and its negation cannot both be true at the same time, written as

$$P \text{ and } \bar{P} = \text{FALSE}$$

Say that P stands for the proposition

"all swans are white"

then this statement and its negation $\bar{P}$

"not all swans are white"

cannot both be true at the same time. Either P or $\bar{P}$ must be false, and consequently the outer proposition P and ¬P, which links the two with an AND, must itself be false.

But in SQL, the existence of NULLs means that we cannot always **know** whether a given proposition is true or false.

Say that, (after connecting to the Garage database in Interactive SQL), we want to answer the request

"find the *jobs* carried out on Ford cars, where the time taken for the job was 2.5 hours or more"

The *job* table contains the data

reg_no	date_start	job_description	make	date_end	hours
AQ12CDE	2016-01-04	12,000 service	Ford	2016-01-04	2.5
AQ12CDE	2016-01-04	Front pads & discs	Ford	2016-01-04	1.5
MN03TSK	2016-01-04	Replace clutch & gbox	VW	2016-01-05	6.0
QP11ABC	2016-01-05	20,000 service	Ford	NULL	NULL
VD09BVC	2016-01-05	Replace exhaust	Renault	NULL	NULL
VI14PPK	2016-01-05	Timing belt	Citroen	NULL	NULL

If we execute the query

```
SELECT * FROM job
WHERE make = 'Ford'
AND hours >= 2
```

the result will be the single row

reg_no	date_start	job_description	make	date_end	hours	surname	postcode
AQ12CDE	2016-01-04	12,000 service	Ford	2016-01-04	2	Ellis	BV3 4RT

Query 61: Jobs on Ford cars taking 2 hours or more

We can see that Query 61 does not, in fact, answer the request

"find the *jobs* carried out on Ford cars, where the time taken for the job was 2 hours or more"

Instead, it answers the request

"find the **completed** *jobs* carried out on Ford cars, where the time taken for the job was 2 hours or more"

Sensibly enough, perhaps, our database only gives the time taken for a job once the job has been completed, but this means there may be ongoing jobs on Ford cars which have already taken 2 hours or more but which won't appear in our results. This is because for those jobs, the time taken is NULL, and Query 61 cannot evaluate whether NULL is ">= 2", because it isn't a value.

The reason that the dbms doesn't explode in despair, when it looks at the row in the above table which starts QP11ABC, and is asked whether the *hours* column is more or less than 2, is that it doesn't have to choose whether that proposition is TRUE or FALSE – something which would be impossible to decide. And this is because SQL departs from the TRUE or FALSE requirement of traditional logic. Instead it offers *three* possible values for a proposition:

TRUE

FALSE

UNKNOWN

And when given a proposition which requires the evaluation of a value, but the value is missing (NULL), it evaluates the proposition as UNKNOWN. We can't know whether the time taken for the job in that row starting QP11ABC is more or less than 2, because we don't have a value for it.

Further, as in classical logic we know that any proposition containing a proposition which is false must itself be false, so this *three-valued* logic of SQL tells us that any proposition containing something which is unknown, must itself be unknown.

So when the dbms looks at that row starting QP11ABC, and is asked

```
WHERE make = 'Ford'
AND hours >= 2
```

it evaluates

```
WHERE make = 'Ford'
```

as TRUE, but

```
hours >= 2
```
as UNKNOWN, and consequently the full WHERE proposition linked by AND is also evaluated as UNKNOWN. For a row to appear in the results, the overall query needs that row to meet the proposition in the WHERE clause as TRUE; this row does not do so, and therefore does not appear.

This may be all well and good for users of the *garage* database, as long as they understand that time taken is only recorded for completed jobs, but as we shall see in the next section, the three-valued logic may have unexpected consequences when it comes to constraint definition and enforcement.

e) *Other column constraints*

Apart from participation and uniqueness, we can use CHECK to enforce specific constraints on column values. We have so far defined columns on the basis of data type, but we haven't attempted to create limits on the values which can be contained within those data types, and that kind of limit is almost always needed, to preserve data integrity.

For example, the *nat_ins_no* column in *driver* is defined as CHAR(9), but National Insurance numbers have a fixed format (two letters, six numeric digits and a letter). In order to ensure values stay within that format, we could include a CHECK in the column definition, thus:

```
CREATE TABLE driver (
        nat_ins_no CHAR(9)
                CHECK( (SUBSTR(@value, 1, 2)
                    BETWEEN 'AA' AND 'ZZ')
                AND (SUBSTR(@value, 9,1)
                    BETWEEN 'A' AND 'Z')
                AND (CAST(SUBSTR(@value, 3, 6) AS
    INTEGER)
                    BETWEEN 000000 AND 999999)),
```

Similarly, we might want to ensure that our drivers are all of a certain age

```
CREATE TABLE driver (
        .
        .
        dob DATE CHECK YEARS(@value,today()) >=
    18,
```

But great care needs to be taken to understand the three-valued logic, when defining constraints. This is because a constraint is only violated if the result of evaluation is FALSE; an item which evaluates as TRUE or UNKNOWN will pass the constraint.

Our last new CHECK constraint is applied to values of the *dob* column of *driver*, but so far we left that column as the default ALLOWED NULL. This means that if a *dob* value has been omitted in any row of *driver*, the dbms will evaluate the YEARS function for that row as UNKNOWN, and the row will be allowed. This can of course be overcome by defining the *dob* column as NOT NULL, and the situation will not then arise.

f)   General constraints

So far, we have looked at primary key constraints, column constraints, referential constraints, and constraints on the degree and participation conditions of a relationship, as well as on inclusivity and exclusivity of relationships. But the ability of an SQL dbms to enforce integrity through constraints goes well beyond that. In fact, any description of data which can be validly requested by a SELECT statement, can be used as a definition of data which either must be allowed or must be prohibited.

We can use the *wyvernbuses* database requirement in order to demonstrate this, so make sure you're now connected to that database again.

We first need to remove the potentially troublesome participation constraint on *driver*, which we created in Query 60, and we can then populate the tables with some test data.

```
ALTER TABLE DRIVER
        DROP CONSTRAINT
driver_must_have_assignment;


INSERT INTO bustype(type,maker,seats)
        VALUES ('B7TL','Volvo',68);
INSERT INTO bustype(type,maker,seats)
        VALUES ('B5LH','Volvo',90);
INSERT INTO bustype(type,maker,seats)
        VALUES ('Europolis','Iveco',49);
INSERT INTO bustype(type,maker,seats)
        VALUES ('CLE','VDL',70);
INSERT INTO bustype(type,maker,seats)
```

```sql
        VALUES ('CityPacer','Optare',25);
INSERT INTO bustype(type,maker,seats)
        VALUES ('Tourneo','Ford',8);


INSERT INTO bus(regno,type)
        VALUES ('AQ12CDE','B7TL');
INSERT INTO bus(regno,type)
        VALUES ('MN03TSK','B5LH');
INSERT INTO bus(regno,type)
        VALUES ('VD09BVC','Europolis');
INSERT INTO bus(regno,type)
        VALUES ('VD09BVE','Europolis');
INSERT INTO bus(regno,type)
        VALUES ('VD09BVF','Europolis');
INSERT INTO bus(regno,type)
        VALUES ('QP11ABC','CLE');
INSERT INTO bus(regno,type)
        VALUES ('VI14PPK','CityPacer');
INSERT INTO bus(regno,type)
        VALUES ('VI17LFK','Tourneo');


INSERT INTO driver(nat_ins_no,name,dob)
        VALUES
('UD987234A','Khan','1997/06/18');
INSERT INTO driver(nat_ins_no,name,dob)
        VALUES
('DQ435721A','Wilson','1990/01/07');
INSERT INTO driver(nat_ins_no,name,dob)
        VALUES
('FV546890B','Smith','1991/08/20');
INSERT INTO driver(nat_ins_no,name,dob)
        VALUES
('QQ525687D','Robinson','1980/12/10');
INSERT INTO driver(nat_ins_no,name,dob)
        VALUES
('VF219787C','Desai','1972/06/12');
INSERT INTO driver(nat_ins_no,name,dob)
        VALUES
```

```
('VU241367D','Winston','1983/02/07');
INSERT INTO driver(nat_ins_no,name,dob)
     VALUES
('QQ978764D','Desai','2000/12/07');


INSERT INTO assignment
(nat_ins_no,regno,timedate,route)
VALUES ('QQ525687D','AQ12CDE','2019-11-08
07:00',23
     );
INSERT INTO assignment
(nat_ins_no,regno,timedate,route)
VALUES ('UD987234A','MN03TSK','2019-11-08
07:30',23
     );
INSERT INTO assignment
(nat_ins_no,regno,timedate,route)
VALUES ('DQ435721A','VD09BVC','2019-11-08
06:30',15
     );
INSERT INTO assignment
(nat_ins_no,regno,timedate,route)
VALUES ('FV546890B','QP11ABC','2019-11-08
07:00',9
     );
INSERT INTO assignment
(nat_ins_no,regno,timedate,route)
VALUES ('VF219787C','VI14PPK','2019-11-08
08:00',11
     );
INSERT INTO assignment
(nat_ins_no,regno,timedate,route)
VALUES ('VU241367D','VI14PPK','2019-11-09
08:00',11
     );
```

Query 62: new data for Wyvern Buses

Now execute the following query, to find whether any driver has been allocated to more than one different bus on the same day:

```
SELECT *
FROM assignment a, assignment b
WHERE a.nat_ins_no=b.nat_ins_no
AND DATE(a.timedate)=DATE(b.timedate)
AND a.regno <> b.regno;
```
Query 63: drivers allocated twice on same day

We can now turn this same SELECT statement into a constraint definition, using the NOT EXISTS operator, to prevent drivers being allocated to different buses on a single day:

```
ALTER TABLE assignment
    ADD CONSTRAINT no_second_assignment
        CHECK
        (NOT EXISTS
            (SELECT *
            FROM assignment a, assignment b
            WHERE a.nat_ins_no=b.nat_ins_no
            AND
DATE(a.timedate)=DATE(b.timedate)
            AND a.regno <> b.regno)
        )
```
Query 64: drivers may not be allocated twice on same day, as CHECK constraint

g)   The problem with CHECK constraints

If you executed Query 64 and then tried to insert a row into *driver* giving a driver a second allocation on the same day, you may have been surprised to find that the dbms happily allowed the row to be inserted, despite the constraint being in place. If you then went on to insert a row giving the same driver a third allocation on that same day, you may have been even more surprised to find that the constraint prevented that insertion, while of course leaving the first offending row in place.

There is a general problem with CHECK constraints, which has nothing to do with the three-valued logic which we looked at in Subsection d) above. It is simply the question of *when* the constraint is to be checked by the system. The CHECK constraint itself is such a general tool that it has within itself no mechanism for defining when it is to be checked, and so this is a matter which has to be defined by each dbms implementation.

In the case of SQL Anywhere, it seems that CHECK constraints on a table are normally evaluated *before* an update to that table takes place. So in the case of our Query 64 constraint, it would be checked before each new row was inserted; and if the only data in the table was that added in Query 62 above, it would find that all was well and allow an insertion to go ahead, even though the insertion violated the constraint definition. When it came to a further offending row, the system would then "notice" the offending row which was already there.

Sometimes a workaround can be found to overcome this problem. Take as an example the Hospital requirement, which we looked at in Section 3 above. It is likely that the hospital would want to ensure that patients were only allocated to a ward if the ward had a bed available. A CHECK constraint on the *patient* table to achieve that might look like this:

```
CHECK
(NOT EXISTS (
        SELECT p.ward, COUNT(p.patient_id),
    w.beds
        FROM patient p, ward w
        WHERE p.ward = w.name
        GROUP BY p.ward, w.beds
        HAVING w.beds < COUNT(p.patient_id)
                        )
                );
```

As you would expect having looked at the age constraint on *driver* just now, in SQL Anywhere this constraint would allow a first patient to be added to a ward which was already full, and would only prevent the addition of a second excess patient. So a workaround for this would be to make the CHECK think the ward was one bed smaller than it actually was, by using

```
HAVING (w.beds-1) < COUNT(p.patient_id)
```

- however this is hardly a perfect solution.

On top of this, the proposed constraint is on the *patient* table, so it will certainly only be evaluated when a change is made to that table. Unless we also put a constraint on the *ward* table, removing a bed from a ward which was apparently full would offend against the meaning of the constraint without causing any error.

For all of these, and other reasons, there is a widespread perception that CHECK constraints are really not suitable for much beyond simple attribute constraints, and indeed some major dbms implementations only support CHECKs for the most simple expressions, advocating instead the use of **triggers**, which we will look at next.

But in any case, with any implementation, it is essential to thoroughly test any constraint, to ensure that it actually performs as expected.

h)   *Triggers*

Unlike a CHECK constraint, a trigger is defined with a very specific instruction as to when it is to operate, or *fire*. The instruction defines

- the trigger's **subject table**, i.e. the trigger will fire only on a change to data in that specific table

- the kind of change (insert, update or delete) which will make it fire, and

- whether the trigger is to fire **before** or **after** the change.

The general form of a trigger is:

```
CREATE TRIGGER <trigger name>
      {BEFORE|AFTER} {INSERT|DELETE|UPDATE|
                OF <column name> [, <column name>,
...]}
                ON <table name>
REFERENCING [OLD AS <old name>] [NEW AS <new
name>]
FOR EACH {ROW|STATEMENT}
[WHEN (<condition>)]
<atomic compound statement>
```

Let's now create triggers to replace the CHECK constraint in Query 64. Since a driver could be given a second assignment on the same day if an existing assignment is updated, we have to create triggers for UPDATE as well as INSERT.

```
ALTER TABLE assignment
      DROP CONSTRAINT no_second_assignment;
```

```
CREATE TRIGGER no_second_assignment
      AFTER INSERT ON assignment
      FOR EACH ROW
      WHEN
      (EXISTS
            (SELECT *
            FROM assignment a, assignment b
            WHERE a.nat_ins_no=b.nat_ins_no
            AND
DATE(a.timedate)=DATE(b.timedate)
            AND a.regno <> b.regno))
      BEGIN
            DECLARE
no_second_assignment_violation
                  EXCEPTION FOR SQLSTATE
'99999';
            SIGNAL
no_second_assignment_violation;
      END;


CREATE TRIGGER no_second_assignment_u
      AFTER UPDATE ON assignment
      FOR EACH ROW
      WHEN
      (EXISTS
            (SELECT *
            FROM assignment a, assignment b
            WHERE a.nat_ins_no=b.nat_ins_no
            AND
DATE(a.timedate)=DATE(b.timedate)
            AND a.regno <> b.regno))
      BEGIN
            DECLARE
no_second_assignment_violation
                  EXCEPTION FOR SQLSTATE
'99999';
            SIGNAL
```

```
        no_second_assignment_violation;
                    END;
```
Query 65: 'drivers may not be allocated twice on same day', as triggers

If you now try to give driver DQ435721A a second assignment on 8.11.2019:

```
INSERT INTO
assignment(nat_ins_no,regno,timedate,route)
VALUES
('DQ435721A','VI14PPK','2019-11-08
08:00:00.000',11
          );
```
Query 66: second assignment for same driver

- you will find that an error message is issued, and the new row is not added to the table.

Triggers can be used to do a great deal more than just enforce constraints. Since the statement following the WHEN clause can be any valid SQL statement, they can be used, for example, to insert, delete, update or even create another table, perhaps to maintain a summary or create a snapshot table.

Although every trigger has its subject table, a trigger is not part of the definition of a table, and so the command to delete a trigger is simply

```
DROP TRIGGER <trigger_name>
```

i)   *Domains*

You will remember that, in the relational model, every attribute had to be defined on some domain, and that attributes were only comparable if defined on the same domain.

SQL is much less restrictive in this respect. It supports domains with the full level of flexibility envisaged in the relational model, but there is no compulsion to include them in a database definition at all; columns can be individually defined, as we've done up until now in this book, and column values are comparable as long as they are defined on the same or *compatible* data types (e.g. an integer can be compared with or multiplied by a decimal).

However, if you consider the eventual definition I proposed for the *nat_ins_no* column in the *driver* table:

```
nat_ins_no CHAR(9)
              CHECK( (SUBSTR(@value, 1, 2)
                  BETWEEN 'AA' AND 'ZZ')
              AND (SUBSTR(@value, 9,1)
                  BETWEEN 'A' AND 'Z')
              AND (CAST(SUBSTR(@value, 3, 6) AS
        INTEGER)
                  BETWEEN 000000 AND 999999)),
```

and remember that we would have to write the same column definition for every column that needs to be comparable with it – for example the *nat_ins_no* column in the *assignment* table – then you will probably appreciate the advantage of being able to write such a definition once, in a domain, and then define all necessary columns on that domain. Apart from saving quite a lot of typing, this removes any inconsistency between definitions that might be caused by typing errors, and enables any change to the definition which might become necessary over time, to be made in just one place.

The general form of definition of a domain is

```
CREATE DOMAIN <domain name> AS <data type>
    [[NOT] NULL]
    [DEFAULT <default value>]
    [CHECK (<condition>)]
```

You can find examples of domain definitions at the start of the installation script for the *garage* database (Garage_database_SQLAnywhere.sql):

```
CREATE DOMAIN nat_ins_nos AS CHAR(9)
        CHECK( (SUBSTR(@value, 1, 2) BETWEEN
  'AA' AND


              'ZZ')
        AND (SUBSTR(@value, 9,1) BETWEEN 'A' AND
  'Z')
        AND (CAST(SUBSTR(@value, 3, 6) AS
    INTEGER)
                              BETWEEN 000000
```

```
AND 999999));
CREATE DOMAIN names AS CHAR(30) ;
CREATE DOMAIN grades AS CHAR(12)
      CHECK (@value IN('Fitter','Chargehand',
                  'Apprentice','Receptionist')
);
CREATE DOMAIN dates AS DATE;
CREATE DOMAIN dl_nos AS CHAR(16)
      CHECK( (SUBSTR(@value, 1, 5) BETWEEN
'AAAAA' AND
                        'ZZZZZ')
      AND (SUBSTR(@value, 12,2) BETWEEN 'AA'
AND 'ZZ')
      AND (SUBSTR(@value, 15,2) BETWEEN 'AA'
AND 'ZZ')
      AND (CAST(SUBSTR(@value, 6, 6) AS
INTEGER) BETWEEN

      000000 AND 999999)
      AND (CAST(SUBSTR(@value, 14, 1) AS
INTEGER)

      BETWEEN 0 AND 9)
      );
CREATE DOMAIN postcodes AS CHAR(8);
CREATE DOMAIN addresses AS VARCHAR(50);
CREATE DOMAIN phone_nos AS CHAR(15);
CREATE DOMAIN discounts AS SMALLINT
      CHECK (@value BETWEEN 0 AND 99);
CREATE DOMAIN descriptions AS VARCHAR(120);
CREATE DOMAIN makes AS VARCHAR(20);
CREATE DOMAIN hours AS DECIMAL(2,1);
CREATE DOMAIN reg_nos AS CHAR(7)
      CHECK( (SUBSTR(@value,1,2) BETWEEN 'AA'
AND 'ZZ')
      AND (SUBSTR(@value, 5,2) BETWEEN 'AAA'
AND 'ZZZ')
      AND (CAST(SUBSTR(@value, 3, 2) AS
```

```
                INTEGER)

              BETWEEN 00 AND 99));
```

Of course, a domain must be defined before any column is defined on it. It's customary, for ease of interpretation, to define all of the domains at the start of an installation script, before any of the table definitions.

Once relevant domains are set up, it's a simple matter to define the columns of a table on those domains, instead of directly on data types, for example, in the *garage* database:

```
        CREATE TABLE employee (
              nat_ins_no nat_ins_nos,
              surname names,
              grade grades,
              date_joined dates,
              dl_no dl_nos,
              manager nat_ins_nos,

              .

              .
```

Exercise 12

Create an SQL schema script to implement the Wyvern Trains requirement, as shown in the model solution to Exercise 7. Use domains for all columns. Implement all of the necessary referential and participation constraints, but don't attempt the Additional Constraints. Compare your result against the model answer.

Exercise 13

Now create a new database *wyverntrains*, using SQL Central, then exit from SQL Central, and using Interactive SQL connect to this new database, and run the prepared script *WyvernTrains_database_SQLAnywhere.sql* (which is the model answer to Exercise 12) to implement the database (if you get a dialogue box asking you to select an encoding method, choose UTF8). Create and test expressions to implement the Additional Constraints; use CHECK constraints wherever possible, but be aware of their limitations, and where necessary use triggers instead.

You should now drop and re-create the *wyverntrains database*, and execute *WyvernTrains_constraints_SQLAnywhere.sql* (which is the model answer to Exercise 13) as a query. Then execute *WyvernTrains_data_SQLAnywhere* to complete preparation of this database, ready for some further work in Chapters 15 and 16.

Chapter 13: Normalisation, and why it matters

Normalisation is an important concept to master in order to ensure that a database represents a requirement in the most efficient way.

"Normalisation is a technique for producing a set of relations with desirable properties, given the data requirements of an enterprise. Normalisation is a formal method that can be used to identify relations based on their keys and the functional dependencies among their attributes." Connolly and Begg (2010)

Less formally, we might say: Normalisation **eliminates redundancy** by ensuring that each table represents a single indivisible entity and contains no duplicated information.

You will notice that Connolly and Begg are talking about *relations* again here, rather than tables. This is because, in theirs as in other database textbooks you may read, normalisation is something we do to a relational schema, not to an SQL database. But a relational schema, like the ones we created in Chapter 5 as a means of explaining the relational theory underlying SQL databases, is not something anyone would actually create as part of developing a real world database. We would instead simply create a conceptual model to represent the data requirement, and then implement that model in SQL, as we did in Chapter 12; so we wouldn't have any relational schema to normalise. Fortunately however, it's perfectly possible to create the SQL tables and then, as necessary, carry out normalisation.

1   *Why we need to normalise*

As a simple example of normalisation and the reason we need to do it, look back at the initial bus table we created for Wyvern Buses in Section 2 of Chapter 12.

Bus			
regno	maker	type	seats
AQ12CDE	Volvo	B7TL	68
MN03TSK	Volvo	B5LH	90
QP11ABC	VDL	CLE	70
VD09BVD	Iveco	Europolis	23
VD09BVE	Iveco	Europolis	23
VD09BVF	Iveco	Europolis	23
VI14PPK	Optare	CityPacer	25
VI17LFK	Ford	Tourneo	8

Figure 47 – the initial bus table

We can see that the table records a number of what are called *single valued facts*, or *SVFs*, which in this case we write as:

1. for each regno there is just one maker

2. for each regno there is just one type

3. for each regno there is just one number of seats

4. for each bus type there is just one maker

5. for each bus type there is just one number of seats

The way in which SVFs are recorded in Fig. 47 can lead to a loss of data integrity, through three kinds of *update anomalies*.

- **insertion anomaly:** if we were to insert a new bus of type CLE, say, we might make a mistake and record a different maker name than Volvo or a different number of seats; we would then have rows in the table with inconsistent data

- **amendment anomaly:** sometimes a vehicle manufacturer is taken over by another, and in the case of buses sometimes another manufacturer simply takes over the production of a particular model; if this happened in the case of the Europolis, for example, we'd have to change the maker name in each of the three rows where that model appears, and if we didn't do that accurately, once again we'd have inconsistent data

- **deletion anomaly**: unlike the Europolis, the company only has one example of each of the other bus types; if, say, they were to get rid of the elderly MN03TSK, the information that a B5LH is made by Volvo and has 90 seats would no longer be recorded anywhere – a loss of data.

In fact, by a happy chance we already got rid of these problems, and the duplicated data, for the *bus* table, in Section 4(b) of Chapter 12, when we split the *bus* table by creating the new *bustype* table:

regno	type
'AQ12CDE'	'B7TL'
'MN03TSK'	'B5LH'
'QP11ABC'	'CLE'
'VD09BVC'	'Europolis'
'VD09BVE'	'Europolis'
'VD09BVF'	'Europolis'
'VI14PPK'	'CityPacer'
'VI17LFK'	'Tourneo'

type	maker	seats
B5LH	Volvo	90
B7TL	Volvo	68
CityPacer	Optare	25
CLE	VDL	70
Europolis	Iveco	23
Tourneo	Ford	8

Figure 48 – the replacement bus and bustype tables

Splitting tables in this way is just the kind of thing which results from the normalisation process.

But it's most often the case that, if a data requirement is correctly analysed and modelled, the resulting entities in the model will already be correct and incapable of further reduction, so that the tables which are created to implement them won't exhibit updating anomalies at all.

The normalisation procedure acts as a further check, and should always be carried out as part of database development. Now , I'll show how that is done.

2   *The normalisation process*

The process aims to verify that existing tables are in "normal form" - and if not, change them so that they are. Normal form comes in at least six increasingly pure versions, but for all practical purposes we need only worry about the first four:

> First normal form, or 1NF
>
> Second normal form, or 2NF
>
> Third normal form, or 3NF
>
> Boyce-Codd normal form, or BCNF

Working with one table at a time, we check the table against each of these four forms in turn. But the first step is to identify the *functional dependencies*, or FDs, within the table.

a)   *Establishing functional dependencies*

A functional dependency is just a way of expressing a single valued fact. If we take the fourth SVF in Section 1 above, "for each bus type there is just one maker," then we would write that as an FD using an arrow symbol:

> FDa   bus type → maker

We say that bus type is the *determinant* here: bus type *determines* maker, and maker is *functionally dependent* on bus type.

You might well ask why we need this symbolic representation: why don't we just stick with the single valued facts, in common language? The answer will, I hope, become clear when we have to manipulate the original functional dependencies, to see if they reveal the existence of others.

We can visualise the two sides of an FD as entities in an E-R diagram; in this example, they'd look like this:

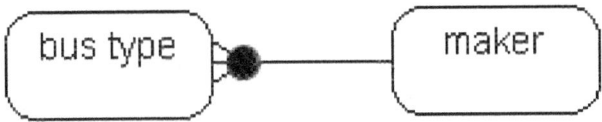

Figure 49 – an FD visualised as an E-R diagram

We say that FDs are not *reversible*; by this we simply mean you can only read them in one direction: in this example, bus type determines maker, but maker doesn't determine bus type.

However, it's quite possible to have another FD which *does* "point the other way." If the makers of buses used by our firm only made one model each, there would be a second FD,

FDb   maker → bus type

Exercise 14

Modify Figure 49 to represent both FDa and FDb

For my explanation of the normalisation process, I'll use a table which might be in the Wyvern Trains database if they ran goods trains as well as passenger services. (For simplicity, I've used the existing domains where possible, but haven't created any new ones.) We will find that the initial analysis which led to the creation of this table, may not have been all that thorough!

```
CREATE TABLE wagon_use (
        wagon_id CHAR(8),
        journey_date datetime,
        wagon_type CHAR(15),
        unladen_wt SMALLINT,
        laden_wt SMALLINT,
        route_id CHAR(4),
        station_from names,
        station_to names,
        loco_id locomotives,
        loco_type types,
        PRIMARY KEY (wagon_id,journey_date)
)
```

Query 67: creating the *wagon_use* table

```
SELECT * from wagon_use
```

wagon_id	journey _date	wagon_type	unladen_ wt	laden_wt	route_ id	station_ from	station _to	loco_id	loco_type

Figure 50 – the columns of wagon_use

From an initial analysis of the company's information, we come up with a list of nine single valued facts:

1   On a given date, a wagon is used on one route.

2   On a given date, a wagon has some laden weight (depending on its load that day).

3   A wagon is constructed as a particular wagon type.

4   A wagon type determines an unladen weight (which is the same for all wagons of that type).

5   A route has a scheduled place of origin.

6   A route has a scheduled place of destination.

7   On a given date, a route has a train pulled by one locomotive.

8   On a given date, a locomotive pulls a train on just one route.

9   A locomotive is of a particular loco type.

Exercise 15

Find the nine functional dependencies which correspond to these nine SVFs.

We next have to see if there are further FDs which can be *derived* from these nine. First, we look to see if any can be derived by *transitivity*. This is how it works:

If there is an FD $A \rightarrow B$

and another $B \rightarrow C$

then we can derive $A \rightarrow C$

and we say that A → C is a *transitive dependency*. However, **IF** it were also true, say, that B → A, then as I mentioned in the solution to Exercise 14, that would mean that A and B were logically the same entity, and A → C would *not* be considered a transitive dependency. The same would be true if C → B existed.

To put this possibly rather difficult concept in another way:

If A → B and B → C, then A → C is also true.

And this is a transitive dependency, unless B → A or C → B.

So let's now take a closer look at our list of nine initial FDs.

From FDs 3 and 4, WagonId → WagonType and WagonType → UnladenWt,

we get

      FD10 WagonId → UnladenWt

From FDs 1 and 5, WagonId, JourneyDate → RouteId and FD5 RouteId → StationFrom,

we get

      FD11 WagonId,JourneyDate → StationFrom

From FDs 1 and 6, WagonId, JourneyDate → RouteId and RouteId → StationTo,

we get

      FD12 WagonId,JourneyDate → StationTo

From FDs 8 and 5, LocoId, JourneyDate → RouteId and RouteId → StationFrom,

we get

      FD13 LocoId,JourneyDate → StationFrom

From FDs 8 and 6, LocoId,JourneyDate → RouteId and RouteId → Destination,

we get

      FD14 LocoId,JourneyDate → StationTo

From FDs 7 and 9, RouteId,JourneyDate → LocoId and LocoId → LocoType,

we get

FD15 RouteId,JourneyDate → LocoType

FDs can also be derived by *augmentation and transitivity*. If we can add an attribute to the "right hand side" of any FD, so that it is the same as the "left hand side" of another, then we potentially have another derived FD.

In this case, if we add JourneyDate to the right hand side of FD1, we get

FD1augmented WagonId, JourneyDate → RouteId,JourneyDate

and we can join that to FD7, RouteId, JourneyDate → LocoId, to get

FD16 WagonId, JourneyDate → LocoId

(It might strike you as odd that we can play around with FDs in this way, adding attributes to FDs at will, but it has a strictly logical basis. If we translate FD1augmented back into an SVF, we find that it means exactly the same thing as the original SVF1:

SVF1augmented   On a given date, a wagon is used on one route)

Similarly, we can join FD1 augmented to FD14 to get

FD17 WagonId,JourneyDate → LocoType

So our full list of FDs is now as follows:

FD1 WagonId, JourneyDate → RouteId

FD2 WagonId, JourneyDate → LadenWt

FD3 WagonId → WagonType

FD4 WagonType → UnladenWt

FD5 RouteId → StationFrom

FD6 RouteId → StationTo

FD7 RouteId, JourneyDate → LocoId

FD8 LocoId, JourneyDate → RouteId

FD9 LocoId → LocoType

FD10 WagonId → UnladenWt

FD11 WagonId,JourneyDate → StationFrom

FD12 WagonId,JourneyDate → StationTo

FD13 LocoId,JourneyDate → StationFrom

FD14 LocoId,JourneyDate → StationTo

FD15 RouteId,JourneyDate → LocoType

FD16 WagonId, JourneyDate → LocoId

FD17 WagonId,JourneyDate → LocoType

I must note here that the two dependencies *derived* by augmentation and transitivity, FD16 and FD17, don't give rise to a *transitive dependency*, because in the derivations

WagonId,JourneyDate → RouteId,JourneyDate → LocoId and

WagonId,JourneyDate → RouteId,JourneyDate → LocoType,

JourneyDate is common to both the combination of attributes. To put that another way, there can be no redundancy in retaining FD16 and FD17, because, to convert FD16 back into an SVF, it would just mean, "on a given date a wagon is used on just one route and that route uses just one locomotive."

b)   *Moving to normal forms*

We now proceed to check the *wagon_use* table against each of the normal forms.

1NF

First normal form is, or normally should be, a very simple step, because we can define a table as being in 1NF if and only if

- there are no duplicate rows

- all values are atomic and

- every non-primary key column is functionally dependent on the primary key

In this case we can certainly take it that *wagon_use* is in 1NF.

2NF

We say that a table is in 2NF if and only if

- it is in 1NF and

- every non-primary key column is functionally dependent on the *whole* primary key

From FDs 1, 2, 11, 12, 16 and 17, we can see that the columns *laden_wt, route_id, station_from, station_to, loco_id* and *loco_type* are all functionally dependent on the whole primary key.

But this leaves us with *wagon_type & unladen_wt*, which are each functionally dependent only on *wagon_id* (FD3, FD10).

So we now need to *decompose* the *wagon_use* table, to produce two or more tables which fully represent the same data, but in which all columns are functionally dependent on the whole primary key.

We do this, in this case, by "moving" FD3 and FD10 into a new table, and removing their right hand side attributes from the original table (the left hand side must remain as it's part of the primary key).

```
DROP TABLE wagon_use;

CREATE TABLE wagons (
        wagon_id CHAR(8),
        wagon_type CHAR(15),
        unladen_wt SMALLINT,
        PRIMARY KEY (wagon_id)
);
CREATE TABLE wagon_use2nf (
        wagon_id CHAR(8),
        journey_date datetime,
        laden_wt SMALLINT,
        route_id CHAR(4),
        station_from names,
        station_to names,
        loco_id locomotives,
        loco_type types,
        PRIMARY KEY (wagon_id,journey_date),
        FOREIGN KEY (wagon_id) REFERENCES
wagons,
);
```
Query 68 decomposing the *wagon* table

We can check that this decomposition was "non-loss", that's to say that all the original data has been preserved, by joining the two new tables, which should give us back our original:

```
SELECT
w.wagon_id,journey_date,wagon_type,unladen_wt,
laden_wt,
route_id,station_from,station_to,loco_id,loco_
type
    FROM wagons w, wagon_use2nf wu
    WHERE w.wagon_id = wu.wagon_id;
```

Query 69 re-joining the decomposed table

wagon_ id	journey _date	wagon_type	unladen_wt	laden_wt	route_ id	station_ from	station _to	loco_id	loco_type

By checking the FDs, we can now see that each of the columns in both *wagons* and *wagon_use2nf* is functionally dependent on the whole primary key of their own table.

3NF

We define a table as being in 3NF if and only if

- it is in 2NF and

- every non-primary key column is *non-transitively dependent* on the primary key.

Taking *wagons* first, we can see that *wagon_type* is non-transitively dependent on the primary key *wagon_id* through our original FDs 3. However *unladen_wt* is transitively dependent, through FDs 3 and 4, so it's FD4 which needs to be removed:

```
DROP TABLE wagon_use2nf;
DROP TABLE wagons;

CREATE TABLE wagon_types (
        wagon_type CHAR(15),
        unladen_wt SMALLINT,
        PRIMARY KEY (wagon_type)
    );
```

```
CREATE TABLE wagons3nf (
      wagon_id CHAR(8),
      wagon_type CHAR(15),
      PRIMARY KEY (wagon_id),
      FOREIGN KEY (wagon_type) REFERENCES
wagon_types
);
```

Query 70: decomposing *wagons* to 3NF

Looking now at *wagon_use2nf*, we see that *laden_wt* and *route_id* are non-transitively dependent on the primary key, through our original FDs 1 and 2.

On the other hand, *station_from* is transitively dependent through FD11, and *station_to* is transitively dependent through FD12)

(*loco_id* (FD16) and *loco_type* (FD17) *appear* to be transitively dependent too, but as I explained when we were deriving the FDs, above, these two do not lead to transitive dependency and so will not be removed.)

To remove transitive dependencies, we remove the right-hand part of the dependency. That's to say, for example, FDs 11 and 12 were derived as

WagonId,JourneyDate → RouteId → StationFrom

WagonId,JourneyDate → RouteId → StationTo

and so we will create a new table with *route_id* as the primary key and *station_from* and *station_to* as the other columns, but leaving *route_id* in the original table, to retain the link between the two.

```
CREATE TABLE routes (
      route_id CHAR(4),
      station_from names,
      station_to names,
      PRIMARY KEY (route_id)
);

CREATE TABLE wagon_use3nf (
      wagon_id CHAR(8),
      journey_date datetime,
```

```
        route_id CHAR(4),
        laden_wt SMALLINT,
        loco_id locomotives,
        loco_type types,
        PRIMARY KEY (wagon_id,journey_date),
        FOREIGN KEY (wagon_id) REFERENCES
    wagons3nf,
        FOREIGN KEY (route_id) REFERENCES routes
    );
```

Query 71: decomposing wagon_use2nf to 3NF

Once again, we can check that this decomposition is non-loss, by joining the new tables back together:

```
SELECT
u.wagon_id,journey_date,w.wagon_type,unladen_wt,lade
n_wt,
u.route_id,station_from,station_to,loco_id,loco_type
FROM wagon_use3nf u, routes r, wagons3nf w,
wagon_types t
WHERE u.wagon_id = w.wagon_id
AND u.route_id = r.route_id
AND w.wagon_type = t.wagon_type
```

Query 72 re-joining the decomposed table

wagon_id	journey_date	wagon_type	unladen_wt	laden_wt	route_id	station_from	station_to	loco_id	loco_type

BCNF

A table is in BCNF if and only if

- it is in 3NF and

- every determinant is a candidate key

There are no defined alternate keys in any of our 3NF tables, so we just need to check that each determinant in each table is the primary key of that table.

wagon_use3nf: the primary key (*wagon_id, journey_date*) is the determinant for all the non-key attributes, *route_id* (FD1), *laden_wt* (FD2), *loco_id* (FD16) and *loco_type* (FD17)

routes: the primary key (*route_id*) is the determinant for both the non-key attributes, *station_from* (FD5) and *station_to* (FD6)

wagons3nf: the primary key (*wagon_id*) is the determinant for the only non-key attribute, *wagon_type* (FD3)

wagon_types: the primary key (*wagon_type*) is the determinant for the only non-key attribute, *unladen_wt* (FD4)

So all of our 3NF tables are already in BCNF (which is in fact very commonly the case).

Chapter 14: Access Control

So far in this book, all the tables which we've used and created have been owned and used by a single user (dba). If a database really had only one user, there would be good reasons for saying that a relational solution would be something of a sledgehammer to crack a nut. The extensive constraints and controls that an rdbms brings, come at the cost of a need for a very large amount of processing power. (You won't notice this during these SQL activities, because of the very small amounts of data in our test databases; but as the size of a database increases, the amount of power needed to check the constraints rises dramatically.) The rdbms really comes into its own in a large, multi-user environment, where the payback is that it addresses all the many problems which can arise when many people are using the same data at the same time.

In order to be able to do this, the dbms must provide some facilities to control which users can access which parts of the database, and what they can do with the data they can access: merely read it, or alter, delete or add to it. We can summarise the aims of access control as follows:

- to restrict each user to only see the parts of the database which concern them, in order to remove unnecessary complexity;

- to prevent users from accessing sensitive data which they do not need, for example the personal information of other users; and

- to reduce the chances of data being corrupted, by only allowing certain people to change data.

1   The user schema

All tables in each database have an owner, who will (apart from the system tables) be the user who created them. Together these tables comprise that user's schema for that database. So far, because we've always been connected as the one user dba and have owned all the tables, we've been able to access them just by the table name, for example:

```
SELECT * FROM employee
```
A user may access another user's table, provided suitable privileges have been granted, but in that case must use the dot notation to show the user schema where they live, e.g.

```
SELECT * FROM dba.employee
```

2   The privileges

Users may grant a range of different privileges on their own tables to other users:

> SELECT
>
> INSERT
>
> DELETE
>
> UPDATE
>
> REFERENCES (bear in mind that because of referential integrity, declaring a foreign key on someone else's table places a considerable restriction on that table – hence the need for a special privilege)

The table owner may grant one or more or any combination of these privileges, or simply

> ALL PRIVILEGES

These are the privileges defined in standard SQL, but some dbms implementations may vary in what they provide.

In general, privileges can only be granted on whole tables, exceptionally the UPDATE privilege may be granted on named columns only. Obviously DELETE and INSERT cannot apply to less than whole rows, but if it is necessary to restrict a user to only SELECT certain columns, this can be done by creating a VIEW (see Chapter 15)

3   The GRANT statement

The format of the statement is

```
GRANT {privilege(s)} ON {owner name.table
name{*column names(s)} TO {user name}
```
* only applies to UPDATE

A powerful addition to the GRANT statement is the addition of WITH GRANT OPTION. This gives the grantee the power to pass on the same privileges to further users, and this includes the ability to also give them the WITH GRANT OPTION. Obviously therefore, this is an option that needs to be used with care. Fortunately, dbms suppliers provide some means of checking which permissions have been granted to whom; in the case of SQL Anywhere, if you look at a table in SQL Central, you'll see there is a tab "Privileges" which will show all the permissions granted to others on that table.

4   The REVOKE statement

This statement allows a table owner, or another user who has been given the WITH GRANT OPTION, to remove a privilege that they have granted. The format is:

```
REVOKE {privilege(s)} ON {owner name.table
name{*column names(s)} FROM {user name}
```

However, note that a user can only revoke privileges which they themselves have granted, not any which have subsequently passed on using WITH GRANT OPTION.

Chapter 15: VIEWs

I've included this as a separate chapter although, as I already mentioned, views are very much part of the access control facilities offered by the dbms. However there's quite a lot to say about them so they deserve a chapter to themselves.

As I said at the start of Chapter 12, in SQL terms the word "table" can mean either a base table or a view, since they each be used in the same way in a query (subject to some restrictions). But unlike a base table, views do not themselves contain any data; they are effectively stored queries which can be used within other queries.

1   Creating views

The general form of the command to create a view is

```
CREATE VIEW {viewname} {optional column names}
AS
        {any valid SELECT statement}
```

Of course, to create a view, a user must have the SELECT privilege for the base table(s) on which it is based, but having done so the view owner can then grant SELECT privilege to others on just the view and not the underlying base tables.

Try creating a view in the Wyvern Trains database, to list out the day's driver allocation details, re-naming the view's columns so as to be more meaningful:

```
CREATE VIEW todays_drivers
        (NINO,Name,Service,Departing,At)
AS
    SELECT d.nat_ins_no,d.name,a.service_no,

station_from,substring(departure_time,12,5)
        FROM driver d, allocated_to a, service s
        WHERE d.nat_ins_no=a.nat_ins_no
        AND a.service_no=s.service_no
```
Query 73: creating the view *todays_drivers*

If we then retrieve data from this view:

```
SELECT * FROM todays_drivers ORDER BY At
```

we get a clear and readable schedule:

NINO	Name	Service	Departing	At
UD987234A	Wilkins	801	Sandy Bay	06:50
DQ435721A	Johnson	711	Central	07:25
VF219787C	Khan	802	Sandy Bay	07:30
FV546890B	Robinson	811	Central	07:40
QQ525687D	Smith	701	Eastend on Sea	07:55
VU241367D	Johnson	311	Thacksbridge Junction	08:15

Figure 51 – "contents" of the view todays_drivers

todays_drivers is an example of a view created to make the data simpler or clearer for the end user.

As I mentioned earlier, views can also be used for access control, by presenting just the columns, and even just the rows, which a given user should be allowed to see. For example, looking at the *garage* database, the chargehand (and let's imagine we've created a user *chargehand*) needs to be able to see details of uncompleted jobs, and to contact the customer concerned if necessary, but s/he should not be shown the customers' addresses. The following view, using both column and row selection, delivers what is needed (remember to use *garage*).

```
CREATE VIEW uncompleted_jobs AS
SELECT
reg_no,date_start,job_description,make,j.surna
me,phone
FROM job j, customer c
WHERE j.surname=c.surname
AND j.postcode=c.postcode
AND date_end IS NULL
```

Query 74: creating the view *uncompleted_jobs*

```
SELECT * FROM uncompleted_jobs
```

reg_no	date_start	job_description	make	surname	phone
'VD09BVC'	2016-01-05	'Replace exhaust'	'Renault'	'Petty'	'407865'
'QP11ABC'	2016-01-05	'20000 service'	'Ford'	'Simpson'	'690513'
'VI14PPK'	2016-01-05	'Timing belt'	'Citroen'	'Wilson'	'881545'

Figure 52 – "contents" of the view uncompleted_jobs

We can even use the dbms special value USER, which returns the name of the current session user, to create one view which would then allow every employee to see just their own details in a personnel database.

Let's create a table *staff* which lists the details of every employee, and includes a column *username* which contains their dbms user names. It doesn't matter which database you use to create this as we won't be relating it to any other tables.

```
CREATE TABLE staff (
     first_name CHAR(30),
     surname CHAR(30),
     dept SMALLINT,
     address1 VARCHAR(30),
     address2 VARCHAR(30),
     postcode CHAR(8),
     phone CHAR(15),
     salary INTEGER,
     username CHAR(10),
     PRIMARY KEY (first_name,surname)
);

INSERT INTO staff
        VALUES('Tony','Williams',3,'12 Windsor
Ave',
                        'Newtown','BV3
4RT','690190',
                        18500,'tony');
INSERT INTO staff
```

```
                    VALUES('Fred','Johnson',3,'9 High St',
                            'Newtown','BV3
        4RT','402973',
                            22000,'fred');
        INSERT INTO staff
                VALUES('Sally','Newman',1,'42 Union St',
                            'Newtown','BV2
        1PO','409111',
                            35000,'sally');
        INSERT INTO staff
                VALUES('Mickey','Mouse',1,'3 Blacksmiths
        Lane',
                            'Newtown','BV2
        9DZ','435675',
                            30000,'dba');
```

Query 75: creating and populating the *staff* table

If we then create the view *my_data*

```
        CREATE VIEW my_data AS
                SELECT * FROM staff
                WHERE username = USER
```

and grant SELECT privilege on it to everyone (PUBLIC is another special value)

```
        GRANT SELECT ON my_data TO PUBLIC
```

then each user who connects to the database and executes

```
        SELECT * FROM my_data
```

will see just the single row containing their own personal details.

2   *Updating views*

The usefulness of views lies primarily in retrieving data to suit the user's needs. Views *can* be updated, but it is the data in the base table(s) on which the view is defined that the updating will take place, and this imposes restrictions on what can be done.

In general, we can say that a view is only updateable if each value in an entry of the view corresponds to exactly one entry of an identifiable underlying base table. SQL provides a set of rules to define what that means in practice for a view to be considered updateable:

    - the FROM clause can refer only to one single updateable base table or view

196

(*i.e. no joins*)

- the SELECT clause can contain only column names (no value expressions and no DISTINCT clause)

- a table cannot appear in both the FROM and the WHERE clause

- there can be no GROUP BY and no HAVING clause, and no subqueries

- two or more queries can only be combined using UNION ALL.

And I should clearly add that the underlying tables impose restrictions of their own:

- an INSERT could only be possible on a view if the view definition included all the NOT NULL columns of the underlying table

- a DELETE or UPDATE would only be possible on data not restricted by a referential constraint

Exercise 16

Is the view *my_data*, defined above, updateable? What about the view *uncompleted_jobs*?

We would be unlikely to grant UPDATE or DELETE privileges on a table like *staff* to any ordinary user, but we might want to allow a user to change just their contact details. We could do this using the *my_data* view, with

```
GRANT UPDATE(address1,address2,postcode,phone)
      ON my_data
      TO public
```

3   Something of a curiosity: the WITH CHECK OPTION

Try the following. Still connected to the same database as user *dba*, execute the following:

```
INSERT INTO my_data
        VALUES('John','Smith',2,'47 Wood St',
                        'Newtown','BV1
4AL','439876',
                        16800,'john');
```
Query 76: inserting into the view *my_data*

As *dba* you are the owner of this view, and we've established that it's updateable, so it should be no surprise that the system doesn't object to this INSERT, which contains valid data. However, now try this:

```
SELECT * FROM my_data;
```
. . and now this:

```
SELECT * FROM staff;
```

The system has allowed the insert of the new row containing John Smith *through the view* to the underlying base table, even though the row does not conform to the view definition and therefore is not visible when you select the view.

To create a view which doesn't behave like this, and instead, as you might hope, only allows people to use the view to change data which is actually visible through it, we need the *with check option*; the view definition would then be simply

```
CREATE VIEW my_data AS
        SELECT * FROM staff
        WHERE username = USER
        WITH CHECK OPTION
```

Chapter 16: SQL control statements

In Section 4(h) of Chapter 12, we looked at triggers, which are a kind of programmable routine. SQL provides other programmable facilities, which we will consider now.

1   *Compound statements*

We encountered the BEGIN .. END loop as part of our discussion on triggers. But we can use this control loop to execute a succession of statements.

In Query 75, we created the *staff* table, and then populated it with a series of INSERT statements. However we could instead have placed all of those statements within a BEGIN .. END loop:

```
BEGIN
CREATE TABLE staff (
    first_name CHAR(30),
    surname CHAR(30),
    dept SMALLINT,
    address1 VARCHAR(30),
    address2 VARCHAR(30),
    postcode CHAR(8),
    phone CHAR(15),
    salary INTEGER,
    username CHAR(10),
    PRIMARY KEY (first_name,surname)
);
INSERT INTO staff
      VALUES('Tony','Williams',3,'12 Windsor
Ave',
                    'Newtown','BV3
4RT','690190',
                    18500,'tony');
INSERT INTO staff
      VALUES('Fred','Johnson',3,'9 High St',
                    'Newtown','BV3
4RT','402973',
                    22000,'fred');
INSERT INTO staff
      VALUES('Sally','Newman',1,'42 Union St',
```

```
                              'Newtown','BV2
1PO','409111',
                              35000,'sally');
INSERT INTO staff
        VALUES('Mickey','Mouse',1,'3 Blacksmiths
Lane',
                              'Newtown','BV2
9DZ','435675',
                              30000,'dba');
END
```

More usefully still, we can use BEGIN ATOMIC:

```
BEGIN ATOMIC

        .

        {series of statements}

        .

END
```

This defines everything within the loop as a transaction: it will either fail completely or succeed completely. That's to say, if any if the statements at any point within the loop fails, none of the statements will succeed.

2   Functions

We have already encountered some of SQL's many *built-in* functions, such as SUBSTRING and CAST, and aggregate functions like AVG and SUM, all of which can be used with any database.

However we are also able to write functions of our own, within a specific database.

The general form of a function definition is:

```
CREATE FUNCTION {name} (parameter 1,. .
parameter n)
                RETURNS {data type}
                BEGIN [ATOMIC]

                .

                {compound statement}

                .

                END
```

The (parameter) section allows us to define the parameter(s) which will be the input to the function, while RETURNS allows us to tell the function how we expect to receive the output. Since the BEGIN . . END loop can contain some relatively complex data manipulations, we can have functions which greatly simplify requests.

As an example, we could create a function in the Wyvern Trains database, to tell us the time of the next train today between any two stations:

```
CREATE FUNCTION my_next_train (station1 VARCHAR, station2
VARCHAR)
    RETURNS CHAR(5)
    BEGIN
        DECLARE my_time TIME;
        SELECT cast(f.time_here as timestamp)
        INTO my_time
        FROM station_on_service f,station_on_service t
        WHERE f.service_no=t.service_no
        AND f.station_name<>t.station_name
        AND f.time_here < t.time_here
        AND CAST(f.time_here AS TIMESTAMP) > NOW()
        AND f.station_name=station1
        AND t.station_name=station2
        AND f.time_here <= ALL
            (SELECT f.time_here
                FROM station_on_service
f,station_on_service t
                WHERE f.service_no=t.service_no
                AND f.station_name<>t.station_name
                AND f.time_here < t.time_here
                AND CAST(f.time_here AS TIMESTAMP) > NOW()
                AND f.station_name=station1
                AND t.station_name=station2)
            ;
        RETURN my_time;
    END
```

Query 77: the *my_next_train* function

The user can then call this function like this, inserting the names of any two stations:

```
select my_next_train('Central','Sandy Bay')
from sys.dummy
```

The time of the next train is returned, unless there is none today, in which case we get a NULL.

(Note: the mechanisms for comparing time values vary across dbms implementations. In this SQL Anywhere example, we have to use CAST . . AS TIMESTAMP because the current time NOW() is returned as system time, which will include any adjustment for daylight saving time, while the values for train times stored in the database are not automatically adjusted in that way.)

3   Procedures

While a user-defined function has to be invoked within a SELECT clause and can only return a single value, a procedure has to be called directly, and can carry out any valid SQL operations, including updates and deletions. It's like a mini application process within a database. Like a function, a procedure can contain some fairly complex code which may need to be be used repeatedly without having to re-write it each time, thus saving work and reducing errors. But procedures also have the considerable advantage that a user authorised to use one does not also have to be given privileges on the actual base tables on which the procedure operates, thus offering finer-grained access control than would otherwise be possible: we can create a procedure to carry out just the specific operations which a user needs to carry out, and give the user privileges on that, rather than on the whole base table(s).

The general structure of the CREATE PROCEDURE statement is:

```
CREATE PROCEDURE <procedure name>
([parameter1, . . ])
        <compound statement>
```

(a procedure can contain just a single statement rather than a compound statement, in which case it's not necessary to use a BEGIN . . END loop)

For each parameter defined for a procedure, we need to say whether it is IN, OUT, or INOUT (depending on whether it's to hold a value we pass to the procedure, or one which is used to return a value, or both), give it a name, and specify its data type.

As a simple example, we could define a procedure to tell us all of the scheduled train services between any two stations for the rest of today, instead of just the next one as with our **my_next_train** function.

```
CREATE PROCEDURE my_next_trains
        (IN station1 VARCHAR, IN station2
VARCHAR)
BEGIN
        DROP TABLE IF EXISTS my_times;
        CREATE TABLE my_times (
        mytime TIME );
        INSERT INTO my_times (mytime)
        SELECT cast(f.time_here as timestamp)
        FROM station_on_service
f,station_on_service t
        WHERE f.service_no=t.service_no
        AND f.station_name<>t.station_name
        AND f.time_here < t.time_here
        AND CAST(f.time_here AS TIMESTAMP) >
NOW()
        AND f.station_name=station1
            AND t.station_name=station2 ;
END

CALL my_next_trains
        ('Central','Sandy Bay')

SELECT * FROM my_times
```

Query 78: the *my_next_trains* procedure

4   *Cursors, loops and SQLSTATE*

Where multiple rows need to be retrieved and processed, the conditions can all be included in a WHERE clause, as in the procedure *my_next_trains*, above. Within a procedure, we can alternatively use a *cursor*, which enables us to hold the results of a query in memory while we carry out further processing on them, row by row.

The following simple example basically does the same job as the *my_next_trains* procedure, but the test which excludes trains which have already left is carried out after the data has been retrieved, rather than as part of the WHERE clause.

```
CREATE PROCEDURE my_next_train_p
    (IN station1 VARCHAR, IN station2
VARCHAR)
    BEGIN
    DECLARE notfound EXCEPTION FOR SQLSTATE
'02000';
    DECLARE t TIME;
    DECLARE all_times CURSOR FOR
        SELECT cast(f.time_here as
timestamp)
    FROM station_on_service
f,station_on_service t
        WHERE f.service_no=t.service_no
    AND f.station_name<>t.station_name
        AND f.station_name=station1
        AND t.station_name=station2;
    DROP TABLE IF EXISTS mytimes;
    CREATE TABLE mytimes (mytime TIME);
    OPEN all_times;
    TimeLoop:
       LOOP
          FETCH NEXT all_times INTO t;
              IF SQLSTATE = notfound THEN
              LEAVE TimeLoop;
              END IF;
      IF  t > NOW() THEN
      INSERT INTO mytimes (mytime) VALUES
(t);
      END IF;
       END LOOP;
    CLOSE all_times;
    END;

CALL my_next_train_p('Central','Sandy Bay');
SELECT * from mytimes;
```

Query 79: a procedure using a cursor

a)　　　　　*Cursors*

The general form of a cursor declaration is

```
DECLARE <cursor name> CURSOR FOR <query
statement>
```
Any form of query is allowed. For example, in the procedure *my_next_train_p* above, the cursor declaration is

```
DECLARE all_times CURSOR FOR
            SELECT cast(f.time_here as
timestamp)
        FROM station_on_service
f,station_on_service t
            WHERE f.service_no=t.service_no
        AND f.station_name<>t.station_name
            AND f.station_name=station1
            AND t.station_name=station2
```
Having declared a cursor, it is used with the *OPEN, FETCH INTO* and *CLOSE* statements.

The OPEN executes the query in the cursor declaration, positioning the cursor at the first row of the results from that query.

FETCH causes the contents of the row to be loaded INTO a predefined variable (in this case *t*) (or variables). At this point the contents of those variables can be further processed (in our example, we test to see if the value of *t* is greater than current time, and if so load it into our temporary table). In order to process all of the results, row by row, we place the FETCH inside a control startement (see next section) so that it is executed repeatedly until some point is reached, which could be some value of the results or, as in this case, the end of the results.

CLOSE stops execution of the cursor.

b)　　　　　*LOOP statements*

The general form of the LOOP is

```
LOOP
        <compound statement>
END LOOP
```

In our case, the loop contains

- a FETCH

- a test to see if nothing was returned (because) the end of results has been reached,

in which case we exit

- a test to see if the results value is greater than current time

- and if all is well, an instruction to write the results value to the temporary table.

c)   *FOR statements*

As an alternative to using LOOP as a control mechanism, SQL provides FOR. The general form of this is:

```
FOR <loop name> AS <cursor name> CURSOR FOR
<statement>
DO
        <statement list>
END FOR
```

With this method, there is no need for explicit OPEN, FETCH or CLOSE statements. Using this method, the body of the procedure at Figure 73 would look like this:

```
BEGIN
        FOR Time_Loop AS all_times CURSOR FOR
                SELECT cast(f.time_here as
        timestamp)
        FROM station_on_service
        f,station_on_service t
                WHERE f.service_no=t.service_no
        AND f.station_name<>t.station_name
                AND f.station_name=station1
                AND t.station_name=station2
        DO
                IF  t > NOW() THEN
                INSERT INTO mytimes (mytime)
        VALUES (t);
```

```
                    END IF;
            END FOR;
      END
```

d)   **SQLSTATE**

We used a test of the value of SQLSTATE in order to see whether the end of results had been reached. SQLSTATE is a global variable set by the dbms after the execution of any statement, which gives the status of that execution. In our case we were testing for 02000, which designates 'row not found'.

An SQLSTATE value consists of two digits which indicate the general type of status (class), followed by three digits which define a specific condition (subclass). Class values and some subclass values are defined by the SQL standard, others are implementation-dependent. A full list of the standard values is at Appendix 3.

Chapter 17: Transaction and Concurrency Management

1   *Transactions*

The need for transaction management is apparent when there are two or more successive operations which are technically discrete but which are semantically interdependent. If any one of that series of operations fails while others succeed on their own terms, then the database may contain inconsistent data or may even become unusable. (Clearly this is something which applies in the main to data updating rather than data retrieval.)

In Section 2 of Chapter 6, I gave the example of a simple banking operation, where a sum is to be debited from one account and then credited to another. Clearly the bank needs to be assured that it will not be possible for one of those operations to succeed unless the other does also.

As I said before, we can define a transaction as

> *a unit of work which either succeeds completely or fails completely*

SQL provides for defining transactions through the COMMIT mechanism. The system session variable AUTOCOMMIT is by default set to ON, meaning that any valid operation will be executed and the result (if any) written to the database. By entering the command

```
SET AUTOCOMMIT OFF
```
we prevent any subsequent operations being fully executed until the command

```
COMMIT
```
is entered.

This means that, by using the SQLSTATE variable or checks of our own design, we can test at each step of the way to see whether things are proceeding correctly, and only if all is well at the end of the series of operations will we issue the COMMIT. If on the other hand anything has failed, we can issue instead the command

```
ROLLBACK
```
which means that the database will be in the same state as it was before the series of operations commenced, and therefore no damage will have been done.

Since a transaction can (hardware constraints aside) contain any number of operations, even the extreme case of an overnight database restructuring, which I also mentioned in Chapter 2, can be handled safely.

2   *Deferred constraint checking*

As we saw in Section 4(b) of Chapter 12, a problem can arise when trying to implement two or more constraints which are part of the data requirement but which conflict with each other.

SQL provides a resolution for this type of problem by enabling a constraint to be defined as INITIALLY DEFERRED, so that the constraint will be suspended until all necessary data has been entered. SQL Anywhere does not fully support this mechanism but does provide deferred constraint checking in the case of referential constraints only, using the WAIT_FOR_COMMIT database option.

So we could use this to resolve the constraint inconsistency problem we identified in the Wyvern Buses requirement:

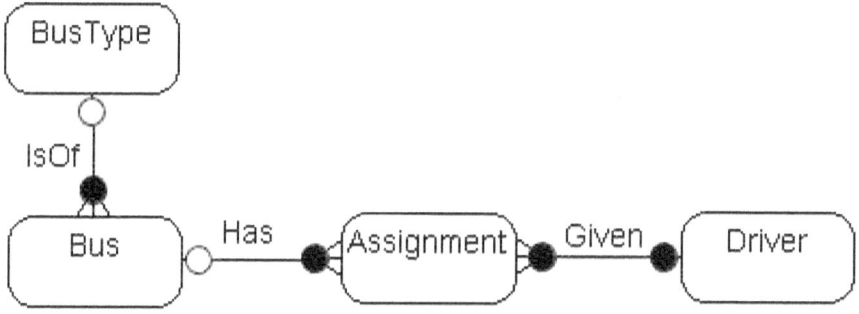

Figure 53 – the Wyvern Buses E-R diagram

The relationship *Given* is mandatory at both ends, and as we saw in Chapter 4, implementing both of those participation constraints would, in the ordinary way, mean that no data could be entered in either *Assignment* or *Driver.*

We can avoid this problem, by using the SQL Anywhere facilities to enter data in both tables within a transaction:

```
SET AUTOCOMMIT OFF;
        .
        .
        .
```

```
BEGIN
SET OPTION WAIT_FOR_COMMIT = ON;
INSERT INTO assignment nat_ins_no regno
timedate route
VALUES('DQ435721A','AQ12CDE','2019-05-25
15:00', 21);
INSERT INTO assignment
VALUES('DQ435721A','AQ12CDE','2019-05-26
15:00', 21);
INSERT INTO driver
VALUES('DQ435721A','Wilson','1990-01-071');
END
  .

  .

COMMIT;
```

Here, two rows are first added to the table at the :n (foreign key) end of the *Given* relationship, the *Assignment* table. This is a mandatory relationship (the foreign key being part of the primary key), but the foreign key values in those new rows are not checked, because of the WAIT_FOR_COMMIT.

A row is then added to the *Driver* table at the :1 end of the relationship to insert driver Wilson. The mandatory participation constraint which applies to each such new row inserted will be satisfied, because two *Assignment* rows are now there for that driver.

At the COMMIT command, the foreign key values in the two new rows just added to *Assignment* will now be checked against the primary key values of the *Driver* table, and that referential constraint will be satisfied because the row for driver Wilson is already there.

3   Concurrency problems

We need to remember that, unlike the small databases you have been using in these activities as the sole user of the dbms, in general relational databases are very large and are used by numbers (potentially very large numbers) of users simultaneously. As long as the hardware and network are sufficiently powerful and efficient, this in itself causes no problems for data retrieval. But where two or more users may be attempting to *update* the same data at the same time, or where a user is updating something which another user is retrieving, problems can arise, and the dbms needs to be able to deal with them. We group these issues in four categories:

- lost update

- uncommitted data

- non-repeatable read

- phantom rows

a)   *Lost update*

Imagine that, in the Garage database, fitter Robinson leaves the company. Any employees he was responsible for managing must now be allocated to a different manager (fitter or chargehand).

Knowing this, user A logs into the database and checks for the employees managed by Robinson; she finds the apprentice Smith. Meanwhile user B also logs into the database to fix the same issue, and finds the same details.

User A now updates the row for Smith, so as to allocate him to fitter Johnson. And then user B updates the row for Smith, to allocate him to chargehand Wilkins.

User A now thinks she has allocated Smith to Johnson, but that update has been lost and in fact the database shows him allocated to Wilkins.

b)   *Uncommitted data (or "dirty read")*

This time let's imagine the same situation, but user A is carrying out the update to the row for Smith as part of a transaction. As before, user B comes along and queries that same row. He sees that Smith has been correctly allocated to another line manager.

However, the transaction does not complete for some reason, possibly because of a system failure, and so the update is rolled back. But User B believes that Smith has been correctly allocated to another line manager, so walks away content.

c)   *Non-repeatable read*

Problems a) and b) involve inconsistent data in the database, but the non-repeatable read problem allows users to obtain inconsistent *results* even when the database itself is always consistent.

User A again checks the database for staff managed by Robinson, and finds the row for Smith. Before she has had time to update it, User C queries the database to list out all staff and their managers, and finds that Smith's manager is Robinson.

User A then successfully completes the task of re-allocating Smith to be managed by Johnson. Meanwhile User C has been carrying out other tasks, returns to query the list of staff and managers again and finds a different answer for Smith.

d) **Phantom rows**

Like problem c), this issue also results in issues of misleading data even though the database is always consistent, but it involves multiple-row queries.

This time User A queries the database to count how many employees are managed by the chargehand Wilkins, and obtains the correct answer which is 3. Then User B carries out the same update as in problem 1, to allocate apprentice Smith to be managed by Wilkins. If User A now carries out her query again, she will get the correct result which is now 4.

4   *Locking and Isolation Levels*

The simplest way for a dbms to address the problems listed above, would be to enforce *serialized[2] execution*, where no two transactions involving any of the data (update or retrieval) would be allowed to execute at the same time. However this is clearly not practicable for any large system.

So the solution instead is to achieve what we call *serializable execution*, where every transaction can execute to completion *as if* it were the only transaction executing in the database. There are various ways of achieving this.

The general solution is to apply *locking*, where all data involved in any transaction is locked, to prevent either update or retrieval of that data while the transaction executes. However, while this is not as extreme a solution as fully serialised execution, if implemented literally it would be a considerable handicap to processing in a large database, because transactions could have to wait for some time for "their" data to be released from another transaction.

Instead, we can consider whether the four concurrency problems are equally serious, or whether some level of concurrent access to locked data could be allowed in some cases. To permit the database designer to make such choices, SQL provides a configurable *isolation level*. In standard SQL (some implementations vary in this respect), the designer has a choice of four settings, which can be implemented with

---

[2]   The American spelling is used here to be consistent with the actual SQL commands

the command

SET TRANSACTION ISOLATION LEVEL <level>

The effects of these settings on each of the concurrency problems are shown in the table below, the default being SERIALIZABLE.

Isolation level	Lost update	Reading uncommitted data	Non-repeatable read	Phantom rows
SERIALIZABLE	Not possible	Not possible	Not possible	Not possible
REPEATABLE READ	Not possible	Not possible	Not possible	Possible
READ COMMITTED	Not possible	Not possible	Possible	Possible
READ UNCOMMITTED	Not possible	Possible	Possible	Possible

Table 4: effects of isolation levels

Chapter 18: Design Choices

Up until now, I have mainly concentrated on describing how to analyse a data requirement, and on the technical steps involved in implementing a database which represents that requirement, and I have tended to let you assume that there is just one way to do the latter.

But because a database has to function in the real world, speed and efficiency of processing, and usability, are aspects which should always be taken into consideration. There are choices we can make to improve those aspects, and sometimes these choices may even involve diverging from the letter of the data requirement (although of course all such choices should be agreed with the end users).

1   Primary keys and surrogates

In Section 1(d) of Chapter 5, I talked about the need for a candidate key to minimally identify tuples and on the effects of choosing multiple attributes to form a key; and in subsequent chapters we just carried on as if all there was to do when we came to the `CREATE TABLE` statements, was to choose primary keys on the same basis. We only ever chose primary keys formed from one or more columns which had been called for by the data requirement.

But consider the *Job* table in the Garage database. The relation heading is

Job(RegNo, DateStart, JobDescription, Make, DateEnd, Hours)

which is perfectly correct in terms of the requirement. But the primary key (RegNo,DateStart,JobDescription) may not be best in terms of identifying a Job from a human perspective. Suppose, as seems quite likely, that we wanted to print out job sheets for the allocated employees, and subequently refer to them, perhaps to ask a fitter how a particular job was progressing. Referring to a job as, for example "AQ12CDE,2016-01-04,12,000 service" is somewhat cumbersome, to say the least; it would seem more natural to be able to refer to a Job by a simple reference, such as its number. But so far, we didn't *give* Jobs numbers, because it wasn't part of the requirement.

Quite apart from this human perspective, if we have to use the system to look up a given Job using that original primary key, then not only does the user have to enter three values (registration number, start date and the possibly lengthy description), but the system has to process three WHERE conditions in order to fnd the row.

So what is frequently done in this type of circumstance, is to create an additional column, probably with a simple and obvious name, such as "JobNo," to serve as the primary key in place of the combined attributes – all of which will still be required anyway, because of the information they contain.

But in doing so, it's important to remember that we've created, and will need to store, data which is additional and redundant (because it simply repeats information which was already there in the form of the combination of RegNo, DateStart, JobDescription). We call this new column a "surrogate key," because it stands in for the existing identifying columns.

We will also need to remember that any necessary constraints implicitly represented by the combined attribute primary key (in this case that only one Job of a given Description can be started on any vehicle on any given date) will have to be enforced instead by explicit additional constraint definitions.

The choice is a trade-off, but often the ease of use of the data, by both humans and the system, will justify abandoning absolute purity of design.

2   Domains

As we saw in Chapter 12, SQL supports the use of domains but does not, like the relational model, insist on their use. It would be perfectly possible (and in fact it's quite common) to have a database which doesn't use domains at all, and where every column definition includes its data type and, if necessary, its range of values and any other applicable constraints. Many other databases make use of domains just for any groups of columns which share the same data type, range and constraint, particularly if the constraint expression is complex; thus saving a lot of typing and ensuring consistency by only storing the definition in one place.

But it would certainly be possible to imitate the relational model by defining every column on some domain. This approach has the advantage of making the schema easier to read, particularly if the domains have clear and meaningful names, because it gives, in one place, a human-readable catalogue of all the data items in the database.

3   Denormalisation

After all the complexity of normalising tables in order to achieve the purest and most elegant representation of the data items in the requirement, with all its advantages of removing redundancy and its resultant processing anomalies, you might well wonder why I would now suggest unpicking all that. But this is another area where the database designer needs to consider processing efficiency and usability.

Consider, for example, the wagon_use table, which we normalised in Section 2 of Chapter 13. We ended up breaking it into four tables, the relation headings of which would look as follows

wagon_types(wagon_type,unladen_wt)

wagons3nf(wagon_id,wagon_type)

routes(route_id,station_from,station_to)

wagon_use3nf(wagon_id,journey_date,route_id,laden_wt,loco_id,loco_type)

But let's say the users of these tables frequently need to list out all the wagons which are available for use at a given station, with their unladen weights, in order to select wagons for another train. The necessary query would look like this:

```
SELECT wagon_id, unladen_wt
FROM wagon_types wt, wagons3nf w, routes r,
                                wagon_use3nf wu
WHERE wt.wagon_type = w.wagon_type
AND wt.wagon_id = wu.wagon_id
AND wu.route_id = r.route_id
AND r.station_to = 'Sandy Bay'
AND wu.journey_date >=ALL
        (SELECT journey_date FROM wagon_use
              WHERE wu.wagon_id =
wagon_use.wagon.id)
```

As we know from the logical processing model, the FROM clause in the outer query would result in a temporary table which would be the cartesian product of the four tables listed, a very large table which would need to be first created and then held in memory while every row was processed against the correlated subquery.

So if this query has to be run often, it *might* be more advisable to de-normalise, and use instead the original wagon_use table, thereby getting rid of all those joins, as long as we are aware of the resultant processing anomalies and can find ways to mitigate the problems they could cause.

In a well run database system, the dba will be continually monitoring system information on the processing of queries and their impact on performance, so as to be able to make informed choices on things like denormalisation.

4   *Constraints*

In Chapter 17, we considered deferred constraint checking as one means of dealing with *processing inconsistency*, that is, the situation where constraints may conflict with each other. Where deferred constraint checking is not available, alternatives may be available, particularly if some of the data is fairly static. Consider again the *Given* relationship between *Driver* and *Assignment*, which I used to illustrate the use of deferred constraint checking.

Figure 54: part of the Wyvern Buses data model

While bus assignments are no doubt created at least daily, the drivers employed by the company probably do not change all that much. So one work-around to avoid the conflict would be as follows:

- create the *Driver* table without its participation constraint, and populate it with details of all the firm's drivers

- create the *Assignment* table, with its referential constraint and participation condition, and insert at least one row for every driver

- alter the *Driver* table to add the participation constraint.

We could then happily add further assignments for each driver, as necessary.

Another reason to reconsider the way we implement the constraints which were called for in the data requirement, is *processing inefficiency*. As I mentioned way back in Chapter 2, relational databases are relatively inefficient, if we compare them, purely on the basis of much power they need to crunch a given amount of data, with the systems which preceded them. The main reason for this is the additional power it can take to process the constraints, which, of course, give us in exchange all the benefits of data consistency.

After all I've said in praise of those benefits, it may sound like sacrilege to be suggesting now that we might not make full use of dbms constraints, but there are situations where we can reduce inefficiency by handling constraints in other ways.

Consider for example a large database where large numbers of users are inputting data. The work the dbms needs to do to check all the constraints may slow the processing considerably. For things like referential constraints, where the acceptability or otherwise of data being input depends on comparing it with data already in the database, it may be inevitable to continue to rely on the dbms to do the checking. But, for example, in checking whether or not the data type and range of an item being input matches the definition of the column for which it is destined, we do not need to look at existing data at all. So, provided we can ensure that data input is only done through application programs, we can do that validation right there in the application program, before the dbms is even involved.

5   *Journaling and backups*

I do not propose, in this book, to describe in any detail the process of database backup and restore, because these aspects are not defined in the SQL standards and the way they are done varies widely between dbms implementations. But whatever the mechanisms, there are decisions to be made about how to use these functions.

It really boils down to how much work or data the organisation can afford to lose, in the event of some kind of software or hardware failure, power cut or other catastrophe. Ideally of course we would wish to never lose any work or data at all, but protecting against loss comes with a penalty.

All organisations will of course take regular *backups*, that's to say full copies of the entire database, and to guard against disaster the backup may be stored remotely. But every time we do this we take up a large additional amount of disk space, and the process of taking the backup itself diverts processing capacity away from operational work, so the organisation may prefer to do this maybe only daily, and perhaps during quiet times.

The backup is in any case something of a blunt instrument. It should enable us to always restore the database back to the point at which it was taken, but it doesn't help with data which was changed in the period *since* it was taken.

So the dbms will also provide some form of *journaling*, which is a system for recording every transaction separately from the database, so that they could be re-applied. In the event of a failure requiring a database restore, the procedure would be to re-create the database, populate it by copying in the last backup, and then apply, from the journal, all the transactions which had taken place since that last backup. In this way we should be able to get fully back to the instant the system failed; but of course the system will not be available to users, possibly for quite some time, while all this is done. And like the backups, the journals take some processing power to create, and some disk space to store.

Where an organisation cannot tolerate either the slightest loss of data or any loss of availability of the system, a further approach which goes well beyond the functionality of the dbms itself, is to replicate the system on one or more other machines, possibly remotely located, on what is often called *hot standby*. In this situation the entire database exists, second by second, on two or more complete systems, and if there is a failure of the live system there will be automatic (and hopefully transparent) switching to a second or further system. Naturally this too comes at considerable cost.

Chapter 19: Data import and export

I already mentioned how dbms suppliers provide functionality above and beyond the SQL language, in order to configure things like physical storage, journaling and database backups.

The SQL standard only provides the INSERT command to add data to a database, and although this can be incorporated into a loop in a program (see Chapter 16 above) to add rows repeatedly, it can be a rather laborious process where large volumes of existing data need to be added to a database. Likewise, the standard only provides commands to take data into another table in the database, and not to pass it out to another kind of application or storage system.

So dbms suppliers also provide functions, which often have SQL-like syntax, to fill these gaps; most commonly these functions are called IMPORT and EXPORT, but they do vary. They may also provide GUI tools to do the same job; SQLAnywhere provides such tools, but only to import data and create a new table at the same time.

The Interactive SQL command provided in SQL Anywhere to import data into an existing is called INPUT. For example, after connecting to the Garage database, the command

```
INPUT INTO customer
FROM '{your path to
SQLpackage}/newcustomers.csv'
FORMAT TEXT
SKIP 1;
```
Query 80: INPUT INTO (SQLAnywhere command)

will insert 6 new rows into the *customer* table (the results pane shows either nothing or the results of the previous query, but if you then SELECT * or use SQL Central, you will be able to see the full table with the inserted rows.).

In this example, the `FORMAT TEXT` tells the system about the format of the file, and `SKIP 1` tells it to ignore the header row in the file.

From that last sentence alone, you will understand that the format of the incoming file has to be known, and in fact it goes much beyond that; the content of the file has to comply with the definition of the table into which it is being inserted, in terms of data types, value ranges, and all other constraints.

However, in general, since the data is being loaded outside of SQL, the constraints defined in SQL in the table definition will *not* be checked at the time. In fact (and if you wish you can play with the *newcustomers.csv* file to show this), the import command will allow all sorts of invalid data to be loaded. Such an invalid value will then normally only be checked the *next time* a user tries to update another value in the affected row, which may well cause surprise.

So although this kind of tool is very useful for loading large amounts of external data (for example from some other type of legacy database), it's essential to write a program to *clean* the data first, to make sure it complies with the definition of the affected table(s), and where necessary to either correct the data automatically or to flag it up for human correction.

Similarly, SQL Anywhere provides the Export wizard in Interactive SQL, as well as the interactive OUTPUT command which is analagous to INPUT, to take data from an SQL table into an external file; for example to enable it to be loaded into a spreadsheet, or to be used to format a report in some suitable external application.

Chapter 20: Connecting applications to the database

So far you have connected with the dbms using either Interactive SQL or SQL Central; these are both general purpose tools, provided by the dbms manufacturer, and which quite naturally work perfectly with their product. But as I mentioned earlier, almost all real world users of an SQL database do so using application programs, which will often have been developed by someone other than the dbms manufacturer. So, given that an SQL dbms understands only SQL, what is the process by which an external application program can "talk to" the dbms?

1   Third generation (3GL) languages

Application programs in third generation languages, such as C, Fortran, Pascal etc, are written in what's called *source code*, and then processed by a *compiler*, which is a piece of software specific to a language and to an operating system, to produce executable *object code*. The reason for this process is that the resultant executable program, which is not in any useful way human-readable or editable, has been transformed into low-level code which is directly readable by the machine and so exploits its performance potential to the full.

But since these languages are quite different from SQL, the programmer has to have some method of sending SQL to the dbms.

a)   *Embedded SQL*

One way to do this is by using is *embedded SQL*. We use the term *hybrid code* to describe such source code containing SQL statements.

What happens is that the programmer writes into the source code program an instruction such as `EXEC  SQL`, followed by whatever SQL code is required, followed by the SQL terminator (usually a semicolon). When the compiler then processes this source code, it recognises the SQL code as needing to be preserved intact in order to be sent to the dbms at some point under control of the program.

Generally (and this is dbms-dependent), a separate DECLARE section is first required in the program in order to create *host variables* which can then be used to store data items which are recognised both by the program and the dbms.

For example, we could write an imaginary C program which collects from the user a registration number, and then uses embedded SQL to run that number against the

Wyvern Buses database, in order to retrieve details of that bus (notice that the names for data types in host languages may differ from those in SQL, although they can usually be easily mapped across):

```
EXEC SQL BEGIN DECLARE SECTION
        preg_no character_string(7)
               pmaker character_string(10)
               ptype character_string(20)
               pseats short
               EXEC SQL END DECLARE SECTION


    {program collects reg no into preg_no}


    EXEC SQL
        SELECT maker,type,seats
               INTO pmaker ptype pseats
               FROM bus,bustype
               WHERE bus.type = bustype.type
               AND regno = preg_no;
```

It's equally possible to use embedded SQL to INSERT, UPDATE or DELETE data in the database

Of course this simple construction could only retrieve from or insert into *a single data item* at a time into the host variables, and that means the SQL query must be of a type which by definition inserts or returns at most a single row of a table (for a SELECT, it must be either, like this example, a query against a primary key value, or one which just returns one aggregate value).

However, it's also possible to create and use a cursor in the embedded SQL, in the same way as described in Chapter 16 in the context of procedures. It would then be possible to insert data from or retrieve it into a pre-defined array within the program.

But things are still one stage more complicated, because although I just implied that the host C compiler would be able to process the kind of hybrid code in my example, in fact this would be of little use because, as it stands, the embedded SQL would still probably not be recognised by the dbms. This is because each dbms has its own *native interface*. So each dbms manufacturer provides a *pre-compiler*, which takes the hybrid code and processes the embedded SQL into a form which the dbms recognises; the output of this pre-compiler can then be fed into the host system's own compiler, to finally produce the object code which can successfully run against the database.

b) ODBC (Open Database Connectivity)

Because of the need to use a dbms-specific pre-compiler, as I described in the last section, a program using embedded SQL is not portable between different makes of dbms. ODBC is a type of application programming interface, which was developed to address that problem.

Given that the dbms has a native interface, in this scenario the host language compiler creates object code which contains calls to ODBC, rather than directly to the dbms. An *ODBC Driver*, which is specific to a dbms and an operating system, makes these calls understandable to the native interface of the dbms. Since each ODBC driver presents the same common interface to the program, such programs can now be portable between db systems.

2 Object-oriented (OO) languages

Connecting an SQL database to a program written in a 3GL language, in one of the ways I just described, is relatively simple, because although those languages make provisions for temporary storage of data in variables during run time, they do not have a structured view of how data is arranged. It's therefore fairly straightforward to have the program work with the table structure of SQL.

OO languages, however, have a very clear idea of how data is structured; the clue is in their name. And objects don't fit comfortably alongside the rigid column-and-row structure of SQL. To describe this difficulty, we borrow a term from electronics: we call it *impedance mismatch*. If an OO program needs to *persist* the data it handles in some way, so that it exists even after the program stops running, then it needs to be able to talk to some kind of database. And given the enormous popularity of OO code for developing applications, and of relational databases for storing data, this is clearly an issue.

Since this is a book about relational databases, I don't propose to give a detailed explanation of object-orientation, but rather to highlight briefly the issues which add up to impedance mismatch, and give some examples of how it can be addressed. I will assume that either you already understand OO concepts, or that this approach is sufficient for you, for the present at least.

OO languages make use of *encapsulated objects*, which are essentially hidden to any external interface such as a database. They consider all data to be inherently either *public* or *private*, which conflicts with SQL where all data is available, subject to access control.

Objects have *classes*, and they support *inheritance* (where one object can assume the characteristics of another without explicity repeating them), and *polymorphism* (where one interface can provide access to differing types of entity). None of these ideas can be easily expressed in terms of columns and rows.

Objects can also be subsets of other objects; you might see this as a way of directly modelling *compound data*, but as we saw in Chapter 11, the kind of relational system we've been looking at deals very differently with compound data.

Relational databases are based on *sets*, and SQL operators are set operators; and an SQL database fully supports physical data independence. OO languages, however, mainly manipulate data through *imperative* operators, often making use of physical paths to access data.

Finally, OO languages have nothing like SQL's all-encompassing notion of *transactions*, which brings with it the possibility of full concurrency support.

a)   Java

Java is an example of an OO language. Like 3GL languages, its programs are compiled into object code, but unlike 3GL, that code runs on a *Java Virtual Machine* or JVM, which is available for all machine environments, so that Java code is fully portable.

b)   JDBC

As its name suggests, JDBC was intended to provide an interface for Java code similar to that provided for 3GL programs by ODBC. And as with ODBC, each dbms environment has its specific JDBC driver, thus extending the portability of Java code to include pretty much universal database connectivity.

A Java class using an SQL database makes use of methods which are provided in the Java class libraries, and which are linked by including the declaration

```
import java.sql.*;
```
in the Java code.

Having done this, JDBC statements are simply included in the program, and compiled with no need for any pre-compiler.

The program loads the JDBC driver and connects through it to the database, and can then directly execute SQL statements.

Within the program, a class is declared as type `ResultSet.` This class comes with a number of methods for processing data to and from the database, including an implicit cursor.

c)   *SQLJ*

SQLJ is effectively embedded SQL for Java, and like embedded SQL it requires pre-compilation, except that, having been developed when JDBC already existed, it uses JDBC, rather than a separate pre-compiler, to achieve that translation. It is now specified as part of the SQL standard.

SQL statements are simply included in the Java code by enclosing them in curly brackets and preceding them with the marker `#sql`. Within the SQL, the only difference is that the Java variables are preceded by a colon.

Our embedded SQL example would look like this in SQLJ:

```
#sql   {SELECT maker,type,seats
        INTO :pmaker :ptype :pseats
        FROM bus,bustype
        WHERE bus.type = bustype.type
        AND regno = :preg_no};
```

As I mentioned when discussing embedded SQL, this type of construction only works when there is at most a single result to be transferred to or from each variable.

To deal with a situation where potentially many rows are to be transferred, SQLJ provides two kinds of *iterator* class: a *positioned iterator* and a *named iterator*.

The positioned iterator is declared with a specified set of data types for the columns in the rows to be transferred. For example, a positioned iterator to retrieve all rows from *bus* and *bustype* would look like

```
#sql iterator BusIterator(string, string,
int);
```

This generates a class named BusIterator. A Java variable can then be created from this class using a Java statement, e.g.

```
BusIterator myBusIterator;
```

and rather like defining a cursor, this is then used to hold the SQL query

```
#sqlj myBusIterator = {SELECT maker,type,seats
                FROM bus,bustype
                WHERE bus.type = bustype.type};
```

Within a control loop in the Java program, the iterator can then be used to fill regular Java variables:

```
#sqlj {FETCH :myBusIterator INTO :pmaker
:ptype :pseats};
```

A *named iterator* is similarly declared, except that the specific colum names have to be included, e.g.

```
#sql iterator BusNamIterator(string maker,
                                string type, int
seats);
```

Again we create a variable from this class:

```
BusNamIterator myNamIterator;
```

and assign a query to it:

```
#sqlj myNamIterator = {SELECT maker,type,seats
                FROM bus,bustype
                WHERE bus.type = bustype.type};
```

However, a method is then generated for each column in the results set, with the same name as that of the related column. Each method can then be used to retrieve the value of that column in the current row, e.g.

```
maker = myNamIterator.maker();
```

and the Java method next is used to move to the next row.

d)   *Object-relational mapping*

Another approach, which avoids the need for the OO programmer to know any SQL at all, is to employ a (usually third-party) object-relational mapping tool.

Such a tool is general purpose software, which has to be configured for each database and each application using it, in order to map the SQL data items to classes in the program. Thereafter the program can, via the tool, use existing rows and columns as if they were instance variables within the program. It does not, of course, mean that the program can insert new OO types into the database if they conflict with the relational structure, at least as long as we are talking about a traditional SQL database; see the next paragraph.

e) *Object-relational databases*

Since SQL:1999 (often referred to as SQL3), the ANSI standard has supported a number of object-oriented features, such as structured types, within an SQL database. Clearly this is a considerable divergence from the true relational model, because it departs entirely from the principle of all values being atomic. While a database which uses these new features can be much more easily interfaced with an OO application, the sacrifice of relational principles means some loss of integrity protection, and because of that and the availability of the other methods already mentioned, the features have not been widely adopted.

f) *Object oriented databases*

Finally, dbms products are available which are based entirely on an OO, rather than a relational model, and which therefore can be a very good fit with OO programs; so an organisation could choose such a solution instead of using an SQL dbms at all. Because they don't have to enforce the built-in integrity rules of the relational model, OO databases generally also provide faster performance where all else is equal. But as I've mentioned before, integrity is often the motivation for using a dbms at all, and so despite their advantages, these systems have not been widely adopted.

3   *Scripting languages*

Despite what I said in the first section of this chapter, about the relatively superior performance of a program which the computer can read in its own internal language, the same forward march of increasingly powerful and cheap processors which enabled the growth of relational systems, has also made more attractive the use of languages which exist only in human-readable form, and which can therefore be more easily and rapidly produced, tested and if necessary edited. The improvements in computer performance mean that the overhead of the system having to translate human-readable into machine-readable, every time it runs, is no longer that important.

This is by no means to say that object code is dead, but for many applications, particularly, it would seem, where it is necessary to interface a web application with a relational database, these *scripting languages* have become very popular.

Examples of these languages include Python, PHP and Ruby. As with the other types of language, a language-and-dbms specific driver is needed, in each case, to link the program with the database.

An extremely popular route to developing web systems using a scripting language is the so-called *AMP stack* (Apache, MySQL, PHP) – on which, for example, the widely used open source WordPress package is based. It's available for Linux (LAMP), Windows (WAMP) and even Mac (MAMP).

Exercise 17

Look back at the list of Codd's eight dbms functions (Chapter 6), and the three further functions which I added to that list. How, and to what extent, do SQL systems implement those functions?

Section IV:
Further Developments in SQL Database Functionality

In this final section of the book, I will describe some further major developments of SQL-based systems. As you will see, they each depart in some way from the relational model, while retaining many of its familiar central features.

It would not be practical for you to experiment with these features on your standalone system, so this section does not include any practical activities.

Chapter 21: Distributed data management

So far in this book, I have ignored the possibility that a database might be logically distributed over more than one single physical (or virtual) machine. After all, the three schema model allows for just one logical schema, and the SQL model which we've looked at so far has just the one database schema.

As we know, SQL doesn't define a storage schema, but certainly some (if not all) dbms suppliers permit physical storage to defined in a distributed way, whether across different disk controllers in a single machine or across separate machines on a network. However this would be done generally to improve performance; so long as there is one single database schema, it doesn't in any useful way affect *logical* distribution.

But there are three reasons why we might want the database to be *logically* separated in some way:

- to enable several existing or planned discrete database systems to be viewed from a single central position as if they were one system;

- to separate data within the database of a large organisation having several bases, so that it is located where it is most used, to reduce network performance issues;

- to keep live copies of all or parts of a large database in more than a single location, to improve either performance or resilience or both.

We will shortly look in turn at how each of these issues can be addressed.

Of course, this kind of arrangement departs from the relational model by introducing redundancy (where there are multiple copies of the same data), and by no longer having just one relatively simple database schema to define all the data.

1   *Date's Rules*

Chris Date (Date C.J. 1987) listed a set of twelve rules which should be followed by an ideal distributed system; they were intended to match Codd's rules for relational systems which we discussed earlier (Codd E.F. 1982). They can be summarised as follows:

a) Local autonomy

Each site within the system should, to the maximum extent possible, be able to operate independently of any other site.

b) No reliance on a central site

All sites must be treated as equals – for example there must not be any reliance on some central "master" site.

c) Continuous operation

The system should, by comparison with a single non-distributed system, show greater *reliability* (the probability that it is up and running at any given moment) and *availability* (the probability that it is up and running continuously throughout any given period). Both features are always subject to unplanned shutdowns, but there should be no planned shutdowns.

d) Location independence

Users should not need to know where data is stored, and should be able to operate – at least from a logical standpoint - as if it were all stored at their own local site.

e) Fragmentation independence

Where data has been split in order to be stored where it is most used, this should have no effect on user access.

f) Replication independence

Where data has been replicated on more than one site, the user should not need to specify which copy to access, or to specify to which copies their updates should apply.

g) Distributed query processing

The user should be able to execute a query which requires data from more than one site, without being aware that multi-site acccess is taking place.

h) Distributed transaction management

The system should take care of transaction management both locally and globally *i)*　　　　　*Hardware independence*

The system should be capable of running on a range of different hardware

j)　　　　　*Operating system independence*

The system should be capable of running on a range of different operating systems

k)　　　　　*Network independence*

The system should be capable of running on a range of different network environments

l)　　　　　*DBMS independence*

It should be possible for the system to maintain a homogeneous user interface, even if it actually employs a range of different dbms software.

As you might imagine, and as you will see as we consider the three main types of data distribution, this list is somewhat optimistic.

2   *Client-multiserver systems*

A client-multiserver system allows a single client (although there could be many such single clients) to connect to several independent database systems, so that they may to some extent be presented to a user as one single system. There might be a number of existing systems which have to remain separate, such as the national vehicle registration systems in European countries, but a desire to connect them so as to trace vehicle ownership across the continent, for example. Or a single organisation, such as a local authority, might provide each of the schools in its area with a standalone database system for local management, but might still need to be able to view them as a single system for some purposes. These two examples pose separate problems, because in the first case we can assume the different national systems may keep their data in differing formats and structures, whereas in the second the local databases are probably uniformly structured.

a)　　　　　*Connection management*

SQL provides connection to a database using a CONNECT command, e.g.

```
CONNECT garage USER dba
```
and the means to switch between multiple connected databases, e.g.

```
SET CONNECTION wyvernbuses
```
Only one connection can be current, so when the client application needs to extract data from more than one database, it has to do so one at a time. If the data is not uniformly structured, then the application will have to reformat some of it after retrieval so that it produces coherent output.

It's fairly easy to see how this can work for retrieval of data, but updating is not so simple. Preserving uniqueness of a primary key for a student, for example, across similar tables which each record a group of students separately in each of a number of local school databases, may be very difficult.

b)   *Transaction management*

Staying with the school example, let's imagine that the central client application, in the local authority offices, needs to transfer a student from one school to another. Clearly integrity requires that the removal of the student from one school, and the addition of that student to another, must both succeed, or both fail; in other words we need to incorporate both actions in a transaction, but the actions are taking place on logically and physically separate systems, so ordinarily one system would commit just its own change without taking any notice of what the other system does.

This can be solved using the *two-phase commit* process.

We assume that all systems have AUTOCOMMIT OFF

The central client application sends a DELETE command to the school from which the student is moving and an INSERT command to the school to which s/he is moving. It then sends a request to both schools, asking them to get ready to commit the changes.

Only if both schools reply with a yes within a timeout period, will the central application send the final COMMIT to them both; otherwise it will tell them both to ROLLBACK.

If and when both schools report that the COMMIT has been completed, the central application can set the correct SQLSTATE value for its overall operation.

Naturally this whole process involves a number of network communications, which can slow it considerably. So this kind of distribution solution may not be suitable for a situation where any large numbers of update operations are needed.

A client-multi-server system should support Date's first and second rules (local autonomy and no reliance on a single site), as well as the ninth tenth and eleventh (hardware, operating system and network independence). It might support the twelfth (dbms independence) if all sites ran compatible versions of SQL. However it is very unlikely to support any of the others, particularly because the potential differences in data content across sites will tend to be obvious.

3   *Distributed databases*

In the distributed database management system (ddbms) approach, unlike the client-multiserver configuration, the whole database system appears to users (whether humans or application processes) to be a single database, even though in reality it is distributed across several systems. This is Date's fourth rule: *location independence.* We are considering a single, centrally designed database system, which however comprises several distinct, geographically distributed database systems, which can each function independently in respect of the data they hold; this is Date's first rule, *local autonomy.* A good example could be a chain of supermarkets. From time to time the central system will need to know about individual employees, or specific stocks of goods, held at each location, but for the most part, most of the data will only be used in the individual supermarkets it relates to, so it makes sense to just store the data where it is most used.

Because each local system is a self-sufficient dbms, each will have its own database schema, but on top of that there is a single *global schema*, which defines all the data in the distributed system. And there is also a copy of the *distribution schema*, which defines in which individual system each part of that data is held; so that it's possible for users of a local system to access data in other local systems.

Data defined in the global schema can be broken into fragments for distributed storage, as defined in the distribution schema. There are two forms of fragmentation, reflecting the row and column structure of tables:

- horizontal fragmentation, where rows of a table are separated; for example, a local supermarket might hold only the rows of a *stock* table relating to stocks actually held at that store; and

- vertical fragmentation, where columns of a table are separated; for example, only the central system might hold the columns of a *staff* table relating to salary and other personal information.

Clearly, a user wishing (with suitable permissions) to access the whole or a large part of a fragmented table will need to make use of the distribution schema, and will use a query including *union*, where there is horizontal fragmentation, or *join*, where there is vertical fragmentation.

Some of the fragments might be stored on more than one local system, in which case the user system will need to decide which copy to use in order to optimise performance. Such a decision will normally always use local fragments as far as possible, and then ideally choose other fragment locations based on minimising network traffic and preferring remote systems which are lightly loaded. This process is called *distribution optimisation*. There is an absence of database products which can comprehensively and dynamically optimise queries based on current conditions, so optimisation of stored distributed queries will often require a manually defined execution plan.

a)   *Updating*

So far so good, perhaps, with some reservations, when it is only a question of *retrieval* of distributed data. But as in the client-multiserver scenario, it's *updating* which poses greater problems, because of the need to maintain data integrity when there is more than one copy of a data fragment, or where separated fragments must only be updated at the same time.

I described the two-phase commit protocol, in the previous section. In a distributed database, it is the ddbms, not the local system, which is responsible for ensuring integrity, and this can pose problems because of network or local system delays or failures. If a COMMIT is sent to a local system and receives no response, the central system has to try to discover whether the network or the local system is down, or whether there are just delays in either case. This can make the whole process sluggish.

b)   *Replication*

I already touched on the possibility that a ddbms might hold more than one copy of a distributed fragment, and this could be either to improve performance by offering a choice of a more local fragment, or to improve resilience in the event that one or other copy is unavailable. This of course poses its own integrity problem because the copies have to be kept consistent.

An approach to this is to designate one of the copies as a *primary copy*. This is then the copy which must be handled first in any update, it is then a question of locking any other copies until they have been made consistent with the primary copy. Of course, this is, again, a source of potential system inefficiency.

I've already explained how Date's first and fourth rules are always supported by a true ddbms. In theory, hardware, operating system and network independence ought to be possible too. However, many of the other rules are difficult to implement fully, and in particular, distributed transaction processing and continous operation are difficult to achieve. The potential processing delays and inconsistencies involved in distributed updates means that there will always be a trade-off between performance and absolute consistency across the system.

4   *Replication systems*

I have already described replication of fragments in a ddbms, but another possibility is a system which is not in fact at all distributed in the sense that data is fragmented, but consists of a number of entirely separate, complete copies of the database, in different locations, for reasons of performance or resilience.

In this scenario, each replicated system will contain a *replication server*, which is responsible for passing on updates from its local database to the other sites, and for collecting and applying locally any updates from the other sites.

Because of its very nature, a replicated system will always comply with four of Date's rules (local autonomy, no reliance on a central site, location independence and replication independence), and a further two (fragmentation independence and distributed query processing) don't apply. The last four (hardware, operating system, network and dbms independence) may be achievable depending on implementation. But the third (continuous operation) will not be complied with any more than on any standalone system, because there is no provision for other sites to help out in the case of local failure. And the eighth (distributed transaction processing) can present a problem: while two-phase commit can be used to ensure a level of integrity, the processing and network delays involved in replication between servers mean that, while each local system should maintain its own integrity, it will frequently be the case that there are differences between the versions of data held at each site. Whether this matters will of course depend on the use of the data.

Chapter 22: Multimedia data

From the perspective of a dbms, multimedia data includes images, and sound or video recordings, but also documents when they are stored in a binary format such as .pdf or .doc There are various technologies available to support multimedia storage and retrieval within a database, but these clearly step outside the basic concept of the relational database, where rows can only contain values of clearly defined string or numeric data types.

This kind of data has four notable characteristics:

- a single value, such as a word processing document, can contain a complete set of information about a subject; this contrasts with the relational database approach, where an entity occurrence (represented by a row) has a number of attributes which are stored separately as atomic values.

- a multimedia file type, such as .jpeg, .avi, .mp3, .xlsx and so on, defines not only the general type of the file but also the kind of processing necessary to access its data (and hence the specific application software which can be used to do that)

- single files can be very large, particularly in the case of video, which can run to many gigabytes

- the file usually contains not only a picture, document, or whatever, but also information *about the contents* of the file, such as the author, date of creation, subject and so on, which we call *metadata*. Sometimes, as with word processing documents, the format of that metadata is defined by the proprietary office application that created them, but there is a more general metadata standard for multimedia, known as the Dublin Core (named for the 1995 international workshop in Dublin, Ohio, where it originated). The standard goes into considerable detail about what can be specified and how, but the original version named fifteen elements:

Title, Creator, Subject, Description, Publisher, Contributor, Date, Type, Format, Identifier, Source, Language, Relation, Coverage and Rights.

All of this information is stored within each specified file type, in such a way that the application able to open that file type can extract it as separate from the main contents.

1   Querying

If a document stored in a database is in text format (unlike most word processed documents), the SQL string operators can be used to query it. This can also apply to, for example, xml and html documents, although these also contain formatting and SQL has no facilities for querying that; so it is not possible to specify whether one is searching for words within a title or other specific part of the document. And while database queries can be speeded up by applying an index to the contents of specific columns, this is not appropriate when columns include documents containing formatting as well as text.

When it comes to multimedia other than documents, the situation is even more difficult. Specialist application software is available which can search for particular image features in photographs or motifs in a piece of music, but if we want to search for author of a video or the language of a document, we need to use the metadata I described just now.

2   Using external files

a)   Direct references

One approach to storing multimedia in a database is just, well, not to actually store it there at all. If a multimedia file is held on a local machine or network then it can be accessed using the file path; if it's further afield it may be possible to access it using a URL. So we could just store that access information in the database, rather than the file itself.

This simple approach could be useful where searchable information about the multimedia file is stored in the database anyway. For example, we might have a table containing lots of information about each member of staff in a company, and just include with that the link to the file containing their photograph. For this to work, the application process used to retrieve the textual and numeric information about a staff member, would also have to be able to use the link information to retrieve and display the photograph.

Another approach, for a different purpose, would be to extract metadata from the multimedia files, and copy it into a table alongside the link to the files themselves, so that the multimedia could be retrieved (using an appropriate application) based on a textual SQL search of that metadata.

The obvious problem with this approach is that the SQL dbms has no way to check whether the link being stored is valid, or whether it points to an actual multimedia file which relates to the metadata it is storing alongside the link, or, even if it ever did that, whether the file still exists or has instead been moved or deleted.

b) Datalink references

Fortunately, SQL has a partial solution to this problem, and this is the predefined data type DATALINK. A link in this format represents the file in question as either FILE: or HTTP: It comes with the function DLVALUE, which is used to construct a datalink, given a valid file reference, and with other functions to access the datalink. Queries using these functions can extract an embedded access token, which provides the process with permission to access the file.

A datalink can optionally be created with write permission or read only permission on the file, and with other useful conditions, including:

FILE LINK CONTROL, which means that, when the datalink is assigned to a column, there is a check that the file exists, and

INTEGRITY ALL, which means that a linked file cannot be deleted or renamed.

DATALINK and its associated functions are defined in the SQL Standard for Management of External Data (SQL/MED).

There is, however, no check on whether the linked file is of any particular multimedia format, or whether it can be read by appropriate software.

Using external files, whether with a direct reference or a datalink, obviously means that the potentially large amounts of multimedia data don't have to be stored in the database, and that multimedia applications can if necessary access the data directly, without having to go through the database, giving faster access, e.g. for streaming. On the other hand, programs accessing the data through the database have to be specially written so that they can integrate results from the database with specialised access to the multimedia itself.

3 Using internal tables

Or, we could store the multimedia data directly in a row of a database table. For this purpose, SQL provides specific data types, known as LOBs (large object data types).

There are two kinds of LOB:

CHARACTER LARGE OBJECT (CLOB) for character data; and

BINARY LARGE OBJECT (BLOB) for binary data.

The DBMS stores LOBs separately within the database, with the value in the column consisting of just a pointer to the data itself; however the data remains entirely within the database and cannot be accessed externally, as is the case with external files.

Logically enough, a LOB value in a row cannot be used as a value in operations such as GROUP BY, ORDER BY, DISTINCT, JOIN, UNION, etc.

However, a CLOB value can be treated much as any other string value, for example it can be searched using LIKE and SUBSTRING.

Access to a LOB stored in a database needs to take account of the potential size of the object. Only an application process can be used to retrieve a LOB, because a direct human user logged into a database would have no way to handle the output. But the application process has to retrieve the LOB into a host variable, which needs to be large enough to handle the data returned, before calling a multimedia program to handle the data itself. This, and the need to retrieve a potentially very large object through the dbms, can create issues for memory size, processing speed and possibly network performance.

However, a dbms which supports LOBs will normally include, as part of its IMPORT and EXPORT facilities, the ability to load LOBs directly into tables, and to write them out directly into files, avoiding the need for dbms processing and for large host variables to temporarily store the data.

Secondly, SQL additionally provides the locator data type, which caters for the fact that multimedia files (especially sound and video) often don't need to be processed all at once, so that the size of the necessary host variable can be considerably reduced. In this case, instead of the whole LOB value being retrieved into the host variable, it receives only a pointer. The application process can then use this pointer to access the file, one part at a time.

Thirdly, LOBs can be processed by the dbms using stored procedures and functions. Specific functions are provided to access known types of metadata from a LOB; but beyond that, with a dbms which supports user-defined data types, types and suitable functions can be created to cater for the various kinds of multimedia data.

Finally, multimedia packages exist, which can be provided either by the dbms supplier or by a third party. The definition of the package is stored in a database (which must also support user-defined data types and related functions), and the package itself can be called by the dbms in the process of handling the data. Using a specialised function provided by the package appears no different from using any other function within the dbms.

Choosing between these various ways of accessing LOBs within a database, like most database design choices, calls for a consideration of how the data will be used, and how frequently.

4   *Multimedia databases*

Instead of storing multimedia data in any of these ways in an SQL database, or in external files linked to it, we can instead use a specialised multimedia dbms, and link that in some way to an SQL database, so that the multimedia itself doesn't need to be handled by SQL at all. Multimedia databases are used for such things as video and sound on demand, geographic information systems and digital libraries.

a)   *Using proxy tables*

An application using an SQL dbms to access multimedia data can of course only use SQL queries, just as for any other SQL database access. A proxy table within the SQL database will contain (at least) a column holding a searchable identifier for the data, and another representing the data itself, and possibly others containing searchable metadata. Of course, the column representing the data doesn't actually contain the data itself, and is only activated when queried to retrieve the data, so in that sense it's rather like a view.

This means that, from the user point of view, there appears to be only the one database involved. However, the SQL dbms has to know how to execute a query which addresses both regular table data and multimedia data, so it has to be aware of the capabilities of the multimedia dbms involved, and how (and if) it should handle the various types of multimedia data. This can involve considerable modification to the SQL dbms, and considerable processor loading.

b)   *Using foreign tables*

As an alternative way of linking an SQL database with a multimedia database, SQL/MED (which I mentioned in the context of DATALINK, above), specifies a particular type of proxy table known as a *foreign table*.

It is first necessary to define a *wrapper*, using the CREATE FOREIGN DATA wrapper statement. This defines the name of the wrapper and the library containing the routines it must use. Then, we would use CREATE SERVER, which gives a name for the external server, its type, and the name of the wrapper to be used. Finally, we use CREATE FOREIGN TABLE, to define the table columns and the name of the server holding that table's data.

(Although I am describing this in the context of a connection to a multimedia database, in fact foreign tables can be used to link to any kind of server, it doesn't even have to be a database server).

The key here is the use of a library of specialised routines. Only these routines need to know about the interface of the external server and its capabilities, removing the need for the dbms to be modified as described in the last section.

Chapter 23: Data warehousing and decision support systems

Data warehousing breaks with the traditional relational database model by involving redundant duplication – massive amounts of it. Why?

The classic example used to explain data warehousing is the supermarket system. An operational supermarket system is primarily concerned with dynamically recording the current situation. It holds details of the level of stock of each product line, its price, its location in the store and no doubt its description. When a customer's purchases are processed through a till, it adds up the customer's bill, and subtracts the items purchased from its stock count, and once that has happened the transactions themselves disappear.

So it can't normally be used to tell us what the stock levels were yesterday or the day before, or what the customer bought last week or what the prices were then; those things are of no interest to day-to-day operations. But these things are of great interest to the supermarket company, which would very much like to know about changes in stock levels over time (and whether they are affected by things like weather), about which items customers buy at the same time and whether their purchases are affected by moving things around the store or by price changes, and (especially when customers can be identified through the use of loyalty cards) how an individual's buying habits change.

To find the answers to those questions involves the continual **extraction** of records from the operational database, to give a complete record of how all the things it records *change over time*. Doing this inevitably means repeatedly storing the same information about the price and location of a product, for example, which is why I started by mentioning redundant duplication. However, the main problem with duplicated danger in operational systems is the inconsistency which can arise when some copies are updated and not others. This does not arise in a data warehouse, because the data is all historical and is not updated.

You can no doubt think of many other situations where such data storage would be useful. Weather forecasting systems rely very largely on tracking patterns in massive amounts of data on previous weather. Ditto stock market systems. Health services are (or anyway should be) very interested in patterns of illness, treatment and survival. And as we well understand, internet companies and the advertisers who support them are very keen on knowing which pages each user likes to visit and when, and where they go next.

The kind of systems used to manipulate data from a data warehouse, in order to provide that kind of information, are known as **decision support systems.** The process of extracting the new information from existing data is called **data mining.**

And the manipulation done by those systems is known as **on-line analytical processing (OLAP),** to distinguish it from routine day-to-day processing of operational data, which we call **on-line transactional processing** (OLTP).

The requirements of the two kinds of system are very different. Operational OLTP systems typically involve relatively small levels of processing (such as scanning items at a supermarket till and adding the price to a bill), but they require very fast response times (neither the customers nor the store want a long wait at the till while the bill is produced). By contrast, OLAP systems involve the processing of very large amounts of data in order to answer the kinds of questions I've described above; but there is no great requirement for speed (store management would probably be perfectly happy to wait overnight, or even for several days, for an answer as to the most profitable aisle in which to locate their bakery). The heavy processing load of OLAP operations would be likely to slow down OLTP operations, if they were both hosted on the same server; for this reason they are normally kept separate.

1   The multi-dimensional data model

The multi-dimensional data model is, like the E-R model we encountered earlier in this book, a kind of conceptual data model. But as the name suggests, it is *un*like the two-dimensional E-R model in having additional dimensions, including *time.* It is therefore represented as a cube, or multiple cubes, depending on how many dimensions there are.

Consider, first of all, a partial E-R model of the data requirements for the operational database of a supermarket chain, Wyvern Stores.

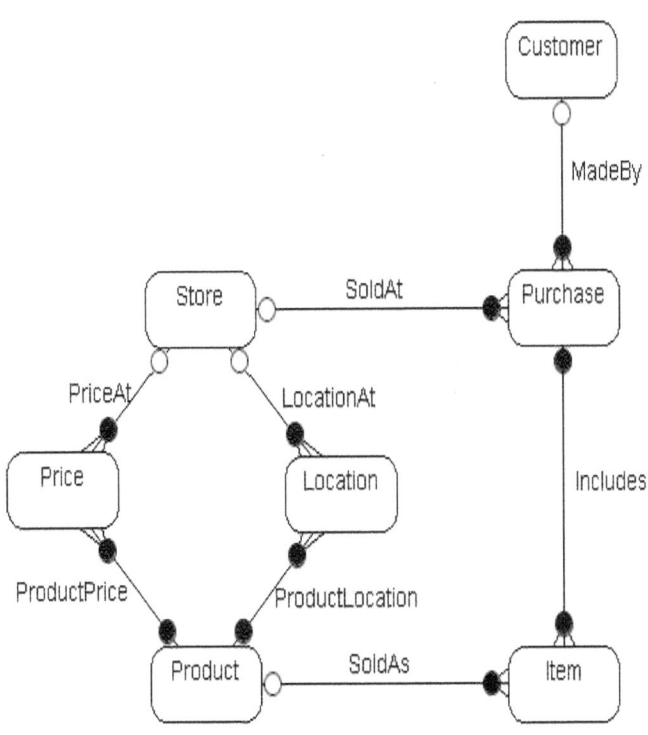

Entity types

Store (<u>StoreCode</u>, Name,Address)

Product(<u>BarCode</u>,Name,Description,Type,Size)

Customer
(<u>LoyaltyCardNo</u>,Name,Address,PostCode,DoB,Sex,Occupation,AnnualIncome
,NoOfChildren,NoOfCars,ReceiveMailShots?,TotalPoints)

Purchase (<u>StoreCode,LoyaltyCardNo,Date,Time,</u>PointsAdded)

Item (<u>StoreCode,LoyaltyCardNo,Date,Time,ProductCode,</u>Quantity)

Price (<u>BarCode,StoreCode,</u>Price)

Location (<u>BarCode,StoreCode,</u>Location)

Figure 55: part of a data model for Wyvern Stores

Let us imagine that this model has been transformed into an SQL database, with one table representing each of the above entities, and that we then execute the following query:

```
SELECT
c.loyalty_card_no,s.name,l.location,p.product_
code,p.type,p.price,    u.time
FROM customer c, store.s,location l,product
p,purchase u,item          i,price r
WHERE p.loyalty_card_no=c.loyalty_card_no
AND p.store_code=s.store_code
AND i. store_code,loyalty_card_no,date,time=
          u. store_code,loyalty_card_no,date,time
AND i.product_code=p.product_code
AND l.product_code=p.product_code
AND l.store_code=s.store_code
AND r.product_code=p.product_code
AND r.store_code=s.store_code
```

This would produce, in part, the following output:

loyalty_card_no	s.name	l.location	p.product_code	p.type	p.price	u.time
6547789	Sandy Bay	R6B3	584099153279	Vegetables	0.60	1013
6547789	Sandy Bay	R4B10	6389554951117	Meat	3.40	1013
6547789	Sandy Bay	R1B7	5402120107020	Nuts	0.25	1013
6547789	Sandy Bay	R1B7	1017213452549	Nuts	0.30	1013
6547789	Sandy Bay	R10B3	2830452488259	Alcohol	18.50	1013
6547789	Sandy Bay	R9B5	3033190926475	Dairy	2.50	1013
6547789	Sandy Bay	R5B7	8949113174845	Salads	1.20	1013
6547789	Sandy Bay	R5B7	7345530760899	Salads	2.00	1013
6547789	Sandy Bay	R5B7	9305873030019	Salads	1.80	1013
6547789	Sandy Bay	R8B2	2324449896207	Pizza	4.50	1013
6547789	Sandy Bay	R9B7	8837432228380	Bakery	2.50	1013
6547789	Sandy Bay	R9B6	2737041654135	Dairy	5.00	1013
6542127	Southville	R6B2	4586938928761	Spices	0.80	1024
6542127	Southville	R6B3	584099153279	Vegetables	0.60	1024
6542127	Southville	R4B10	6389554951117	Meat	3.40	1024
6542127	Southville	R9B5	6277911667743	Dairy	3.00	1024
6542127	Southville	R9B7	7616168717235	Bakery	4.50	1024
6542127	Southville	R10B3	7500399770131	Alcohol	15.00	1024
6542127	Southville	R5B7	7345530760899	Salads	2.00	1024
6542127	Southville	R5B7	9305873030019	Salads	1.80	1024
6542127	Southville	R8B2	2324449896207	Pizza	4.50	1024
6542127	Southville	R6B3	6170869010916	Vegetables	1.10	1024
6542127	Southville	R1B7	5697550433652	Nuts	0.35	1024

Figure 56: part of a data model for Wyvern Stores

We can already see that this *extracted* data, unlike the operational database from which it came, contains a lot of redundancy; as just one example, the fact that item 2324449896207 cost 4.50 in both the stores in this output (at least on the day in question), is recorded twice. However this data is a snapshot; if we put it together into a data warehouse with data from all the stores, and did that again every day, some of these facts would change *over time*, enabling us to investigate how or whether some changes seemed to be associated with others.

The multi-dimensional data model enables us to represent such amalgamated data in terms of *facts* and *dimensions*. Consider now such a possible model for some of the data shown above:

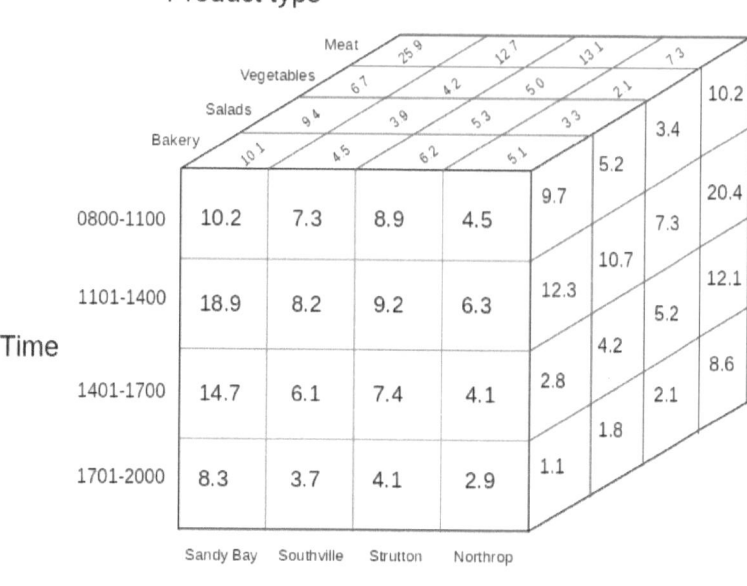

Figure 57: **Sales** at Wyvern Stores branches, by £000s

In this model, the cube represents a *fact*: sales at Wyvern Stores branches. This fact has three **dimensions**: location, product type and *time*.

Note that creating this simple example has already included *aggregation* of the original data shown in Figure 56. *Customer* has not, for example, been included as a dimension, so the sales to individual customers have been aggregated in terms of the remaining three dimensions. Similarly, the time dimension in the model is expressed only in terms of three-hour periods, so all the data has been simplified into those terms. In a data warehouse the data will almost always be aggregated along at least some of the dimensions, depending on the kinds of analysis required.

The model can be realised in three ways. Multi-dimensional database systems exist, which implement it directly as a matrix. Processing the data using this kind of system is known as MOLAP, for obvious reasons. It can also be implemented using a relational approach, and by a hybrid of the two, HOLAP. But since this book is chiefly about *relational* systems, the remainder of this chapter describes how it can be implemented instead as a series of *fact* and *dimension* tables, and how the data is then processed using *relational* on-line analytical processing (ROLAP). SQL makes provisions, known as SQL/OLAP, for this processing.

2   OLAP systems

OLAP systems use a three-tier architecture consisting of presentation, processing and storage layers.

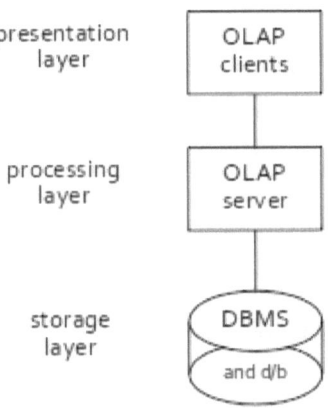

Figure 58 An architecture for OLAP systems.

The presentation layer provides interfaces to other applications, and includes in-built tools for data analysis, reporting and so on. The processing layer provide an interface between OLAP clients and the storage layer, which in turn interacts with the database.

In ROLAP systems, the ROLAP server will satisfy request from OLAP clients by issuing SQL statements to the relational DBMS, and formatting the resultant tables as a multidimensional array.

a)   ROLAP schemas

Here, the multidimensional model is represented in the form of a *fact table* and *dimension tables*. In a simple multidimensional model, such as the single cube in Figure 57, the relational approach would be to use a *star schema*, such as the one in Figure 59 below.

253

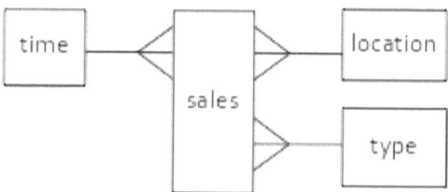

sales (time_code,store_code,type_code,quantity,cost)
time (time_code,date, day, week, month, quarter, year)
location (store_code,name,address)
type (type_code,name)

Figure 59: A relational implementation of the model at Figure 57

A variant of the star schema, called a **snowflake schema**, can represent dimensions as a hierarchy. Figure 60 shows a snowflake schema representation of the star schema given in Figure 59

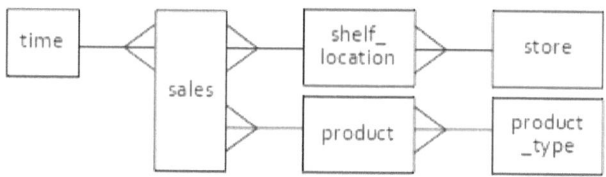

sales (time_code, shelf, store_code, product_code, quantity, cost)
time (time_code, date, day, week, month, quarter, year)
shelf_location (shelf, store_code)
store (store_code, name, address)
product (product_code, description, product_type)
product_type (type_code, name)

Figure 60 A snowflake schema diagram for Wyvern Store sales data.

Another variation, called a **galaxy schema**, covers the situation where multiple *fact* tables may be required, possibly sharing one or more of the same dimension tables, to cover multiple subjects of interest. An example is shown in figure 61

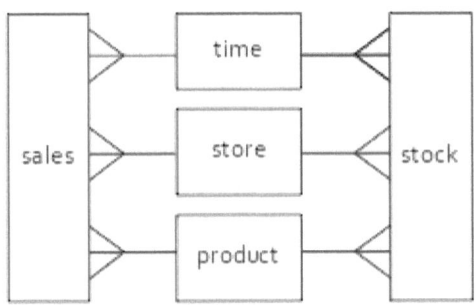

sales (<u>time code</u>, <u>store code</u>, <u>product code</u>, quantity, cost)
stock (<u>time code</u>, store_code, product_code, quantity)
time (<u>time code</u>, date, day, week, month, quarter, year)
store (<u>store code</u>, store_name, store_address)
product (<u>product code</u>, description, product_type)

Figure 61 A galaxy schema for Wyvern Store sales and inventory data.

b)   *SQL/OLAP*

Extensions to the GROUP BY clause in SQL/OLAP allow the use of the *aggregate functions* to summarise the raw data in the fact table.

Roll-up

The *roll-up* operation performs an aggregation. This is can be done with the normal GROUP BY clause, using the dimensions as grouping columns. The aggregation is then done with aggregate functions in the SELECT clause.

For example, the following SQL query, run against the database described by the star schema given in Figure 59, will produce a roll-up of Wyvern Stores' sales data according to the dimension of *location*.

```
SELECT location.name, SUM(cost) AS
total_revenue_in_thousands
FROM sales, time, location
WHERE sales.time_code = time.time_code
  AND sales.store_code = location.store_code
  AND time.year = 2019
GROUP BY location.name
```

location.name	total_revenue_in_thousands
Sandy Bay	52.1
Southville	25.3
Strutton	29.6
Northrop	17.8

Figure 62

There is also a ROLLUP option to the GROUP BY clause, which produces additional rows, called super aggregate rows, because they further aggregate rows already aggregated by the values in each group.

```
SELECT location.name, time.quarter,
  SUM AS total_revenue_in_thousands
  FROM sales, time, location
  WHERE sales.time_code = time.time_code
    AND sales.store_code = location.store_code
    AND time.year = 2019
  GROUP BY ROLLUP (location.region_code,
  time.quarter)
```

location.name	time.quarter	total_revenue_in_thousands
Sandy Bay	Q1	10.1
Sandy Bay	Q2	12.6
Sandy Bay	Q3	10.5
Sandy Bay	Q4	18.9
Sandy Bay	NULL	52.1
Southville	Q1	5.8

location.name	time.quarter	total_revenue_in_thousands
Southville	Q2	5.2
Southville	Q3	5.6
Southville	Q4	8.7
Southville	NULL	25.3
Strutton	Q1	6.7
Strutton	Q2	6.8
Strutton	Q3	6.3
Strutton	Q4	9.8
Strutton	NULL	29.6
Northrop	Q1	3.9
Northrop	Q2	4.1
Northrop	Q3	3.9
Northrop	Q4	5.9
Northrop	NULL	17.8
NULL	NULL	124.8

Figure 63

In each super aggregate row, one or more of the grouping columns are NULL, the others have the value of the group from which the group is derived.

Cube

There is also a CUBE option that can be included with the GROUP BY clause. In the SQL query below, the output includes further super aggregate rows, created for every combination of the grouping columns.

```
SELECT location.name, time.quarter,
        SUM(cost) AS total_revenue_in_thousands
  FROM sales, time, location
  WHERE sales.time_code = time.time_code
    AND sales.store_code = location.store_code
    AND time.year = 2019
  GROUP BY CUBE(location.name, time.quarter)
```

location.name	time.quarter	total_revenue_in_thousands
Sandy Bay	Q1	10.1
Sandy Bay	Q2	12.6
Sandy Bay	Q3	10.5
Sandy Bay	Q4	18.9
Sandy Bay	NULL	52.1
Southville	Q1	5.8
Southville	Q2	5.2
Southville	Q3	5.6
Southville	Q4	8.7
Southville	NULL	25.3
Strutton	Q1	6.7
Strutton	Q2	6.8
Strutton	Q3	6.3
Strutton	Q4	9.8
Strutton	NULL	29.6
Northrop	Q1	3.9
Northrop	Q2	4.1
Northrop	Q3	3.9
Northrop	Q4	5.9
Northrop	NULL	17.8
NULL	Q1	26.5
NULL	Q2	28.7
NULL	Q3	26.3
NULL	Q4	43.3
NULL	NULL	124.8

Figure 64

Drill-down

The *drill-down* operation gives a more detailed view of the data along one or more dimensions. It can't produce any *new* data, because it's impossible to produce more detailed data from summary data. It requires the data to be already available, otherwise it has to be produced from more detailed data using the *roll-up* operation.

3   Constructing a data warehouse

Data warehouses fall into three broad categories:

an *enterprise data warehouse,* which comprises information about all subjects of interest to an organisation, constructed by integrating all the relevant data from an organisation's operational information systems;

a *data mart,* which contains information relating to a specific group of users, such as a marketing department, or, for example, to a specific product or group of products;

and a *virtual data warehouse,* which as the name suggests contains no data of its own, but gives access to operational data through a series of views; obviously, given what I've already said about the processing load of OLAP systems, there are limitations to its use (but see below).

A data warehouse often needs to be constructed from various separate systems within an organisation, in order to include all of the information useful for decision making. These systems may store their data in heterogenous formats, so the various structures, naming conventions, attribute data formats and ranges need to be *integrated.*

This involves *extracting* the data from each information source, *translating* it to resolve any incompatibilities, *cleaning* it to remove errors and inconsistencies, and then *combining* it.

The *virtual data warehouse,* which I mentioned above, can play an intermediate role here; the information it "contains" can be extracted, and if necessary rolled-up or drilled-down to produce a final, physical warehouse.

Exercise 1. We couldn't use *RegNo* as the primary key of *Job*, because its uniqueness property would mean we could only record one single job against any vehicle. A possibility might be the combination of *(RegNo, StartDate)*, but the problem with that is that it would mean we could only do one job on a vehicle on any given date; and as we can see from Fig. 8, we do sometimes carry out two jobs on a single vehicle on the same date. So I've chosen *(RegNo, StartDate, JobDescription)*, which imposes the quite sensible restriction that we couldn't carry out the same job twice on the same vehicle on any given date. The only possible alternative would be *(RegNo, EndDate, JobDescription)*, but the problem there might be that presumably the garage would like to record jobs when they start, when the end date may not be known, and they could not, in that case, leave EndDate as NULL, because it would be part of the primary key. (But see also Section 1 of Chapter 18.)

Exercise 2. No, we couldn't represent the relationship between *Job* and *Employee* by posting the primary key of *Job* into *Employee*. As we can see from Fig. 9 (and as we would expect), an employee carries out more than one job. So if the foreign key were in *Employee*, it would have to contain, in each tuple, the primary key values of all the jobs that employee had carried out. And as we can see from the first property of a relation, that would not be allowed: all values have to be *atomic*. This is absolutely fine (at least for the moment) when we put the foreign key in *Job*, because we want to show the one single employee who carries out each job.

Exercise 3. Since the *Employee* attribute of *Job* is, like all other attributes except the primary key, allowed by default to be NULL, to make it represent a mandatory participation condition requires that, in the relational schema, wed explicitly define it as not being allowed to contain NULLs.

Exercise 4. Yes, we can validly represent a 1:1 relationship by using a foreign key at either end. In each case it will be referencing a candidate key. However, from a design point of view, we need to consider the problems created by NULLs. If a foreign key is placed in a relation which has optional participation in the relationship which that key represents, the foreign key attribute will contain NULLs. If a 1:1 relationship is optional at one end but mandatory at the other, we would place the foreign key at the mandatory end, thus avoiding NULLs in the foreign key altogether. If, on the other hand, the relationship is optional at both ends, we should look to see which of the two relations has less tuples not participating in the relationship, and place the foreign key there.

Exercise 5. No, because like every other attribute, a foreign key is allowed to contain NULLs unless its constrained not to; and does so, in the situation where it represents an optional relationship. So we could instead say, "*IF* a foreign key contains a value, that value much match some actual value of the candidate key it references."

Exercise 6. "Without duplication, list the registration numbers of all the vehicles which have been worked on."

Exercise 7. A data model of the Wyvern Trains requirement

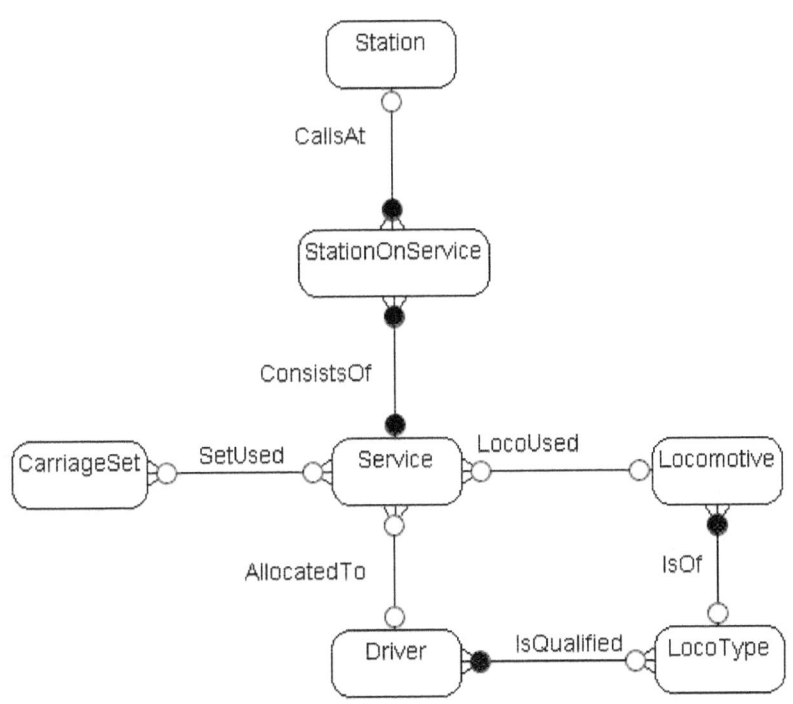

Entity types

Station (<u>Name</u>, PlatformLength)

StationOnService(<u>ServiceNo,StationName</u>,TimeHere)

Service (<u>ServiceNo</u>,StationFrom,StationTo,DepartureTime,ArrivalTime)

CarriageSet (<u>SerialNo</u>,LadenWeight)

Locomotive (<u>SerialNo</u>)

LocoType (<u>Type</u>,MaxLoad)

Driver (<u>NatInsNo</u>, Name)

Additional constraints

C1   Names of stations and of drivers can have up to 25 characters

C2   The length of a platform is either 'Long' or 'Short'

C3   Carriage set serial numbers are between 000000 and 999999

C4   Locomotive serial numbers are between 0000 and 9999

C5   Locomotive types are between 00 and 99

C6   Loads (in tonnes) are between 0 and 9999

C7   A National Insurance Number consists of two letters followed by six numerals and one letter

C8   A service number has three numeric digits

C9   Trains are made up of either one or two sets of coaches

C10   A train made up of two sets of coaches cannot be scheduled to call at a station with a short platform

C11   A locomotive cannot be allocated to a train having two sets of coaches unless its maximum load exceeds 500 tonnes

C12   A driver cannot be allocated to a train unless s/he is currently qualified to drive a locomotive of the class allocated to that train

C13   A driver cannot be assigned to drive for more than 6 hours in any day

Further constraints needed to preserve data integrity:

C14   Where carriages are assigned to a train less than 2 hours after the scheduled completion of a previous assignment in any day, they must already be in the correct starting location.

C15   Where locomotives are assigned to a train less than 2 hours after the scheduled completion of a previous assignment in any day, they must already be in the correct starting location.

C16   Where drivers are assigned to a train less than 2 hours after the scheduled completion of a previous assignment in any day, they must already be in the correct starting location.

c17   A carriage set cannot be assigned to more than one train at the same time

c18   A locomotive cannot be assigned to more than one train at the same time

c19   A driver cannot be assigned to more than one train at the same time

c20   A train can only be scheduled to call at an intermediate station after the original departure time and before the final arrival time of the service

Assumptions

a1   Only the current 24-hour period is recorded

a2   Drivers are only recorded as such if they are qualified to drive some type of locomotive

a3   A service has just one locomotive and just one driver

a4   For the first allocation of the day, all carriage sets, locomotives and drivers are already in the correct location

a5   Each set of coaches weighs 250 tonnes when fully laden

Exercise 8. Each of the foreign keys of Assignment forms part of the primary key of that table. Since a primary key can contain no NULLs, every row of the table will have to contain a valid value for each of the foreign keys.

Exercise 9. It will be impossible to insert a row into either table. The CHECK constraint on *driver* means that a row cannot be inserted before there is a row of *assignment* to reference it, but the mandatory foreign key of *assignment* means that a row of that table could not be created until the relevant row of *driver* was already in place.

Exercise 10. The CHECK statement means that an Apprentice MUST be supervised by *someone* – either a Chargehand or a Fitter. S/he cannot be unsupervised. (This use of OR is known in classical logic as the "strong or.")

Exercise 11. No CHECK constraint would be required. If a row of a table must participate in all of two or more relationships, this can achieved by simply making the relationships mandatory: the respective foreign key columns can either form part of the primary key of their table, or will be explicitly declared

NOT NULL.

Exercise 12.

```
/* Create domains
         */

/* c1 Names of stations and of drivers can
have
                         up to 25 characters
         */
CREATE DOMAIN names AS CHAR(25) ;

/* c2 The length of a platform is either
'Long' or
         'Short'     */
CREATE DOMAIN platforms AS CHAR(5)
     CHECK (@value IN('Long','Short'));

CREATE DOMAIN times AS DATETIME ;
/* SQLAnywhere doesn't support datatype TIME
     */

/* c3 Carriage set serial numbers are between
                         000000 and
999999           */
CREATE DOMAIN carriage_sets AS CHAR(6)
     CHECK( CAST (@value AS INTEGER) BETWEEN
0 AND

     999999);

/* c4 Locomotive serial numbers are between
0000
                         and 9999
             */
CREATE DOMAIN locomotives AS CHAR(4)
     CHECK( CAST (@value AS INTEGER) BETWEEN
0 AND
```

```
                    9999);


/* c5 Locomotive types are between 00 and 99
        */
CREATE DOMAIN types AS CHAR(2)
        CHECK( CAST (@value AS INTEGER) BETWEEN
0 AND 99);


/* c6 Loads (in tonnes) are between 0 and 9999
*/
CREATE DOMAIN loads AS SMALLINT
        CHECK (@value BETWEEN 0 AND 9999);


/*c7  A National Insurance Number consists of
2 letters followed by 6 numerals and 1 letter
*/
CREATE DOMAIN nat_ins_nos AS CHAR(9)
        CHECK( (SUBSTR(@value, 1, 2) BETWEEN
'AA' AND


            'ZZ')
        AND (SUBSTR(@value, 9,1) BETWEEN 'A' AND
'Z')
        AND (CAST(SUBSTR(@value, 3, 6) AS
INTEGER)
                             BETWEEN 000000
AND 999999));


/*c8  A service number has three numeric
digits     */
CREATE DOMAIN service_nos AS CHAR(3)
        CHECK( CAST (@value AS INTEGER) BETWEEN
0 AND

999);
```

```
/* Create tables implementing the entity types
   */

CREATE TABLE station (
     station_name names,
     platform_length platforms,
     PRIMARY KEY (station_name)
     );

CREATE TABLE service (
     service_no service_nos,
     station_from names,
     station_to names,
     departure_time times,
     arrival_time times,
     PRIMARY KEY (service_no),
     );

CREATE TABLE station_on_service(
     station_name names,
     service_no service_nos,
     time_here times,
     PRIMARY KEY (station_name,service_no),
     CONSTRAINT calls_at
     FOREIGN KEY (station_name) REFERENCES
station,
     CONSTRAINT consists_of
     FOREIGN KEY (service_no) REFERENCES
service
);

CREATE TABLE carriage_set(
     serial_no carriage_sets,
     PRIMARY KEY (serial_no));

CREATE TABLE set_used(
     serial_no carriage_sets,
```

```
        service_no service_nos,
        PRIMARY KEY (serial_no,service_no),
        CONSTRAINT carriage_set
        FOREIGN KEY (serial_no) REFERENCES
carriage_set,
        CONSTRAINT carriage_on_service
        FOREIGN KEY (service_no) REFERENCES
service
);

CREATE TABLE loco_type(
        loco_type types,
        max_load loads,
        PRIMARY KEY (loco_type)
);

CREATE TABLE locomotive(
        loco_type types,
        serial_no locomotives,
        PRIMARY KEY (loco_type,serial_no),
        CONSTRAINT is_of_type
        FOREIGN KEY (loco_type) REFERENCES
loco_type
);

CREATE TABLE loco_used(
        service_no service_nos,
        loco_type types,
        serial_no locomotives,
        PRIMARY KEY
(service_no,loco_type,serial_no),
        CONSTRAINT locomotive
        FOREIGN KEY (loco_type,serial_no)
REFERENCES

locomotive,
        CONSTRAINT service
        FOREIGN KEY (service_no) REFERENCES
```

```
        service
    );

    CREATE TABLE driver(
            nat_ins_no nat_ins_nos,
            name names,
            PRIMARY KEY (nat_ins_no)
    );

    CREATE TABLE allocated_to(
            nat_ins_no nat_ins_nos,
            service_no service_nos,
            PRIMARY KEY (nat_ins_no,service_no),
            CONSTRAINT service_on
            FOREIGN KEY (service_no) REFERENCES
    service,
            CONSTRAINT driver
            FOREIGN KEY (nat_ins_no) REFERENCES
    driver
    );

    CREATE TABLE qualification(
            nat_ins_no nat_ins_nos,
            loco_type types,
            PRIMARY KEY (nat_ins_no,loco_type),
            CONSTRAINT has
            FOREIGN KEY (nat_ins_no) REFERENCES
    driver,
            CONSTRAINT relates_to
            FOREIGN KEY (loco_type) REFERENCES
    loco_type
    );

    COMMIT;
        WyvernTrains_database_SQLAnywhere.sql
```

Exercise 13.

```
/* Constraints on table set_used */

/* c9 Trains are made up of either one or two
sets
          of coaches
/* c10     A train made up of two sets of
coaches cannot be scheduled to call at a
station with a short platform */
CREATE TRIGGER constraint_c9_10
     BEFORE INSERT ON set_used
     REFERENCING NEW AS new_set_used
     FOR EACH ROW
     WHEN
     (EXISTS
     (SELECT su.service_no /* this part
enforces c10 */
     FROM station s, station_on_service sos,
set_used su
     WHERE s.station_name=sos.station_name
     AND sos.service_no=su.service_no
     AND platform_length='Short'
     AND
su.service_no=new_set_used.service_no
UNION
     SELECT su.service_no /* this part
enforces c9 */
     FROM set_used su
     WHERE
su.service_no=new_set_used.service_no
     GROUP BY su.service_no
     HAVING COUNT(service_no) >1 )
     )
     BEGIN
     DECLARE constraint_c9_10_violation
EXCEPTION FOR
                              SQLSTATE
```

```
        '99999';
            SIGNAL constraint_c9_10_violation;
END;
/* No update trigger required for this */



/* c14       Where carriages are assigned to a
train less than 2 hours after the scheduled
completion of a previous assignment in any
day, they must already be in the correct
starting location */
/* c17       A carriage set cannot be assigned
to more than one train at the same time */
CREATE TRIGGER constraint_c14_17
        AFTER INSERT ON set_used
        FOR EACH ROW
        WHEN
        (EXISTS
                (SELECT su1.serial_no FROM
set_used su1, service s1, set_used su2,
                    service s2 /* c 14 */
            WHERE su1.service_no=s1.service_no
            AND su2.service_no=s2.service_no
            AND su1.serial_no=su2.serial_no
            AND su1.service_no<su2.service_no
            AND
(DATEDIFF(MINUTE,s2.arrival_time,
                        s1.departure_time))
<120
            AND s2.station_to <>
s1.station_from
        UNION
            SELECT su1.serial_no   /* c17 */
            FROM set_used su1, service s1,
                        set_used su2,
service s2
            WHERE su1.service_no =
```

```
s1.service_no
            AND su2.service_no = s2.service_no
            AND su1.serial_no = su2.serial_no
            AND s1.service_no <> s2.service_no
            AND
            (s1.arrival_time BETWEEN
s2.departure_time
                                          AND
s2.arrival_time
            OR s1.departure_time BETWEEN
                  s2.departure_time AND
s2.arrival_time))
      )
      BEGIN
      DECLARE constraint_c14_17_violation
                  EXCEPTION FOR SQLSTATE
'99999';
      SIGNAL constraint_c14_17_violation;
END;

CREATE TRIGGER constraint_c14_17u
      AFTER UPDATE ON set_used
      FOR EACH ROW
      WHEN
      (EXISTS
            (SELECT su1.serial_no FROM
set_used su1,
            service s1, set_used su2, service
s2 /* c14*/
            WHERE su1.service_no=s1.service_no
            AND su2.service_no=s2.service_no
            AND su1.serial_no=su2.serial_no
            AND su1.service_no<su2.service_no
            AND
(DATEDIFF(MINUTE,s2.arrival_time,

      s1.departure_time)) <120
            AND s2.station_to <>
```

```
                s1.station_from
        UNION
                SELECT su1.serial_no
                FROM set_used su1, service s1,
                            set_used su2, service
        s2 /* c17 */
                WHERE su1.service_no =
        s1.service_no
                AND su2.service_no = s2.service_no
                AND su1.serial_no = su2.serial_no
                AND s1.service_no <> s2.service_no
                AND
                (s1.arrival_time BETWEEN
        s2.departure_time
                                            AND
        s2.arrival_time
                OR s1.departure_time BETWEEN
                    s2.departure_time AND
        s2.arrival_time))
            )
        BEGIN
        DECLARE constraint_c14_17u_violation
        EXCEPTION FOR
                                            SQLSTATE
        '99999';
        SIGNAL constraint_c14_17u_violation;
        END;


        /* +++++++++++++++++++++++++++++++++++++++++++++++
        ++++++ */

        /* Constraints on table loco_used */

        /* c11      A locomotive cannot be allocated
        to a train having two sets of coaches unless
        its maximum load exceeds 500 tonnes        */
        /* c15      Where locomotives are assigned to
```

a train less than 2 hours after the scheduled
completion of a previous assignment
        in any day, they must already be in the
correct starting location
                              */
/* c18   A locomotive cannot be assigned to
more than one train at the same time
                              */
CREATE TRIGGER constraint_c11_15_18
        AFTER INSERT ON loco_used
        FOR EACH ROW
        WHEN
        (EXISTS
        (
        /* c_11   */
        SELECT s.service_no FROM loco_used l,
loco_type lt, service s, set_used su
                WHERE l.service_no = s.service_no
                AND s.service_no = su.service_no
                AND l.loco_type = lt.loco_type
                AND max_load <500
                GROUP BY s.service_no
                HAVING count(su.serial_no) >1
        UNION
        /* c_15 */
        SELECT a.serial_no FROM loco_used a,
service b, loco_used c, service d
                WHERE a.service_no=b.service_no
                AND c.service_no=d.service_no
                AND a.serial_no=c.serial_no
                AND a.service_no<c.service_no
                AND
(DATEDIFF(MINUTE,d.arrival_time,b.departure_ti
me)) <120
                AND d.station_to <> b.station_from
        UNION
        /* c_18 */
        SELECT lu1.serial_no FROM loco_used lu1,

```
service s1, set_used lu2, service s2
          WHERE lu1.service_no =
s1.service_no
          AND lu2.service_no = s2.service_no
          AND lu1.serial_no = lu2.serial_no
          AND s1.service_no <> s2.service_no
          AND
          (s1.arrival_time BETWEEN
s2.departure_time AND s2.arrival_time
               OR s1.departure_time BETWEEN
s2.departure_time AND s2.arrival_time) )
     )
     BEGIN
     DECLARE constraint_c11_15_18_violation
EXCEPTION FOR SQLSTATE '99999';
     SIGNAL constraint_c11_15_18_violation;
END;

/* NB trigger for update also required, as
follows */
CREATE TRIGGER constraint_c11_15_18u
     AFTER UPDATE ON loco_used
     FOR EACH ROW
     WHEN
     (EXISTS
     (
     /* c_11     */
     SELECT s.service_no FROM loco_used l,
loco_type lt, service s, set_used su
          WHERE l.service_no = s.service_no
          AND s.service_no = su.service_no
          AND l.loco_type = lt.loco_type
          AND max_load <500
          GROUP BY s.service_no
          HAVING count(su.serial_no) >1
     UNION
     /* c_15 */
     SELECT a.serial_no FROM loco_used a,
```

```sql
        service b, loco_used c, service d
                WHERE a.service_no=b.service_no
                AND c.service_no=d.service_no
                AND a.serial_no=c.serial_no
                AND a.service_no<c.service_no
                AND
(DATEDIFF(MINUTE,d.arrival_time,b.departure_ti
me)) <120
                AND d.station_to <> b.station_from
        UNION
        /* c_18 */
        SELECT lu1.serial_no FROM loco_used lu1,
service s1, set_used lu2, service s2
                WHERE lu1.service_no =
s1.service_no
                AND lu2.service_no = s2.service_no
                AND lu1.serial_no = lu2.serial_no
                AND s1.service_no <> s2.service_no
                AND
                (s1.arrival_time BETWEEN
s2.departure_time AND s2.arrival_time
                        OR s1.departure_time BETWEEN
s2.departure_time AND s2.arrival_time) )
        )
        BEGIN
        DECLARE constraint_c11_15_18u_violation
EXCEPTION FOR SQLSTATE '99999';
        SIGNAL constraint_c11_15_18u_violation;
END;



/* +++++++++++++++++++++++++++++++++++++++++++++
+++++++++++++++++++++++++++++++++++++++++++++++++
+++++++++++++++++++++++++++++++++++++ */

/* Constraints on table allocated_to */

/* c12      A driver can't be allocated to a
```

train unless currently qualified to drive a
loco of the class allocated to that train */
ALTER TABLE allocated_to
        ADD CONSTRAINT constraint_c12
        CHECK (service_no IN
                (SELECT service_no
                FROM loco_used l, qualification q
                WHERE allocated_to.nat_ins_no =
q.nat_ins_no
                AND l.loco_type = q.loco_type)
                );

/* c13   A driver cannot be assigned to
drive for more than 6 hours in any day
                                        */
/* c16 Where drivers are assigned to a train
less than 2 hours after the scheduled
completion of a previous assignment
        in any day, they must already be in the
correct starting location
                            */
CREATE TRIGGER constraint_c13_c16
        AFTER INSERT ON allocated_to
        FOR EACH ROW
        WHEN
        (EXISTS
        /* c13 */
        (SELECT a.nat_ins_no
                FROM allocated_to a,service s
                WHERE a.service_no=s.service_no
                GROUP BY a.nat_ins_no
                HAVING
SUM(DATEDIFF(MINUTE,departure_time,arrival_tim
e))>360
        UNION
        /* c16 */
        SELECT a1.nat_ins_no

```
      FROM allocated_to a1, service s1,
allocated_to a2, service s2
      WHERE a1.nat_ins_no=a2.nat_ins_no
      AND a1.service_no=s1.service_no
      AND a2.service_no=s2.service_no
      AND s1.arrival_time<s2.departure_time
      AND s1.station_to<>s2.station_from
      AND
(DATEDIFF(MINUTE,s1.arrival_time,s2.departure_
time)) <120
      AND s2.station_from <> ALL
            (SELECT station_to
            FROM allocated_to a, service s
            WHERE a.service_no=s.service_no
                AND
a.nat_ins_no=a1.nat_ins_no
                GROUP BY
s.station_to,s.arrival_time
                HAVING s.arrival_time
=MAX(arrival_time))))
      BEGIN
      DECLARE constraint_c13_c16_violation
EXCEPTION FOR SQLSTATE '99999';
      SIGNAL constraint_c13_c16_violation;
END;

CREATE TRIGGER constraint_c13_c16_u
      AFTER UPDATE ON allocated_to
      FOR EACH ROW
      WHEN
      (EXISTS
      /* c13 */
      (SELECT a.nat_ins_no
            FROM allocated_to a,service s
            WHERE a.service_no=s.service_no
            GROUP BY a.nat_ins_no
            HAVING
SUM(DATEDIFF(MINUTE,departure_time,arrival_tim
```

```
e))>360
      UNION
      /* c16 */
      SELECT a1.nat_ins_no
      FROM allocated_to a1, service s1,
allocated_to a2, service s2
      WHERE a1.nat_ins_no=a2.nat_ins_no
      AND a1.service_no=s1.service_no
      AND a2.service_no=s2.service_no
      AND s1.arrival_time<s2.departure_time
      AND s1.station_to<>s2.station_from
      AND
(DATEDIFF(MINUTE,s1.arrival_time,s2.departure_
time)) <120
      AND s2.station_from <> ALL
            (SELECT station_to
            FROM allocated_to a, service s
            WHERE a.service_no=s.service_no
                 AND
a.nat_ins_no=a1.nat_ins_no
                 GROUP BY
s.station_to,s.arrival_time
                 HAVING s.arrival_time
=MAX(arrival_time))))
      BEGIN
      DECLARE constraint_c13_c16_u_violation
EXCEPTION FOR SQLSTATE '99999';
      SIGNAL constraint_c13_c16_u_violation;
END;

/* c19      A driver cannot be assigned to
more than one train at the same time */
ALTER TABLE allocated_to
ADD CONSTRAINT constraint_c19
CHECK
(NOT EXISTS
      (SELECT *
      FROM allocated_to a1, service s1,
```

```
allocated_to a2, service s2
      WHERE a1.service_no <> a2.service_no
      AND a1.nat_ins_no=a2.nat_ins_no
      AND a1.service_no=s1.service_no
      AND a2.service_no=s2.service_no
      AND s1.departure_time BETWEEN
s2.departure_time AND s2.arrival_time)
);


/* ++++++++++++++++++++++++++++++++++++++++++
++++++++++++++++++++++++++++++++++++++++++++++
++++++++++++++++++++++++++++++++++++ */


/* Constraints on table station_on_service */

/* c20     A train can only be scheduled to
call at an intermediate station after the
original departure time and before the final
arrival time of the service */
CREATE TRIGGER constraint_c20
      AFTER INSERT ON station_on_service
      FOR EACH ROW
      WHEN
      (EXISTS
      (SELECT *
            FROM station_on_service s1,
service s2
            WHERE s1.service_no=s2.service_no
            AND s1.time_here NOT BETWEEN
s2.departure_time AND s2.arrival_time))
      BEGIN
      DECLARE constraint_c20_violation
EXCEPTION FOR SQLSTATE '99999';
      SIGNAL constraint_c20_violation;
END;

CREATE TRIGGER constraint_c20u
      AFTER UPDATE ON station_on_service
```

```
        FOR EACH ROW
        WHEN
        (EXISTS
        (SELECT *
            FROM station_on_service s1,
service s2
            WHERE s1.service_no=s2.service_no
            AND s1.time_here NOT BETWEEN
s2.departure_time AND s2.arrival_time))
        BEGIN
        DECLARE constraint_c20u_violation
EXCEPTION FOR SQLSTATE '99999';
        SIGNAL constraint_c20u_violation;
END;

COMMIT;
WyvernTrains_constraints_SQLAnywhere.sql
```

Exercise 14.

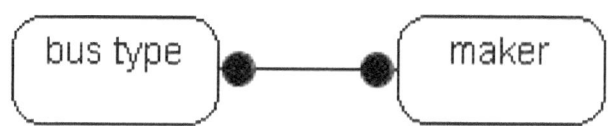

(Note that we would probably not, in a real database, have two tables in a 1:1 relationship where they both had mandatory participation. It would mean the two entities were logically inseparable, and as you'll see, this kind of relationship has a bearing on the normalisation process. The only reason for keeping them as separate tables might be for performance reasons: if one of the two were used much more often than the other, it might be more efficient to keep it separate so that less data has to be retrieved each time.)

Exercise 15.

  FD1 WagonId, JourneyDate -> RouteId

  FD2 WagonId, JourneyDate -> LadenWt

FD3 WagonId -> WagonType

FD4 WagonType -> UnladenWt

FD5 RouteId -> StationFrom

FD6 RouteId -> StationTo

FD7 RouteId, JourneyDate -> LocoId

FD8 LocoId, JourneyDate -> RouteId

FD9 LocoId → LocoType

Exercise 16.

my_data is updateable, a row in the view definition corresponds to exactly one row in the underlying base table.

uncompleted_jobs is not updateable since there is a join in the SELECT clause

Exercise 17.

Data storage, retrieval, and update

> The SQL INSERT function enables persistent data to be stored in tables in a pre-defined format. The SELECT function allows it to be retrieved, and the DELETE and UPDATE functions allow it to be changed.

A user-accessible catalog for data description

> The table definitions (CREATE TABLE statements) provide a full description of all the data which the database will hold.

Transaction support to ensure that all or none of a sequence of database changes are reflected in the pertinent databases

> Transactions are defined using AUTOCOMMIT OFF, COMMIT and ROLLBACK

Recovery services in case of failure (system, media, or program)

> The SQL standards do not define recovery services but all SQL dbms implementations provide them in some form.

Concurrency control services to ensure that concurrent transactions behave the same way as if run in some sequential order

Serializable execution can be controlled using the SET TRANSACTION ISOLATION LEVEL command, which allows a choice between various levels of locking.

Authorisation services to ensure that all access to and manipulation of data be in accordance with specified constraints on users and programs

Data in tables owned by a given user can by default only be retrieved or altered by the owner of those tables; however the owner can control access by others using the GRANT command

Integration with support for data communication

The SQL standards provide only the SQL DML and DDL as methods of communicating with a database, but a variety of other tools, whether provided by the dbms supplier (such as ODBC drivers and pre-compilers) or by others (such as JDBC and object-relational mappers) enable a wide variety of application software to communicate with a database using SQL statements. Further SQL-like commands, provided by the dbms supplier, allow data to be transferred to and from the database without using SQL statements.

Integrity services to ensure that database states and changes of state conform to specified rules

SQL provides for the creation of integrity constraints, including primary keys and UNIQUE indexes, and referential, column and domain constraints. Constraints can be defined in triggers and procedures as well as in table definitions. The timing and conditions under which constraints in table definitions are activated is somewhat dependent on the type of constraint and the dbms implementation, but can be user-specified in triggers and procedures.

Restructuring

Restructuring involves changes to the *logical* structure of the database, such as the addition or removal of columns or tables. It is provided for by SQL commands including CREATE TABLE (or VIEW), ALTER TABLE, DROP TABLE (or VIEW), etc.

Re-organisation

Re-organisation involves changes to the *physical* structure of the database. Since SQL does not provide for a storage schema to map the logical to the physical, each dbms manufacturer provides its own facilities to place tables, etc, onto physical storage, and to make changes as necessary.

Data manipulation

The SQL DML provides facilities well beyond the simple storage, retrieval and update envisaged in Codd's first listed feature. The SELECT command permits the use of logical and arithmetical operators to manipulate existing data while it is being retrieved, and SELECT . . INSERT means it can be transformed using those operators before being returned to the database. This means that any logically possible inquiry can be made of the data without need for external programs.

ANSI/SPARC (1975) Interim Report. FDT, ANSI/X3/SPARC Study Group on Data Base Management Systems: ACM SIGMOD bulletin. Volume 7, No. 2, 1975

Codd E.F. (1970) A Relational Model of Data for Large Shared Data Banks. Communications of the ACM Volume 13 Number 6 June, 1970

Codd E.F. (1979) Extending the data base relational model to capture more meaning. ACM Transactions on Database Systems (TODS): Volume 4 Issue 4, Dec. 1979

Codd E.F. (1982). The 1981 ACM Turing Award Lecture: Relational Database: A Practical Foundation for productivity. Communications of the ACM: Volume 25 Issue 2, Feb 1982

Codd E.F. (1990) The Relational Model for Database Management, Version 2. Addison Wesley ISBN 0-201-14192-2

Connolly and Begg (2010) Database Systems: a Practical Approach to Design, Implementation and Management, Fifth Edition. Addison Wesley ISBN 0-321-52306-7

Date C.J. (1987) Twelve Rules for a Distributed Database. Computer World, 8 June, 75-81; also in Date C.J. (2004) , An Introduction to Database Systems, 8th edition, 552-560, Pearson Education ISBN 0-321-19784-9

Date C.J. (1982) Null Values in Database Management. Proceedings of the Second British National Conference on Databases, Bristol 1982; also published in Relational Database Selected Writings, Addison-Wesley 1986 ISBN 0-201-14196-5

DB-engines (2019) DBMS popularity broken down by database model https://db-engines.com/en/ranking_categories

Navathe S.B. & Fry J.P. (1976) Restructuring for Large Databases: Three Levels of Abstraction. ACM Transactions on Database Systems. Vol. 1, No. 2, June 1976, Pages 138-158.

Tsichritzis, Dennis and Klug. Anthony, editors (1977). The ANSI/X3/SPARC DBMS Framework; Report of the Study Group on Data Base Management Systems. AFIPS Press, 210 Summit Avenue, Montvale, New Jersey 07645.1977.

Yao S.B., Das K.S. & Teorey T.J. (1976) A Dynamic Database Reorganization Algorithm. ACM Transactions on Database Systems, Vol. 1. No. 2, June 1976, Pages 159-174.

Appendix 1: Data types

Character string types	
CHARACTER(len) (or CHAR(len))	Fixed-length character strings of length len
VARCHAR(max_length)	Variable-length character strings, up to length max_length
Numeric data types	
INTEGER (or INT)	Integer numbers
SMALLINT	Small integer numbers
BIGINT	Big integer numbers
DECIMAL(p, s) (or DEC(p, s))	Decimal numbers containing at least p digits altogether, with s digits after the decimal point
NUMERIC(p, s)	Decimal numbers containing exactly p digits altogether, with s digits after the decimal point
FLOAT	Single precision floating-point number
REAL	Single precision floating-point number
DOUBLE PRECISION	Double precision floating-point number
Bit string types	
BIT(len)	Fixed-length bit string of length len
BIT VARYING(len)	Variable-length bit string up to length len
Date–time types	
DATE	Calendar date
TIME(p)	Clock time of precision p
TIMESTAMP(p)	Date and time of precision p
INTERVAL	Time interval
Large object string types	
CHARACTER LARGE OBJECT(size) (or CLOB(size))	Character data of size up to size
BINARY LARGE OBJECT(size) (or BLOB(size))	Binary data of size up to size

Appendix 2: SQL Operators

1   Arithmetic operators

Operator	Meaning	L/H expression	R/H expression	Result
+	Add	Integer	Integer	Integer
		Integer	Decimal	Decimal
		Decimal	Integer	Decimal
		NULL	Any	NULL
		Any	NULL	NULL
		Date	Time	DATESTAMP
		Time	Date	DATESTAMP
		Date or time	Integer or decimal	Invalid
		Integer or decimal	Date or time	Invalid
		String	Any	Invalid
		Any	String	Invalid
-	Subtract	Integer	Integer	Integer
		Integer	Decimal	Decimal
		Decimal	Integer	Decimal
		NULL	Any	NULL
		Any	NULL	NULL
		Date	Time	DATESTAMP
		Time	Date	Invalid
		Date or time	Integer or decimal	Invalid
		Integer or decimal	Date or time	Invalid
		String	Any	Invalid
		Any	String	Invalid

Operator	Meaning	L/H expression	R/H expression	Result
*	Multiply	Integer	Integer	Integer
		Integer	Decimal	Decimal
		Decimal	Integer	Decimal
		NULL	Any	NULL
		Any	NULL	NULL
		Date or Time or String	Any	Invalid
		Any	Date or Time or String	Invalid
/	Divide	Integer	Integer	Integer (truncated if necessary)
		Integer	Decimal	Decimal
		Decimal	Integer	Decimal
		NULL	Any	NULL
		Any	NULL or zero	NULL
		Date or Time or String	Any	Invalid
		Any	Date or Time or String	Invalid

2   Comparison operators

Operator	Meaning	L/h expression	R/h expression	Result
=	Equal to	Integer	Integer	TRUE or FALSE
>	Greater than	Decimal	Decimal	TRUE or FALSE
<	Less than	Integer	Decimal	TRUE if the right hand expression is an integer in a decimal type, otherwise FALSE

Operator	Meaning	L/h expression	R/h expression	Result
>=	Greater than or equal to	Decimal	Integer	TRUE if the left hand expression is an integer in a decimal type, otherwise FALSE
<=	Less than or equal to	NULL	Any	UNKNOWN
!=	Not equal to	Any	NULL	UNKNOWN
<>	Not equal to	Any	NULL	UNKNOWN
!>	Not greater than	Any	NULL	UNKNOWN
!<	Not less than	Any	NULL	UNKNOWN

Appendix 3: Standard SQLSTATE values

SQLSTATE	Cat.	Class	Class Text	Subclass	Subclass Text
00000	S	00	successful completion	000	(no subclass)
01000	W	01	warning	000	(no subclass)
01001	W	01	warning	001	cursor operation conflict
01002	W	01	warning	002	disconnect error
01003	W	01	warning	003	null value eliminated in set function
01004	W	01	warning	004	string data, right truncation
01005	W	01	warning	005	insufficient item descriptor areas
01006	W	01	warning	006	privilege not revoked
01007	W	01	warning	007	privilege not granted
01009	W	01	warning	009	search condition too long for information schema
0100A	W	01	warning	00A	query expression too long for information schema
0100B	W	01	warning	00B	default value too long for information schema
0100C	W	01	warning	00C	result sets returned
0100D	W	01	warning	00D	additional result sets returned
0100E	W	01	warning	00E	attempt to return too many result sets
0100F	W	01	warning	00F	statement too long for information schema
01010	W	01	warning	010	column cannot be mapped
01011	W	01	warning	011	SQL-Java path too long for information schema
01012	W	01	warning	012	invalid number of conditions
0102F	W	01	warning	02F	array data, right truncation

SQLSTATE	Cat.	Class	Class Text	Subclass	Subclass Text
02000	N	02	no data	000	(no subclass)
02001	N	02	no data	001	no additional result sets returned
07000	X	07	dynamic SQL error	000	(no subclass)
07001	X	07	dynamic SQL error	001	using clause does not match dynamic parameter specifications
07002	X	07	dynamic SQL error	002	using clause does not match target specifications
07003	X	07	dynamic SQL error	003	cursor specification cannot be executed
07004	X	07	dynamic SQL error	004	using clause required for dynamic parameters
07005	X	07	dynamic SQL error	005	prepared statement not a cursor specification
07006	X	07	dynamic SQL error	006	restricted data type attribute violation
07007	X	07	dynamic SQL error	007	using clause required for result fields
07008	X	07	dynamic SQL error	008	invalid descriptor count
07009	X	07	dynamic SQL error	009	invalid descriptor index
0700B	X	07	dynamic SQL error	00B	data type transform function violation
0700C	X	07	dynamic SQL error	00C	undefined DATA value
0700D	X	07	dynamic SQL error	00D	invalid DATA target
0700E	X	07	dynamic SQL error	00E	invalid LEVEL value
0700F	X	07	dynamic SQL error	00F	invalid DATETIME_INTERVAL_CODE
08000	X	08	connection exception	000	(no subclass)
08001	X	08	connection exception	001	SQL-client unable to establish SQL-connection
08002	X	08	connection exception	002	connection name in use
08003	X	08	connection exception	003	connection does not exist

SQLSTATE	Cat.	Class	Class Text	Subclass	Subclass Text
08004	X	08	connection exception	004	SQL-server rejected establishment of SQL-connection
08006	X	08	connection exception	006	connection failure
08007	X	08	connection exception	007	transaction resolution unknown
09000	X	09	triggered action exception	000	(no subclass)
0A000	X	0A	feature not supported	000	(no subclass)
0A001	X	0A	feature not supported	001	multiple server transactions
0D000	X	0D	invalid target type specification	000	(no subclass)
0E000	X	0E	invalid schema name list specification	000	(no subclass)
0F000	X	0F	locator exception	000	(no subclass)
0F001	X	0F	locator exception	001	invalid specification
0K000	X	0K	resignal when handler not active	000	(no subclass)
0L000	X	0L	invalid grantor	000	(no subclass)
0M000	X	0M	invalid SQL-invoked procedure reference	000	(no subclass)
0N000	X	0N	SQL/XML mapping error	000	(no subclass)
0N001	X	0N	SQL/XML mapping error	001	unmappable XML name
0N002	X	0N	SQL/XML mapping error	002	invalid XML character
0P000	X	0P	invalid role specification	000	(no subclass)

SQLSTATE	Cat.	Class	Class Text	Subclass	Subclass Text
0S000	X	0S	invalid transform group name specification	000	(no subclass)
0T000	X	0T	target table disagrees with cursor specification	000	(no subclass)
0U000	X	0U	attempt to assign to non-updatable column	000	(no subclass)
0V000	X	0V	attempt to assign to ordering column	000	(no subclass)
0W000	X	0W	prohibited statement encountered during trigger execution	000	(no subclass)
0W001	X	0W	prohibited statement encountered during trigger execution	001	modify table modified by data change delta table
0X000	X	0X	invalid foreign server specification	000	(no subclass)
0Y000	X	0Y	pass-through specific condition	000	(no subclass)
0Y001	X	0Y	pass-through specific condition	001	invalid cursor option
0Y002	X	0Y	pass-through specific condition	002	invalid cursor allocation
0Z000	X	0Z	diagnostics exception	000	(no subclass)
0Z001	X	0Z	diagnostics exception	001	maximum number of stacked diagnostics areas exceeded
0Z002	X	0Z	diagnostics exception	002	stacked diagnostics accessed without active handler
10000	X	10	XQuery error	000	(no subclass)

SQLSTATE	Cat.	Class	Class Text	Subclass	Subclass Text
20000	X	20	case not found for case statement	000	(no subclass)
21000	X	21	cardinality violation	000	(no subclass)
22000	X	22	data exception	000	(no subclass)
22001	X	22	data exception	001	string data, right truncation
22002	X	22	data exception	002	null value, no indicator parameter
22003	X	22	data exception	003	numeric value out of range
22004	X	22	data exception	004	null value not allowed
22005	X	22	data exception	005	error in assignment
22006	X	22	data exception	006	invalid interval format
22007	X	22	data exception	007	invalid datetime format
22008	X	22	data exception	008	datetime field overflow
22009	X	22	data exception	009	invalid time zone displacement value
2200B	X	22	data exception	00B	escape character conflict
2200C	X	22	data exception	00C	invalid use of escape character
2200D	X	22	data exception	00D	invalid escape octet
2200E	X	22	data exception	00E	null value in array target
2200F	X	22	data exception	00F	zero-length character string
2200G	X	22	data exception	00G	most specific type mismatch
2200H	X	22	data exception	00H	sequence generator limit exceeded
2200J	X	22	data exception	00J	nonidentical notations with the same name
2200K	X	22	data exception	00K	nonidentical unparsed entities with the same name
2200L	X	22	data exception	00L	not an XML document
2200M	X	22	data exception	00M	invalid XML document
2200N	X	22	data exception	00N	invalid XML content
2200P	X	22	data exception	00P	interval value out of range

SQLSTATE	Cat.	Class	Class Text	Subclass	Subclass Text
2200Q	X	22	data exception	00Q	multiset value overflow
2200R	X	22	data exception	00R	XML value overflow
2200S	X	22	data exception	00S	invalid comment
2200T	X	22	data exception	00T	invalid processing instruction
2200U	X	22	data exception	00U	not an XQuery document node
2200V	X	22	data exception	00V	invalid XQuery context item
2200W	X	22	data exception	00W	XQuery serialization error
22010	X	22	data exception	010	invalid indicator parameter value
22011	X	22	data exception	011	substring error
22012	X	22	data exception	012	division by zero
22013	X	22	data exception	013	invalid preceding or following size in window function
22014	X	22	data exception	014	invalid argument for NTILE function
22015	X	22	data exception	015	interval field overflow
22016	X	22	data exception	016	invalid argument for NTH_VALUE function
22017	X	22	data exception	017	invalid data specified for datalink
22018	X	22	data exception	018	invalid character value for cast
22019	X	22	data exception	019	invalid escape character
2201A	X	22	data exception	01A	null argument passed to datalink constructor
2201B	X	22	data exception	01B	invalid regular expression
2201C	X	22	data exception	01C	null row not permitted in table
2201D	X	22	data exception	01D	datalink value exceeds maximum length
2201E	X	22	data exception	01E	invalid argument for natural logarithm
2201F	X	22	data exception	01F	invalid argument for power function
2201G	X	22	data exception	01G	invalid argument for width bucket function

SQLSTATE	Cat.	Class	Class Text	Subclass	Subclass Text
2201H	X	22	data exception	01H	invalid row version
2201J	X	22	data exception	01J	XQuery sequence cannot be validated
2201K	X	22	data exception	01K	XQuery document node cannot be validated
2201L	X	22	data exception	01L	no XML schema found
2201M	X	22	data exception	01M	element namespace not declared
2201N	X	22	data exception	01N	global element not declared
2201P	X	22	data exception	01P	no XML element with the specified QName
2201Q	X	22	data exception	01Q	no XML element with the specified namespace
2201R	X	22	data exception	01R	validation failure
2201S	X	22	data exception	01S	invalid Query regular expression
2201T	X	22	data exception	01T	invalid Query option flag
2201U	X	22	data exception	01U	attempt to replace a zero-length string
2201V	X	22	data exception	01V	invalid Query replacement string
2201W	X	22	data exception	01W	invalid row count in fetch first clause
2201X	X	22	data exception	01X	invalid row count in result offset clause
22021	X	22	data exception	021	character not in repertoire
22022	X	22	data exception	022	indicator overflow
22023	X	22	data exception	023	invalid parameter value
22024	X	22	data exception	024	unterminated C string
22025	X	22	data exception	025	invalid escape sequence
22026	X	22	data exception	026	string data, length mismatch
22027	X	22	data exception	027	trim error
22029	X	22	data exception	029	noncharacter in UCS string
2202A	X	22	data exception	02A	null value in field reference

SQLSTATE	Cat.	Class	Class Text	Subclass	Subclass Text
2202D	X	22	data exception	02D	null value substituted for mutator subject parameter
2202E	X	22	data exception	02E	array element error
2202F	X	22	data exception	02F	array data, right truncation
2202G	X	22	data exception	02G	invalid repeat argument in a sample clause
2202H	X	22	data exception	02H	invalid sample size
23000	X	23	integrity constraint violation	000	(no subclass)
23001	X	23	integrity constraint violation	001	restrict violation
24000	X	24	invalid cursor state	000	(no subclass)
25000	X	25	invalid transaction state	000	(no subclass)
25001	X	25	invalid transaction state	001	active SQL-transaction
25002	X	25	invalid transaction state	002	branch transaction already active
25003	X	25	invalid transaction state	003	inappropriate access mode for branch transaction
25004	X	25	invalid transaction state	004	inappropriate isolation level for branch transaction
25005	X	25	invalid transaction state	005	no active SQL-transaction for branch transaction
25006	X	25	invalid transaction state	006	read-only SQL-transaction
25007	X	25	invalid transaction state	007	schema and data statement mixing not supported
25008	X	25	invalid transaction state	008	held cursor requires same isolation level
26000	X	26	invalid SQL statement name	000	(no subclass)

SQLSTATE	Cat.	Class	Class Text	Subclass	Subclass Text
27000	X	27	triggered data change violation	000	(no subclass)
27001	X	27	triggered data change violation	001	modify table modified by data change delta table
28000	X	28	invalid authorization specification	000	(no subclass)
2B000	X	2B	dependent privilege descriptors still exist	000	(no subclass)
2C000	X	2C	invalid character set name	000	(no subclass)
2D000	X	2D	invalid transaction termination	000	(no subclass)
2E000	X	2E	invalid connection name	000	(no subclass)
2F000	X	2F	SQL routine exception	000	(no subclass)
2F002	X	2F	SQL routine exception	002	modifying SQL-data not permitted
2F003	X	2F	SQL routine exception	003	prohibited SQL-statement attempted
2F004	X	2F	SQL routine exception	004	reading SQL-data not permitted
2F005	X	2F	SQL routine exception	005	function executed no return statement
2H000	X	2H	invalid collation name	000	(no subclass)
30000	X	30	invalid SQL statement identifier	000	(no subclass)
33000	X	33	invalid SQL descriptor name	000	(no subclass)
34000	X	34	invalid cursor name	000	(no subclass)

SQLSTATE	Cat.	Class	Class Text	Subclass	Subclass Text
35000	X	35	invalid condition number	000	(no subclass)
36000	X	36	cursor sensitivity exception	000	(no subclass)
36001	X	36	cursor sensitivity exception	001	request rejected
36002	X	36	cursor sensitivity exception	002	request failed
38000	X	38	external routine exception	000	(no subclass)
38001	X	38	external routine exception	001	containing SQL not permitted
38002	X	38	external routine exception	002	modifying SQL-data not permitted
38003	X	38	external routine exception	003	prohibited SQL-statement attempted
38004	X	38	external routine exception	004	reading SQL-data not permitted
39000	X	39	external routine invocation exception	000	(no subclass)
39004	X	39	external routine invocation exception	004	null value not allowed
3B000	X	3B	savepoint exception	000	(no subclass)
3B001	X	3B	savepoint exception	001	invalid specification
3B002	X	3B	savepoint exception	002	too many
3C000	X	3C	ambiguous cursor name	000	(no subclass)
3D000	X	3D	invalid catalog name	000	(no subclass)
3F000	X	3F	invalid schema name	000	(no subclass)

SQLSTATE	Cat.	Class	Class Text	Subclass	Subclass Text
40000	X	40	transaction rollback	000	(no subclass)
40001	X	40	transaction rollback	001	serialization failure
40002	X	40	transaction rollback	002	integrity constraint violation
40003	X	40	transaction rollback	003	statement completion unknown
40004	X	40	transaction rollback	004	triggered action exception
42000	X	42	syntax error or access rule violation	000	(no subclass)
44000	X	44	with check option violation	000	(no subclass)
45000	X	45	unhandled user-defined exception	000	(no subclass)
46000	X	46	OLB-specific error	000	(no subclass)
46001	X	46	Java DDL	001	invalid URL
46002	X	46	Java DDL	002	invalid JAR name
46003	X	46	Java DDL	003	invalid class deletion
46005	X	46	Java DDL	005	invalid replacement
4600A	X	46	Java DDL	00A	attempt to replace uninstalled JAR
4600B	X	46	Java DDL	00B	attempt to remove uninstalled JAR
4600C	X	46	Java DDL	00C	invalid JAR removal
4600D	X	46	Java DDL	00D	invalid path
4600E	X	46	Java DDL	00E	self-referencing path
46102	X	46	Java DDL	102	invalid JAR name in path
46103	X	46	Java DDL	103	unresolved class name
46110	X	46	OLB-specific error	110	unsupported feature
46120	X	46	OLB-specific error	120	invalid class declaration
46121	X	46	OLB-specific error	121	invalid column name
46122	X	46	OLB-specific error	122	invalid number of columns
46130	X	46	OLB-specific error	130	invalid profile state

SQLSTATE	Cat.	Class	Class Text	Subclass	Subclass Text
HW000	X	HW	datalink exception	000	(no subclass)
HW001	X	HW	datalink exception	001	external file not linked
HW002	X	HW	datalink exception	002	external file already linked
HW003	X	HW	datalink exception	003	referenced file does not exist
HW004	X	HW	datalink exception	004	invalid write token
HW005	X	HW	datalink exception	005	invalid datalink construction
HW006	X	HW	datalink exception	006	invalid write permission for update
HW007	X	HW	datalink exception	007	referenced file not valid
HV000	X	HV	FDW-specific condition	000	(no subclass)
HV001	X	HV	FDW-specific condition	001	memory allocation error
HV002	X	HV	FDW-specific condition	002	dynamic parameter value needed
HV004	X	HV	FDW-specific condition	004	invalid data type
HV005	X	HV	FDW-specific condition	005	column name not found
HV006	X	HV	FDW-specific condition	006	invalid data type descriptors
HV007	X	HV	FDW-specific condition	007	invalid column name
HV008	X	HV	FDW-specific condition	008	invalid column number
HV009	X	HV	FDW-specific condition	009	invalid use of null pointer
HV00A	X	HV	FDW-specific condition	00A	invalid string format
HV00B	X	HV	FDW-specific condition	00B	invalid handle

SQLSTATE	Cat.	Class	Class Text	Subclass	Subclass Text
HV00C	X	HV	FDW-specific condition	00C	invalid option index
HV00D	X	HV	FDW-specific condition	00D	invalid option name
HV00J	X	HV	FDW-specific condition	00J	option name not found
HV00K	X	HV	FDW-specific condition	00K	reply handle
HV00L	X	HV	FDW-specific condition	00L	unable to create execution
HV00M	X	HV	FDW-specific condition	00M	unable to create reply
HV00N	X	HV	FDW-specific condition	00N	unable to establish connection
HV00P	X	HV	FDW-specific condition	00P	no schemas
HV00Q	X	HV	FDW-specific condition	00Q	schema not found
HV00R	X	HV	FDW-specific condition	00R	table not found
HV010	X	HV	FDW-specific condition	010	function sequence error
HV014	X	HV	FDW-specific condition	014	limit on number of handles exceeded
HV021	X	HV	FDW-specific condition	021	inconsistent descriptor information
HV024	X	HV	FDW-specific condition	024	invalid attribute value
HV090	X	HV	FDW-specific condition	090	invalid string length or buffer length
HV091	X	HV	FDW-specific condition	091	invalid descriptor field identifier

SQLSTATE	Cat.	Class	Class Text	Subclass	Subclass Text
HY000	X	HY	CLI-specific condition	000	(no subclass)
HY???	X	HY	CLI-specific condition	n/a	dynamic parameter value needed
HY???	X	HY	CLI-specific condition	n/a	invalid handle
HY001	X	HY	CLI-specific condition	001	memory allocation error
HY003	X	HY	CLI-specific condition	003	invalid data type in application descriptor
HY004	X	HY	CLI-specific condition	004	invalid data type
HY007	X	HY	CLI-specific condition	007	associated statement is not prepared
HY008	X	HY	CLI-specific condition	008	operation canceled
HY009	X	HY	CLI-specific condition	009	invalid use of null pointer
HY010	X	HY	CLI-specific condition	010	function sequence error
HY011	X	HY	CLI-specific condition	011	attribute cannot be set now
HY012	X	HY	CLI-specific condition	012	invalid transaction operation code
HY013	X	HY	CLI-specific condition	013	memory management error
HY014	X	HY	CLI-specific condition	014	limit on number of handles exceeded
HY017	X	HY	CLI-specific condition	017	invalid use of automatically-allocated descriptor handle
HY018	X	HY	CLI-specific condition	018	server declined the cancellation request

SQLSTATE	Cat.	Class	Class Text	Subclass	Subclass Text
HY019	X	HY	CLI-specific condition	019	non-string data cannot be sent in pieces
HY020	X	HY	CLI-specific condition	020	attempt to concatenate a null value
HY021	X	HY	CLI-specific condition	021	inconsistent descriptor information
HY024	X	HY	CLI-specific condition	024	invalid attribute value
HY055	X	HY	CLI-specific condition	055	non-string data cannot be used with string routine
HY090	X	HY	CLI-specific condition	090	invalid string length or buffer length
HY091	X	HY	CLI-specific condition	091	invalid descriptor field identifier
HY092	X	HY	CLI-specific condition	092	invalid attribute identifier
HY093	X	HY	CLI-specific condition	093	invalid datalink value
HY095	X	HY	CLI-specific condition	095	invalid FunctionId specified
HY096	X	HY	CLI-specific condition	096	invalid information type
HY097	X	HY	CLI-specific condition	097	column type out of range
HY098	X	HY	CLI-specific condition	098	scope out of range
HY099	X	HY	CLI-specific condition	099	nullable type out of range
HY103	X	HY	CLI-specific condition	103	invalid retrieval code
HY104	X	HY	CLI-specific condition	104	invalid LengthPrecision value

SQLSTATE	Cat.	Class	Class Text	Subclass	Subclass Text
HY105	X	HY	CLI-specific condition	105	invalid parameter mode
HY106	X	HY	CLI-specific condition	106	invalid fetch orientation
HY107	X	HY	CLI-specific condition	107	row value out of range
HY108	X	HY	CLI-specific condition	108	invalid cursor position
HYC00	X	HY	CLI-specific condition	C00	optional feature not implemented
HZ???	?	HZ	Reserved for ISO9579 (RDA)	???	

Appendix 4: Software installation – SQL Anywhere

Downloading SQL Anywhere – all systems

To download SQL Anywhere for your system, first go to bit.ly/SAP2Fit

Fill in your details and press Get Started

On the next page, select the link to your operating system (Windows, Linux etc) under the column headed "SAP SQL Anywhere 17". This will enable you to download the installation software to your chosen location.

Further down the same column, you can also choose to download Documentation for SQL Anywhere; however full on-line help is available from within the system, once installed.

Downloading the database scripts – all systems

Go to bit.ly/SQLpacK and download the file SQLpackage.zip to a convenient location. Unzip the file to create a new folder, *SQLpackage,* containing the scripts.

Installation of SQL Anywhere on Linux systems

Navigate to where you saved the downloaded SQL Anywhere file *sqla17developerlinux.tar.gz,* and extract it to a suitable location. This will create a new directory named *sqlany17*

Using a terminal, log in as root, change to that directory and execute the file *setup,* which will open the installation dialogue.

On the first page, press *Forward,* and then in the next page select your geographic location from the pull-down menu, select "I accept the terms of this agreement," and again press *Forward.* Select "Create a new installation," press *Forward,* and then on the Registration Key page just press *Forward* again. On the next page, select "I accept the terms of this agreement," and again press *Forward.*

The next page allows you to choose the components you wish to install. Under Databases, you should select SQL Anywhere for *either* 32-bit or 64-bit systems according to your hardware, but you can safely de-select Ultralite and all of the Synchronisation options. You should also ensure that both SQL Anywhere Monitor and Administration Tools are selected, for your type of system. Unless there are special circumstances you should leave the default installation location as it is, and then press *Forward*.

On the next page, you should choose to create Application Menu items and possibly a desktop shortcut. It's your choice as to whether you want to send your usage information to SAP. Press *Forward* again, and again on the next page. The installation will then proceed, which will take a few minutes. Once it has completed, press *Forward* again.

On the next page, make a note of the instruction for setting up the correct environment variable for SQL Anywhere, and execute it as the user who will be running the software. You do not need to do the same for the SAP-provided sample database, or press the "Check for Updates" button.

Press *Quit*

Depending on which desktop you're using, you should now have an SQL Anywhere item or items in your application menu. The two options you will be using are Interactive SQL and SQL Central (and Interactive SQL can be started either directly, or from within SQL Central).

Installation of SQL Anywhere on Windows systems (version 7 or later)

Navigate to where you saved the downloaded SQL Anywhere file *SQLA17Developer.exe*, right-click on it and select "Run as administrator". In the window which pops up "Do you want this application to make changes to your system?" Select Yes.

This will bring up the SQLAnywhere 17 Installshield Wizard. Select Next, which will bring up the dialogue box "Choose Setup Language"; if necessary change the selection using the drop-down menu, and press OK.

This will return you to the Installshield Wizard; press Next. Now use the drop-down menu to select your location, press the radio button for "I accept the terms of this agreement," and press Next twice. Press the radio button for "I accept the terms in the license agreement," and press Next twice.

On the next page, you should choose to create a desktop shortcut. It's your choice as to whether you want to send your usage information to SAP. Press Install. You can uncheck the boxes on the final page and then press Finish.

You will now have a desktop shortcut for SQL Central, which you can use directly by double-clicking on that shortcut. To start Interactive SQL, select Tools – SQL Anywhere 17 – Open Interactive SQL. Alternatively, in your Applications menu, you will have a heading SQL Anywhere, which opens to give you either Interactive SQL or SQL Central.

Installation of SQL Anywhere on Mac systems (OSX 10.9 Mavericks or later)

Navigate to where (usually Downloads in your own home folder) you downloaded the SQL Anywhere file *sqladeveloperosx.tar.gz*, right-click on it and select Open. This will extract the archive into a new folder, *sqlany17*, in the same location. Double-click on that folder to open it. Locate the file *setup*, right-click on it and select Open. The system asks if you are sure you want to open it – press *Open*.

Now a terminal window will open, inviting you to install SQL Anywhere; press Enter. Select the number for your country and press Enter again. Hold down the Enter key or spacebar to scroll to the bottom of the licensing agreement, type Y and press Enter. Type 1 and press Enter, and then Enter again. Hold down Enter or spacebar to scroll to the bottom of the rights and limitations agreement, type Y and press Enter.

The next page allows you to choose the components you wish to install. You only require SQL Anywhere Server and Client, and the Administration Tools. Start by typing N and pressing Enter, this will de-select all the options. Type 1 and press Enter, then 1 and Enter, and 1 and Enter again, and then 2 and Enter again. Type P and press Enter, and P and Enter again. You will now be back at the top menu.

Type 3 and press Enter, then type S and press Enter to start the installation. Unless there are special circumstances you should leave the default installation location as it is, so just press Enter, and then Y and Enter again.

On the next page, it's your choice as to whether you want to send your usage information to SAP – type Y or N and press Enter, and then Enter again.

When the installation completes it will ask about updates – choose N and press Enter. Up to you whether you want the Read Me file. You can then close the window.

Unless the Java runtime is already installed on your system, you now need to use your browser to visit www.oracle.com/technetwork/java/index.html. Go to the Downloads page, select Java SE and then JDK. Download the .dmg file for Mac OS. Navigate to your Downloads folder, open the Java .dmg file and double-click on the icon to install Java.

You also need to set your environment variables in order to use the software. First open a terminal window, log in as root (sudo -i followed by your password), and enter cd /Applications/SQLAnywhere17/System/bin64. Give the relevant shell file execute permissions by typing chmod +x ./sa_config.sh and pressing Enter (or sa_config.csh if your default shell is c shell). Now log out of the root session (Ctrl-D), navigate back to the directory (enter cd /Applications/SQLAnywhere17/System/bin64 again) and execute the file you just modified (type ./sa_config.sh and press Enter). Close the terminal window.

In the Applications folder on your desktop there will now be a folder SQLAnywhere17, in it you will find icons for InteractiveSQL.app and SQLCentral.app – you can execute them from there, or drag them to the Dock.

Creating the databases - all systems

Creation of the Garage database *(required from Chapter 9 onwards)*

(Notes:

- to remove an empty database entirely: disconnect any open connections and exit SQL Central; open Interactive SQL and connect to *another* database; run the command drop database {full path to database file}

- the following commands to create databases are not part of SQL – obviously, since until you create a database you have nothing which understands SQL - so the method will be quite different in a different dbms)

Start SQL Central

Select Tools – SQL Anywhere 17 - Create Database. This will open the Create Database Wizard.

Select Next 2 times

Enter the location where you want to save the new database file (you can use the Browse button to navigate); give the file the name 'garage' and press Save.

Select Next 3 times

Fill in the user name 'dba' and password also 'dba' (note that this is very poor security practice and you should always use a much more secure password for any real world database; however I have chosen these values for simplicity as there are no security issues with a training database)

Change the Minimum Password Length to 3

Select Finish; this will create the empty database with all the default options.

Select Tools – SQL Anywhere 17 – Open Interactive SQL". Enter the user name and password you just created. On the Action pull-down menu, select "Start and connect to a database on this computer," browse to where you just saved the *garage* database file, and select it. Press Connect.

Select File – Run Script

Navigate to where you saved the downloaded folder SQLpackage, open it and select the file Garage_database_SQLAnywhere.sql

Press Open

The script will create the domains and tables and insert all the test data.

Initial creation of the WyvernBuses database *(required from Chapter 12 onwards)*

Open SQL Central. Select Tools – SQL Anywhere 17 – Create database. This will open the Create Database Wizard.

Select Next twice

Enter the location where you want to save the new database file (you can use the Browse button to navigate); give the file the name 'wyvernbuses' and press Save

Select Next 3 times

Fill in the user name 'dba' and password also 'dba' (note that this is very poor security practice and you should always use a much more secure password for any real world database; however I have chosen these values for simplicity as there are no security issues with a training database)

Change the Minimum Password Length to 3

Select Finish; this will create the empty database with all the default options.

Refer to Chapter 12 for how to populate and use this new database.

Index

320

www.ingramcontent.com/pod-product-compliance
Lightning Source LLC
Chambersburg PA
CBHW020728180526
45163CB00001B/148